park
and
ride

Adventures in
Suburbia

MIRANDA SAWYER

LITTLE, BROWN AND COMPANY

A *Little, Brown* Book

First published in Great Britain in 1999
by Little, Brown and Company

Copyright © Miranda Sawyer, 1999

The moral right of the author has been asserted.

The author gratefully acknowledges permission to quote from the following:
'The English Motorway System'. Words and music by Luke Haines and John Moore.
Copyright © Luke Haines and John Moore, 1999. Reprinted by permission.
'High'. Music by Paul Tucker and Tunde Baiyewu. Words by Paul Tucker.
Copyright © PolyGram Music Publishing Limited, 1997. Reprinted by permission of
Music Sales Ltd. All Rights Reserved. International Copyright Secured.
'Ocean Drive'. Words and music by Paul Tucker. Copyright © PolyGram Music
Publishing Limited, 1994. Reprinted by permission of Music Sales Ltd. All Rights
Reserved. International Copyright Secured.
Ken and Me by William Roache. Copyright © William Roache, 1993. Reprinted by
permission of Simon & Schuster, London.
Max Power. Copyright © *Max Power.* Reprinted by permission.
The *Guardian.* Copyright © The *Guardian.* Reprinted by permission.
Every effort has been made to trace the copyright holders and to clear reprint
permissions for the following: Extract from the *Mail.*

A CIP catalogue record for this book is available from the British Library.

ISBN 0 316 64575 3

Typeset in Horley OS by M Rules
Printed and bound in Great Britain by
Clays Ltd, St Ives plc

Little, Brown and Company (UK)
Brettenham House
Lancaster Place
London WC2E 7EN

For my family
and because of Gavin Hills

contents

Thank you to everyone who features in this book, especially Keith, Clint, Lizanne, Phil, Flo, Harry, Jen, Dick and Granny. Special thanks to David Godwin, also Heather and Penny. Thank you to Sally, Sarah, Ali, Richard, Peter, Debbie and Miles at Little, Brown. Polly at Best Est. Ernesto, Sonia and Ziggy at Arthrob. Thanks to David Eldritch at Senate for the cover. Mark Whelan at iD for locating the Most Average Town In Britain. Craig Melvin and Janine Glasspole for Brighton. Mike and Jeanette Hursey for Center Parcs. Richard Benson for suggestions. Luke Haines and John Moore for permission. Jamie Hewlett for the almost-zombies. Thank you to Louise, David, Toby, Jonathon, Michael, Keeney, Bernie, Carol, Richard: without whom etc etc. And to John for everything.

I come from suburbia. Personally I don't ever want to go back. It's the one place in the world that's further away from anywhere else.
Frederick Raphael, *The Glittering Prizes*, 1977

The English motorway system is beautiful and strange
Black Box Recorder, 'The English Motorway System', 1999

1

coming out of nowhere

When I was growing up, Wilmslow was a pink jumper, white stilettos kind of a town. Flash. Flashy. It was where Mancunians moved to once they'd made a bit of money: it had plenty of large, squat, thirties-era houses, with garages, gardens, gables, porches. Pretty fields clustered round its southern perimeter. More importantly, to its residents, Wilmslow had a Porsche garage, and a Benetton, and its very own department store, Finnigan's. Finnigan's had a china department described by every local grandmother as 'lovely', and an exclusive hair salon called Steiners that would do you a feather cut and highlights for a price that would straighten Granny's shampoo and set. Wilmslow had pubs where work boots were not allowed, and expensive shoe shops that stocked every kind of court shoe available. As long as Madam wanted them in white.

And Madam always did. Wilmslow girls lived in white stilettos. They wore them everywhere: at school, at party, at pub, at it on the bench outside Barclays Bank. In fact, aside from the pink jumper (slung and knotted around the shoulders), Wilmslow girls wore white everything. White shoes, white mini-skirt, white plastic earrings, white streaks in mousy hair, white Consulate cigarettes, white convertible Golf GTI with matching white spoilers. You could spot the odd tinge of colour – turquoise mascara, luminous nail varnish, Marbella-orange legs topped up with brick-red fake tan – but the overall effect was of a poodle that had been put in the washer with Tipp-Ex as well as Persil. And then subjected to an eye-wateringly vigorous fur-tonging afterwards.

Wilmslow girls could tong for Britain. They wielded their hair tongs like light sabres. You know that coffee advert where the attractive young thing tearfully plugs her portable heating element into the car cigarette-lighter to heat up her lonely Nescafé? That was the kind of thing that Wilmslow girls could never understand. Why didn't she just plug in her hairtongs? Sort out some of life's real problems, the silly ninny? Well, *honestly.* Coffee before curling? Sustenance before a scrunch-dry? No wonder the girl was crying. She'd be weeping in shame. In Wilmslow, a half-hour's hard tonging, plus full slap and appropriately co-ordinated jumpsuit were required just to put out the bins. On Saturday afternoons, when Wilmslow girls tripped gigglingly along Grove Street, tinkling their car-keys, tossing their root-perms, swinging their Ravel bags, it was as if an army of Barbies had come to life, eaten cream buns for a week, and then decided to invade Cheshire. Armed only with hair tongs and bright white stilettos.

White, white, white. White was so dominant a wardrobe staple, such a uniform of desirable femininity, that my friend Tracey and I joined the tennis club when we were thirteen, simply because it was a good opportunity to wear white a lot. We swanned about with our rackets on our shoulders, bobble socks abobbling, wristbands afluff, poised for a game; but we never got on that well, because we hadn't yet worked out what a tennis club was for.

We'd thought it was a place for playing tennis and working up to all-day snow-hued casualwear. It wasn't. It was a place for picking up tennis players. That was why all the men – burly and blokish, even in their wussy pink tank tops – made all that noise, thumping each other in the biceps, trumpeting scores, snorting like hay-fevered rhinoceri at the punchline to some joke you would never understand. We were too young for them to bother with, but we could see the change when a real lady was present. Then, the roaring, phwoarring boys with the flamboyant hip-thrusts froze into grinning statues who jingled the change in their shorts pockets.

The lady tennis enthusiasts, though less demonstrative (just a quick nip to the loo for retong and lip-gloss whenever a man hove into view), certainly weren't any quieter than the men. They never, ever stopped talking. Despite this, they seemed . . . not prim, but contained, feminine, neat, tucked in, braceleted, cross-ankled, without a fleck of dirt on them. (I still don't know how they managed this. The tennis courts were covered in red sand, which I couldn't help kicking up when I walked on them. I played in a dust cloud, like Pigpen in *Peanuts*. My pristine ensemble kept streaking pink with sweat; vanilla charm ruined by splurges of raspberry ripple. Clearly, my world was not yet up to wearable whites.)

The thing that Tracey and I had failed to understand was that white was the preferred colour for a Wilmslow girl's wardrobe because – despite her seeming independence: her flighty car, her fluffy chatter, her feather earrings – every Wilmslow girl was practising for her wedding day. The *Wilmslow World* was stuffed with pictures of unblushing brides in swathes of satin-feel polyester. Each looked like a living marquee. And judging by the fierce smile, each was proud to do so. The groom's mood was more difficult to read. Still, if you searched a photo carefully you could usually just spot the lucky man, a tiny speck in the background suffocating under several miles of snowy petticoat.

Of course, the joke was that white wouldn't be right once you'd got to your wedding day, ha ha. At least not if those wild Wilmslow boys had anything to do with it. And as I got older and could read those one-thought expressions beneath those fearsome flicker fringes, the intention in the Action Man grip of those soap-smooth hands, I understood that the wild Wilmslow boys were not the marrying kind. Well, not until they were in their twenties, anyway. Wild Wilmslow boys had wild jobs, in 'business', which usually meant they spent their days photocopying or doing deliveries for their dad's firm. They had wild names: John, Mike, Darren. And they had a wild song which they sang on wild occasions, like on the way to

4

The Swan or The King's Arms every single Friday night. It went: *Dr Martens, yellow laces/Levi jeans with clip-on braces/We're the ones who'll smash your faces/We're the Wilmslow boot boys.*

Which was strange because every Wilmslow boy I knew wore a pink jumper. And pulled that chase-me pink jumper over the tidgiest hint of a Boddingtons' belly to tuck smoothly into the waistband of pale blue stonewash jeans. And probably straight into the waistband of his pale blue stonewash Y-fronts too. True, a Wilmslow boy strutted with the dick-first swagger of a man from the north-west – what is it about that walk? Is every male born within twenty miles of Manchester taught to toddle like that by law or something? – but he never strutted in *braces*. Also, if a Wilmslow boy was going to smash your face in, no way would he do it in Doctor Martens. No work boots allowed: he'd never get into the pub for a pint afterwards.

Wilmslow, in those days, was suburbia's wet dream. (Plopped slap bang on the Cheshire plain, where the clouds stream their Atlantic tears before hoisting themselves over the Pennines; the rain sluiced down on us in a way unimaginable to those born in sunnier environs, like Harrogate. My mother's leisure time was spent in an exciting whirl of hanging out and bringing in the washing.) My parents moved there in 1967. When my brother and I were in our teens, and one or other of us was moaning about living so far out of Manchester, away from exciting city diversions like buses and the Arndale Centre, my mum would get defensive and say:

'Well, flower, when we moved here we couldn't afford Manchester rates. Anyway, your father likes the countryside.' Then her look would turn frantic and she'd gallop out of the back door into a sudden, whipping thunderstorm, yelping helplessly about the sheets.

I used to watch the rain course down the picture window in the back extension, have bets with my brother on which drop would reach the sill first. The weather didn't bother us: it wasn't until I moved away that I realised how well watered my life had been up until then. In Wilmslow, when it wasn't raining, the clouds stacked up like a pile of sodden tea-towels; when it wasn't raining, it was just about to. When ELO released 'Mr Blue Sky', we thought it was a ludicrous Red Indian weather chant (with cod-opera middle eight). Blue skies? When we gazed upwards, it was at a firmament the colour of boil-washed vests. It was like living inside Tupperware.

But not even the dull drear of a north-west sky could stop Wilmslow dreams from shining. They glittered like money. They gleamed like money. They *were* money. Say it loud: we're *nouveaux riche* and we're proud. There was a TV programme made about it in the 1980s. In Wilmslow, giggled the commentator, the 'house without the swimming pool is the odd one out'; then there were lots of shots of fur shops and car showrooms. I watched the programme: I was miffed by it. Not because we didn't have a swimming pool, I didn't care about that; but because I knew the other, darker side of Wilmslow. I knew that it wasn't all designer labels and ditsy housewives. There were charity shops (two of them), and a council estate (with an unfortunately wimpy name. The local hoolies came staight outta Lacey Green). There was crime too: one time I came home from school to find a policewoman taking notes in our kitchen. Some pervert had stolen my mum's bras off the washing line. Either that, or the thief was just worried about them getting rained on.

Now, I look back on Wilmslow in those cocksure, cash-happy, pool-and-paying-school days, and I consider that telly programme and I think: fair enough. I mean, in the eighties, Wilmslow was flaunting it big style. Wilmslow was flaunting it with such dedication, such desperate determination, that it had its very own, gold-coloured credit card. The Wilmslow Card. Imagine that. A suburb so convinced of its staggering superiority that it invents its own in-town identification, its own *currency*. What did Wilmslow think it was? Monaco? Anyway, the Wilmslow Card was available to those residents whose incomes were rated chunky enough to deserve one. It could be flexed within several Wilmslow outlets, to buy sunspecs, or china fruit. It proved such a success that if you were on an aeroplane due to land at Manchester Airport, when the hostess came round with the duty-free trolley, the airflight announcer would say: 'All our duty-free goods are available for purchase by cash or credit card. We are sorry but the Wilmslow Card is not acceptable.' That still makes me laugh.

Then, Wilmslow was so desirable an area, so riotously, famously, fabulously bourgeois that celebrities were proud to bring their families there, to shop for china fruit, or even to live. It was where footballers resided, like Man City's Asa 'Hole In The' Hartford, and telly stars, like Gordon 'Krypton Factor' Burns and William 'Ken Barlow' Roache. In fact, telly stars queued up to pick Wilmslow not only as their home, but as their point of existential crisis also: vis, Stuart Hall, cleared of shoplifting sausages from Safeways in 1991 (apparently he thought the cashier knew he'd be back to pay later). Alex 'Hurricane' Higgins, who lived down the road in Prestbury, was married in Wilmslow Parish Church, and all his snooker chums held up their cues in a triumphal wedding arch. I remember the picture on the front page of the *Wilmslow World*. But the marriage didn't last.

I left Wilmslow when I was eighteen, went to university and moved to London. There I discovered that, although everyone in Manchester had told me I was posh, in fact, I wasn't at all. In Manchester, if you earnt enough money to buy a comfortable house, you were to the manor born; in London, if you decorated it with pastel flowered sofas and matching stick-on wall borders, you were common. Worse: you were suburban.

Which, of course, is what I was. And try as I did to disguise it – by going to scummy gigs and snotty art galleries, continental cafés and capital parties, by drinking in bars the size of toilets in a city the size of the world – my bourgeois background would keep bubbling up. There I'd be, Ms City-Slick, discussing films or trousers as though I knew an iota about either, when my mind would be overtaken by a dreadful home movie of my adolescent self, shrink-wrapped in pale pink New Man stretch corduroy, queuing to see Kramer Vs Kramer. Such flashbacks could occur at any moment, so I made every effort to avoid my past. I'd recoil from wheel-along suitcases, run from ruched blinds. I'd play deaf to code-words like 'time-share',

'XJS', 'Martinique', I'd flinch when I heard Shakatak or Sade or Freeez. I refused point blank to go to garden centres or ever to learn to play golf. I burnt every photo of my teenage root perm. But, sometimes, at home, in private, I'd slap on the fake tan and day-dream of a soft-top Mercedes.

And after a while, I discovered that there were plenty of others like me. You'd be chatting to some London sophisticate about politics or music or telly, and they'd suddenly let slip that they came from the outskirts of Swindon, or from Croydon, or Surbiton, or Sutton Coldfield. But when I asked them for specifics, they'd get all embarrassed and start making jokes about twitching curtains and two-point-four Volvos.

I began to wonder: what was so terrible about coming from suburbia? More to the point: how would you find your way back again? None of the ex-suburbanites seemed to know where suburbia was, exactly, other than it included the particular town that they'd run away from. But if you wanted to be accurate about it, then the suburbs are just outside the outer city, so that Withington is a suburb of Manchester, Brixton one of London's. And clearly, those lively, interesting, mixed-up places were not what we were refusing to talk about.

Perhaps we meant satellite towns: ones that had been joined to the city by motorways and housing developments. That fitted in with Wilmslow, but what about Droylsden, or Rochdale? In the end, suburbia didn't seem to be a geographically distinct place at all. It was instead a manner of living, an attitude to life, an atmosphere. And it was a mirage. It was like the true North Pole: you could be standing on it and you'd never know unless you had the right instruments, because –

well, because it looked just like everywhere else. It blended into the background.

Still, there were a few clues. For a start, it wasn't just ex-suburbanites who hated the place. Everyone did. Every time it was mentioned – on the news, in newspapers or magazines – it was referred to sneeringly, snottily. Suburbia was looked down upon, except in sitcoms, and even then it had the mickey thoroughly hoovered out of it. The press made nasty comments about Neighbourhood Watch and wife-swapping; cultural commentators laughed at its small 'c' conservatism; audiences gave canned titters at its transparent snobbery. If it was illustrated, the picture was of row upon row of modern, semi- or fully-detached houses that all looked exactly the same.

I thought that suburbia might, in fact, be Middle England (although I'd talked to Scottish people and they'd recognised the place. Interestingly, not a single Welsh or Irish person, northern or southern, said they came from suburbia). So I read a few articles about it. The two certainly sounded like the same spot. Neither seemed to be easily pin-pointed (no precise map co-ordinates), but both were effortlessly, endlessly caricatured.

Middle England, said the *Guardian*, is 'Neighbourhood Watch, Gordon's Gin, Enid Blyton, framed pictures of botanical illustrations, Ford Mondeo, Antiques Roadshow, Watchdog, Scouts and Brownies, collecting silver, or Victoriana, or china dolls'. Suburbia, said the *Mail*, is a place with 'gardens for their children to play in, potting sheds where Dad can propogate his cacti, decent schools for the kids, easy access to the city where they have their jobs'. Which certainly narrowed it down.

10

For a time, I forgot about suburbia. Then one day, in the late 1990s, when I was over thirty and over caring what other people thought of me, I woke up in a mucky London flat and got up and walked to the mirror and this is what I saw.

A woman whose hair was dyed a little too blonde; whose dress-sense was a little too young; who was wearing blue nail varnish and a good slather of self-tanning lotion; who drove a turquoise soft-top car; who had given up on black clothes years before in favour of pastel-hued sportswear; who wore pink pearly lipstick and read celebrity biographies and loved ickle puppies and thought it would be brilliant to have a smart kitchen. And I thought: look at you, woman, your roots are showing. You better go and reclaim your past.

So l drove up to Wilmslow and stayed for a time and had a good nosy around. I holed up in my old room, in amongst the pink and the grey and the flowered curtains and the white wardrobe; and I went out, into the recently pedestrianised centre, to the shops and the bars, and onto the new bypass, away into the countryside.

It was 1997. I'd left home in 1985. Things had changed. Like everywhere else, Wilmslow had suffered in the recession of the early nineties. It had taken the slump very badly, because it had believed so wholeheartedly in Maggie's dream – small businesses, big cars, paying schools, credit cards, mortgage living. It had been shattered when that dream had disappeared. Or more specifically, when the dream backfired.

During the high-living eighties, snotty little Wilmslow had refused to let several chainstores locate in its centre: too

common, not 'villagey' enough. One of those it refused was
Marks and Spencer. But in 1995, Marks and Spencer built its
biggest store outside London, on the new bypass, just outside
Wilmslow. Traffic poured there, and to the other mega-mar-
kets – John Lewis, Tesco, B&Q – that joined M&S; traffic that
streamed along the freeway, straight to the free parking without
even troubling Wilmslow's outskirts, let alone its cliquey, bou-
tiquey centre. People travelled from as far away as Leeds.

My mum told me about the new Marks's; though she seemed
far more fascinated by the swathes of tarmac that surrounded it.
'There's all those spaces and yet, still, sometimes you have to
park in Tesco's next door and walk over,' she said. 'And you
know Tesco's had that twenty-four hour shopping, just for the
Christmas week? Well I went on the Monday night at about ten
o'clock and it was chock full. The security guards linked arms
across the front of the shop because there were so many people
inside. The twenty-four hours shopping's permanent now. Do
you think it's starting to spit? I might just nip and bring the
sheets in.'

Mum said that she didn't mind the new shops, but that she
felt sorry for the old ones, so she tended to shop there.
Supporting local retailers against the overblown corporate new-
comers: a commendable decision. Except that the shops she
felt sorry for were Wilmslow's Safeway's and Sainsbury's supermarkets – 'They're almost morgues, these days' – which seemed
misplaced sympathy to me, like sending your pension to Sporty,
as opposed to Posh, because she hasn't got a millionaire under
her duvet just at the minute.

My dad, however, has no qualms about bypass shopping.

He worships B&Q. In fact, in the years since I had left home, he had transformed the garage – once used for, you know, storing a car – into an elaborate shrine to his fave DIY chain. There was no longer room enough even for a foldaway Mini: all available space had been taken up by twirly screw drawers and special tool racks; by cupboard upon tiny compartmented cupboard of nifty implements: nails, rulers, saws, hammers, wrenches, yankers, twisters, whackers, filler-inners, knock-em-downers, smash-em-into-little-piecers-and-then-start-all-over-againers. They stretched to the ceiling. They covered the floor space. If a serial killer had been looking for a private workshop with equipment to make that special cupboard-under-the-stairs, with dismembering facilities, my dad could have rented for a handsome profit.

Dad was always a collector of stuff: tools, musical instruments, crossword puzzle solvers, Victorian books with etchings of wafty fairy folk. I'm sure that one of the reasons why my parents were so happy to live in suburbia was that the houses there provided him with space to store his junk, whilst also leaving entire rooms free for my mum to stand in the middle of and worry about the state of the carpet.

I ventured into the garage, to talk to Mum as she loaded the washing machine, which stood on a small oasis of lino in the corner. She was explaining about the instant death of Wilmslow's retail life that the bypass and superstores had caused, about how many shops were boarded up, how the council had tried to revive things by pedestrianising the main shopping street, but it hadn't seemed to work. The Wilmslow Card had long since been abandoned. Mum reeled off a list of shops that had shut – Johnson's the Stationers, the Mac Fisheries, the International Store, Timpson's shoe shop, Gilbert's Sports. As she talked, I looked up, to one of Dad's many high shelves, and caught sight of the long furl of family tent. God, that tent. Symbol of holidays past: home from holiday home. Both my parents had a strong, yet warped, work ethic: for them, toil was never done, even after work, even on vacation. Not for us the lazy pleasure of a hotel or holiday camp. Camping was the only option that afforded my dad the opportunity to continue his home improvements and Mum reassuringly unlimited housework worries.

We'd always stay at a 'family' campsite, meaning it was laid out exactly like a suburban housing estate, down to the gravel driveways, and we'd always take half our real house with us there, under a tarpaulin on the roof-rack of the car. Putting The Tent Up was a ritual that took quite some time. Our tent was an orange and blue number with plastic side windows (curtained) and three zip-up bedroom compartments. Its erection was achieved in long-suffering, pre-Gortex-and-little-whippy-sticks stages. First, construct the roof-frame, checking the little coloured tape on each metal pole and skewering your brother with the pointy end; then hang the canvas and raise the tent to its knees; next, fold your back in half hoiking the whole thing up onto its last legs. Peg out. Find the torch and make huge V-sign shadows on the tent wall at passers-by. Finally, run away with the mallet to inflict pain upon those smaller than yourself instead of helping your mother hang out the washing.

The next two weeks would pass in a joyous blur of Swingball, violent argument and sausages-and-beans-from-the-same-tin. At least, for me and Toby: my parents were usually involved with some tent improvement or other – my dad inventing new ways to make the zip function more smoothly, Mum trying to Shake N Vac the gravel. When they were done, we'd get on with enjoying ourselves. We'd drive for hours to gawk at real-life still-working witch-dunking stools. We bought pet stones from craft fairs. We went to the seaside.

This last me and Toby liked the best, though it did entail Putting The Windbreak Up – similar to Putting The Tent Up, but without the torch. The Windbreak was as essential to sea-side life as a bucket and spade. With it, you could curl up next to its stripey wall, pull all limbs inside your jumper like a hiber-nating tortoise, force meat paste sandwiches through chattering teeth and know you were having a good time. Without it, your belongings would race each other to hurtle away from you, bowling down the beach in a Force Ten gale. You'd spend all afternoon chasing after them and you'd still have died of hypothermia by teatime. We never got much of a suntan on our holidays.

I gazed at the tent for so long that I didn't realise that my mum had whipped back into the kitchen. She was doing the bins. Her voice came wrapped in a bunny bag. 'This bypass is all very well,' she rustled, 'but it's not the hot topic at the moment.' Apparently, the bypass and its superstore charms had had to fight for local front page attention. There'd been far too much else going on. 1997 was turning out to be a red letter year for Wilmslow.

The first thing to happen was that it was bombed by the IRA. That had happened in early spring. No one had been hurt – the bomb had been left at the railway station, and went off in the middle of the night – but, for a brief, heady interlude, national news had begun with a map of the North West and an arrow pointing right to Wilmslow. I thought back to the last act of terrorism to take place in my home town. In the early 1980s, a member of Wilmslow's disaffected youth expressed his small town Cheshire angst by hurling a milk-bottle and a match at a long-standing representative of the ruling establishment, i.e. a tree. Ooh, narky, as we said at the time. That petrol bomb made the headlines of the *Wilmslow World*. The IRA bomb didn't, but that was because the *Wilmslow World* was no more: the *Wilmslow Express and Advertiser* went to town on it, though, understandably enough. Mum said that no one ever found out why the IRA picked Wilmslow station as a strategic target. Trains from London hadn't stopped there for years. 'Perhaps the terrorists just didn't like the hanging baskets,' said my mum, whipping out the Mr Muscle and bearing down upon the cat.

Now, after all that hoo-haa had barely subsided, Swampy had come to town. Mum, between foraying attacks upon the cooker hob, reported that he was holed up in the fields near Manchester Airport, just down the road from my parents' house. He and his partners in grime were trying to delay the building of a new airport runway, through their usual tactics of burrowing and tree-squatting; and, as usual, they trailed cameras and reporters in their wake. It sounded terrifically exciting: the news was all over Wilmslow. I left Mum doing a complicated juggling manoeuvre involving Pyrex bowls, pastoral scene coasters and Safeway's own brand salad dressing, and set out to have a look.

16

I parked up where she'd told me to – 'Opposite what used to be the Valley Lodge Hotel, dear' – and walked straight into a dread-heads vs developers confrontation. It wasn't at all what I expected. Yes, the protestors were dressed according to convention – that is, in eco-guerrilla style: big clumpy boots, big clumpy hair, diddy little earrings in uncomfortable places – and yes, the security guards were also as you'd imagine – big clumpy boots, big clumpy heads, diddy little radios to call up big clumpy reinforcements. But the way the two sides battled was bizarre.

They were gathered in a small dip at the side of a dual carriageway, by a serious-looking fence. A tractor-type digger vehicle was parked there; the security guards had made a silent standing circle around it, facing outwards. The eco-hairies surrounded the guards, in a more disorganised manner: they kept cracking jokes or stepping to the side to smoke a roll-up. But the hairies carried bits of chain, and hand-cuffs, and every so often a few of them would make a run at the security guards, try to break through the circle. It took me a while to realise why: they were trying to get past and clamp themselves to the digger, so that it couldn't be used. It was a very difficult thing to do, because it was all the security guards were trying to stop. Time and time again, a hairy would half-turn his back on the guards, then run for a gap, and the security would just sandwich together, grab the hairy by the scruff of the neck and push him off. It was like that game What's The Time Mister Wolf, except there were about twenty Mister Wolves and they never turned away and it was always Dinner Time. The ecos didn't have much of a chance. One rainbow-tressed girl had managed

17

it: she sat atop the bonnet in triumph, her wrist chained to a side mirror. She shouted for someone to chuck her a roll-up.

The police were there, doing nothing much except filming everyone who wasn't in a security uniform, including me. I waved. Swampy was there, too, looking about twelve years old. He was very pretty and very, very mucky: the filthiest of the lot, a just-dug-up King Edward with straggly roots for hair. He said, 'We know we won't stop them, but we can make it take them a really long time.' What was really surprising was that some local Wilmslow residents were there as well: not quite chaining themselves to diggers, but standing awkwardly by their parked cars, murmuring encouragement to the protestors. Swampy said, 'People come to the site and give us hampers of food.'

I went back home and told Mum about it and she spat out a mouthful of clothes pegs and coloured pens (she's a teacher) to say that Swampy was all very well, but 'It's not what they're really bothered about around here.' Duh. Of course not. It was 1997. It was almost May. The General Election was coming up. And Wilmslow was part of the Tatton constituency. The Battle for Tatton was turning out to be a bloody one, a war for local hearts and local votes between the boyish Neil Hamilton (Con), and the saintly Martin Bell (Indep), with the formidable Christine Hamilton dashing around barking instructions at the bewildered voters like an out-of-control Cuckoo's Nest Nurse Ratchett. Neil and Christine were well respected around Wilmslow. After all, they'd been around long enough to merit several mentions in William 'Ken Barlow' Roache's autobiography, *Ken And Me*. In his book, Ken made it plain that he thinks politics rather trivial – it 'deals with the physical aspects of life and I was always more concerned with the metaphysical'; still, Neil and Christine did make an impression when he first met them at a craft exhibition at Wilmslow Library. Now they are all 'close friends'. Ken Barlow is a man of some local standing. I remember when he had his hair trimmed just before me, and the stylist was still shaking when it was time for my layering.

My mum had done a straw poll amongst her friends. 'Sleaze' Hamilton or 'Please' Bell? They'd all insisted that they would never vote Labour, and that what they really wanted was a Conservative candidate that they could believe in. As my mum said, 'They'd vote for a donkey round here, if it wore a blue ribbon.' But it seemed as though they really had turned against Hamilton. My mum's friends said things like, 'Hamilton's not the kind of person I want to represent me', 'He's arrogant and cynical', 'In any other company, he would have been suspended'. But Martin Bell was 'a credible chap', and, more importantly, he wasn't Labour, so that was all right. Mum reported that they would have preferred Terry Waite as a candidate, though. He was born down the road, in Styal.

My stay in Wilmslow had made me wonder. Everything about it had changed: its politics, its small boutique supremacy, its disdain for grubby Lefties, its glitz, its smugness. Now it was a political hot potato; yet a town without a centre or real purpose, literally bypassed. I thought: was it just Wilmslow, or had all suburbia altered? I decided I would strike out and see. I would tour Britain, travel through the provinces, visit the edge-towns and the new towns, the bypasses and the supermarkets, the almost-countryside, the nearly somewheres. I wanted to find out if any of my – our – long-held, long-in-the-tooth assumptions about Middle Britain held any truth any more.

Besides, I needed to get out of my parents' house. Not because I didn't love them, but because they will keep doing that parent thing: going on about people you can't remember, and hoovering under your feet. Plus, their house was just too cosy. I couldn't stay any longer in its plump-cushioned, repointed, flowery-bordered atmosphere, with its particular scent: cat nibbles and carpet shampoo, mown lawns and Immac-ed legs, regularly Flashed lino. I was starting to smell the same. I was starting to meld with the soft furnishings. I needed to leave, to drive off and breathe in some good strong exhaust fumes or I'd never get up off the sofa again.

2

get your kicks on the B156

I remember learning to drive very clearly. My driving instructor was a mild, balding man called Mr Wilson, who had a nervous blink that you could force into a full-face twitch without too much effort. Initially, though, he gave out the traditional mirror, signal, manoeuvre bit without a trace of impatience; and he wasn't a dirty perv who put his hand on your knee, unlike some driving instructors that my friends had told me about. Mind you, I lagged several years behind many of my friends in that department, being too cheery and pudding-faced to attract much male attention. I had a 'nice personality'. I also had what was then known as a footballer's haircut, which wasn't much cop on a footballer, let alone a seventeen-year-old girl –

blonde-streaked and spikeyish on top, with straggly length at the back. What with that and my turquoise mascara, I can't imagine that I caused respectable Mr Wilson too many sleepless nights.

What I do remember him getting edgy about was my determined refusal to stop. Learner drivers never want to stop. You don't see the point: it took you all that faff to get into fourth gear, all that checking the mirror and releasing the handbrake and finding the biting point (not revving too much, not riding the clutch) and up into second and check that mirror and select third gear whilst steering and putting your left foot down at the same time and oh yes check the bloody mirror again, and third gear is never where you think it is and you keep putting it into reverse by mistake and there's that terrifying grinding noise and . . . you're hardly going to want to go through all that again, are you? I used to approach driving as though I was in a bumper car: just try and wiggle through, just steer and hope for glory. This was incorrect, technically, and dangerous. Mr Wilson applied his special instructor's brakes on many occasions, until I learnt to do so myself. And even then, with a learner's unerring instinct, I usually managed to miss the brake and stomp on the accelerator instead.

Mr Wilson and I would rumble bumpily around Wilmslow: from leafy Pownall Park along past the Post Office and the tricky left turn towards Safeway's and the Parish Church. Sometimes you wouldn't turn but drive up over the traffic lights, past the train station, then head out into the countryside. But mostly, you'd aim wherever there was a roundabout and a quiet cul-de-sac, to practise three-point turns. You were usually interrupted by another car, when you were hovering, gear-grunting, brake-bound, mid-road somewhere around the two-and-a-half point stage.

There was quite a bit of traffic in Wilmslow then. It was several years before the bypass would be built, and the town was thriving: bustling with smart boutiques – Country Casuals, Samuel Cooper's, Jaeger – that attracted well-off women from all over the county, women who wouldn't dream of travelling into Manchester to shop, *Well it's a bit rough and I'm always worried leaving the car.* Most of them only used their car for local journeys anyway: their husband's company car was used for travelling further afield, because the petrol was paid for. Other ladies, whose gents had not made the fleet car brigade, could be spotted every afternoon in the car park in front of the station, waiting to meet their husbands from the train. Each would sit in the vehicle that she drove to the station, sit quite still, hands in lap, not listening to the radio for fear of running down the battery. When her husband arrived, suited, brief-cased, paunched with responsibility, his wife would get out of the car, walk round and swap to the passenger seat so that he could drive home.

Weekends were for longer trips, when the men were free to drive. Off on the motorway (the M56 was just around the corner), out with the family, take the kids to football, or dance class, nip off for shopping expeditions in other satellite towns. And on Sundays, as the day slipped into evening, with the family at home, preparing tea, doing homework, phoning grandparents, the company men would take their company cars on a good long run, along the country lanes to Mobberley, to

Alderley Edge, to Prestbury, beyond. They'd cruise comfortably on leather seats, air-conditioned, toasty-toed, alone, purring through the country miles in company Rovers, company Volvos, company BMWs. They'd drive and drive. But they weren't aimless. They had to keep their mileage up to get their company car tax rebate.

The car is the key to life in the suburbs: there's not much you can do without it. You can get a train to work, but you'll have to drive to the station. You can pop to the corner shop, but you'll end up driving to the supermarket. You can walk to school, but if you're going out later, your mum will have to drive you there. There are buses in suburbia, and trains, to and from; but public transport won't get you to the bowling alley, or that nice little country pub, or to the golf course, or over to Gran's.

Like everyone else I knew, we drove everywhere when I was young. My mum and dad motored for miles, hours to work, in Salford and Whalley Range. Every day, they'd commute for over eighty minutes each. But it wasn't enough. They'd come home, have a cup of tea, and get straight back behind the wheel. The north-west is a viper's nest of motorways. My mum and dad drove them all.

Outside school hours, my brother and I were such regular back-seaters that we could have been substituted with nodding dogs. Our parents drove us to Stockport, for the precinct, to Manchester, for the Arndale, to Altrincham, for the market and the B&Q; and regularly, every holiday, up the M6 to Barrow-in-Furness, to see my mum's mum, and down the M6 to Surrey, to see my dad's parents. They drove together and apart, with one child or two, just up the road to the garage, or the long way round to the supermarket, or away to see the new housing development out by the canal. We'd even drive to go for a walk. Another reason for us to go camping every summer – aside from the DIY and housework thrills – was that it was the holiday option that involved the most time in the car. Up we'd get at 5 a.m. and trundle off to Norfolk, or Cornwall, or Aviemore, or anywhere else in Britain far enough away to involve a good forty-eight hours' hard motoring. We never went to the Lake District, for instance. Call that a holiday? It was scarcely an hour-and-a-half on the motorway.

Eventually, my brother and I developed specific in-car behaviour. Not for us your common-or-garden 'Are we there yet?' choruses, punctuated with quiet times to be sick. No: Toby and I *worked* in the car. We had to. You see, despite all his practice, my dad was a terrible driver. He never seemed to be quite awake – pootling along at 20 m.p.h. in fourth gear, pulling a U-turn across three lanes because he'd spotted an interesting windmill, making harrumphing noises and then suddenly accelerating just to prove he was fully alert. It didn't fool us. We were terrified. So we never, ever shut up. We had to keep yakking to keep him awake. It was life or death. It was talk or walk. It was chat or splat. We did shifts. Subjects like the weather were strung out for days. Entire Abba LPs were sung in the round, with descant and formation dancing. To this day, if you show me a pub sign, I can riff on it for a full half-hour, without repetition, deviation, hesitation or change in high-pitched whiney tone.

I learnt early that a car is a suburban essential. But so are lawn mowers, fridge-freezers, fabric conditioner, worming tablets. Yet a car has always been more, meant more, than any of these. In the suburbs, a car isn't only a necessity, it's the ticket to all your dreams.

Actually, a car is the only one of your dreams you're likely to see come true. I have a little theory of motoring, and this is it. The car is capitalism's sop. The advertising industry spends more money selling us cars than any other durable: over £833 million in Britain in 1997. Advertisers understand that you may not ever run a company or own a mansion or have rails of couture clobber or go to Bali on your holidays – but, for a few hundred quid, you, too, can buy a car. You, too, can spend your way to insta-status. You, too, can find the hero inside yourself (and if you suck in your stomach he might look like Steve McQueen). You, too, can buy your freedom. And then slowly murder it in a traffic jam alongside everyone else.

Through adverts, films, music, photography, through our small ideas of liberty, cars have become our freedom fighters. Drive and you are powerful, unshackled, liberated. Shuck off the office job, the rows at home, that niggling failing feeling, and drive for your life. Oh yes, anyone who's aspirational – and that's everyone in the suburbs – knows the perfect power of the perfect motor. There's no surprise in the middle-class cliché of Washing The Car. Your vehicle is your fantasy. You've got to keep it buffed.

So, of course, at seventeen, I learnt to drive. That's all every out-of-town teenager wants to do. And on 26 June 1984, I passed my driving test, first go. I was inordinately proud of myself, right up until 30 June 1984, when I crashed. I had a

Saturday job in Woolworth's and my mum had lent me her car to drive there as a treat. After work, still dressed in my light blue, wipe-clean overall, I merrily scooted the Strada up the ramp to the top floor of Safeway's multi-storey. I was playing a Monkees' tape at full whack as I whipped into a space, and the tape was still running as I missed. I went straight into the side of a bright red VW that was parked in the bay next to mine.

The owners were inside. They were not best pleased. Out they got, all indignant and in-the-right, and told me that it would cost at least £100 for a new wing. I burst into tears, bluey streaks coursing behind my NHS specs to merge with the collar of my Crimplene overall. 'Daydream Believer' was still wafting from the stereo, and I did so want to believe, but there I was, an overalled gonk in a badly-lit multi-storey, my enveloped earnings all hot in my pocket, a day's work adding up to a tenth of the damage I'd caused in a few lax seconds. It wasn't my idea of glamour.

But still, I didn't lose faith. I was a child of the suburbs: I *knew* that driving was great. My first proper job ambition, at the age of ten, had been to be a long-distance lorry driver. And at seventeen, I wanted to drive myself to places, not just to rely on my parents to do so. I wanted to drive fast to places that my parents didn't know about.

I saw other teenagers, my contemporaries, in Golfs, or Escorts, or Minis, or even BMWs. They revved at the roundabouts, posed composedly, luminous jewellery clattering on wrists, highlights glinting in the traffic lights. I was sick with longing. But I couldn't yet afford my own car. So I borrowed my mum's, and drove all around south Manchester, picking up friends, dropping them off, just driving. I started going to nightclubs in central Manchester, to the recently opened Haçienda, and the Ritz, which was a traditional ballroom with a sprung floor that had an 'alternative' night on Mondays (a pound in and a free bottle of Pils if you got there before 10 p.m.). They were very different from the nightclubs nearer Wilmslow. In Wilmslow, tans were tuned to tikka and night-clubs were in hotels – the Queensgate, the Pinewood, the Valley Lodge – places with flashing dancefloors and ultraviolet teeth and legs like Spanish ham. In the Ritz and the Haçienda, white people were pale and proud. They glistened with ill-health. Their faces were the colour of mashed potato. They kept their overcoats on, coughed a lot and never wore any shade lighter than black.

Sometimes, I drove to the pub, drank a few blackcurrant and sodas (I was saving for contact lenses), and then drove about after closing time. I would drop people off at various houses and then happily motor a long route home. I was driving for driving's sake, for that specific liberation of cruising by myself, along roads I'd never been along alone before. I was at that just-learnt stage where you rejoice that no one has to sit in with you, you revel in your independence and power, *I can go exactly where I like, no one can stop me, I could drive to London if I wanted, I could drive to China if I wanted.*

But it was even better when a few of us were off out, when I beetled halfway into town for a quick drink, picking up a couple of friends on the way; then stuffed the car so full of bodies that it creaked, turned up the music, opened the windows to let out the smoke and hammered through Rusholme and into

Manchester. There's not much that can beat that feeling, even now, of music and motor and people yapping nonsense and knowing that there's stuff to come, that the evening's not even started, that you and this fantastic machine are getting closer, being drawn in, towards the lights and the dark and the possibilities, towards the noise that keeps you up and out, the noise that keeps you awake, that drowns the other noise that won't let you sleep.

And driving like that always leads to other places – other clubs that start when the first ones finish; strange, rammed parties in council flats with no lights except in the kitchen; round the place of some people that you never met before, for a spliff and a chat and music music music. Driving like that opens your life up, flicks the ribbons of new experiences so they stretch out before you like shiny roads, for you to cruise along to who knows where. Eventually, driving like that leads to stopping. Stopping in some lay-by and leaving the tape on and getting into the back seat and pushing the front seats up against the window and grappling with zips and tongues and twisting clothes and limbs because there's nowhere, really, for you to go, because your parents are in and the clubs are all shut and there's only the car that can give you the space to discover what you are and who you like and who you are and what you like.

Now I'm a grown-up, I can pet in indoor comfort and the car that I drive is my own. It's a Peugeot 504 with a soft-top, and it's over twenty-five years old. It's a pain; it has the kind of problems that elderly cars always have, meaning not the type that you can nip into Kwik-Fit to sort out before you go to work. My car is an attention seeker and a money pig. Every month I take a significant portion of my salary and throw it at the car and the car makes an ungrateful coughing sound before hoovering all the cash up and chuffing a sky-high column of black smoke out of its rear in derisive gratitude. But still, I love it. That's my darlin', I think fondly, as an injection pipe cracks and the engine bursts into flames.

But I can't lose my teenage fire over cars. It's warped a little, from panting lust into a love that's more mature, but it's still there. And I know I'm not the only one who feels like this. Not everyone, perhaps, would love my car, but everyone loves their own. To anyone else, a particular motor may just be a rusting old Fiat Panda, but to the owner, it's special. They could pick it out of any number of other rusting Pandas. They know how to operate its tape deck without looking, how to get the sticky boot lid to open, how to make the seat-belts work; they know the exact significance of the sticker in the back window and who left the Quavers packet stuffed into the passenger seat. I think that anti-car campaigners, puffed-up no-bypass proselytisers forget about things like that. They forget that people are senti-mental about their cars, that they love them. You love your car like a teenager, like an adult: because of its romance, its poten-tial and because your car is part of you – well, a good part of your savings, anyway. Not only do you invest it with totemistic power, you invest it with your history, your personality, you hope that it says something about you. Cars are the outer expression of inner go-faster stripes.

Of course, some vehicles show their go-faster stripes more

obviously than others. Some cars want to be noticed. Some motors scream 'MONEYSPEEDPOWERTHRILLS' so deafeningly loud you can hear them in the next street. Even when they're parked up. I'd noticed several such fashion-passion wagons on my recent Wilmslow visit, tearing up the by-roads, screeching from the lights. They were rainbow coloured – pink, lime green, yellow, red – and they were noisy, leaving bystanders with a heart-attack drive-by impression of juddering bass and rumbling engine, of throbbing motor fire. I decided to hunt one down.

And I found it in Northampton, of all places, at half-past nine on a freezing winter night, in a godforsaken no-storey car park. I stood and looked. It was impressive. So impressive, in fact, that Dave, standing next to me, accorded the object of our contemplation the highest of his accolades.

'Now that,' said Dave, in awe, 'is my idea of sex.'

We were gazing upon a car so pink that it made Barbara Cartland seem funereal. Every bit of it, save the windows, lights and wheels, was pinker than a pack of Panthers: the door handles, the headlight surrounds, the sills, the bumpers, the back spoiler – all gleaming like sunburnt Angel Delight, dazzling, obscene. Wow! that back spoiler was really something: vast, flat, jutting, springing from the boot like a big pink coffee table. The bumpers were huge too, plunging so low they'd scrape snails off the road, curving round to fat, deep wheels that left mere millimetres of air between themselves and the chassis. The wheels were snug to their pink rims, which flowed silkily into the wings, the doors, the side skirts, which skimmed the ground. The lines were fluid; everything about the car was smoothed and rounded, scooped in, curved out. The wing mirrors hugged and flexed to their doors. No sharp angles, no nips and tucks. No superfluous chroming or plastic, no badges to tell you what type of car this was, other than a tiny Ford logo at front and back.

I looked harder. Under all the exaggerated curves, the retina-wrecking paintwork, I could see the outline of a car that I knew. A Ford Escort. I asked Dave.

'It's an RS 2000,' he said, not looking at me, not taking his eyes from the pink vision. RS, I knew, stood for Rally Sport. The pink-mobile was a racing version of a Ford Escort.

Dave ran his hand gently along the bonnet. Through the side windows, I could see interior scaffolding poles, running from back shelf to roof to provide a roll-over bar. The poles were painted lime green, and beneath them, where the back seat should have been, were two of the biggest built-in car speakers I had ever seen. Someone opened the boot. It was full of winking, blinking electronica. I counted six amps, aside from all the other flashing boxes.

Dave and I took a step back. We had to. First, we were getting crowded out by the cluster of spectators, goggling respectfully at the big pink beast. Second, someone had pressed the on-switch on the stereo. The bass started shaking my loose change. And this was over the sound of the engine, which was revving and booming like Concorde with a cough. Clearly, someone had spent some money on customising the motor within, as well as the body without.

What a monster! What a car! And what a scene! I left Dave to his worship and walked away to get an overview. God, it was cold! The car park was a third full of parked cars; fuller of revving ones. Opposite me, on the far side of the pay-and-display, were Bar Koda café-bar, Visage nightclub, Aldi supermarket. Behind me was the road, a short burst of one-way between roundabouts. And before me, spread higgledy-piggledy across the car park, in small knots and smoke-breathed clusters, were at least 250 young men. All in sportswear, all in 'just stepped out of the sheep shearer's' crop, all revved up because they'd found some place to go, they'd found something that was going on. Energy fizzed off them like too much aftershave. They were elated, feverish, running from pack to pack, pushing past each other, craning heads to see the action.

And the action? Well, it wasn't the twenty or so women there, though several were dressed for arrest. None of the men gave them a glance. And it wasn't the police, though a squad car was parked, and a lone policeman was surveying the scene as obviously and authoritatively as he could. And it certainly wasn't the prospect of an evening at Visage nightclub. No, what the boys were all worked up about, what they were panting, laughing, crowing over were the trouser-popping, heart-stopping assets of – you guessed it – a load of cars.

Some of the cars, like the pink RS, were stationary. Their owners leant against them with watchful eyes, with the boot open to display stereo hardware that would shame most front rooms, the bonnet up to show the engine – fat-piped, gleaming, chromed. More excitingly, some of the cars were bumping around the car park, accelerating wildly, screeching to a halt, bunny-hopping past the police, music pumping, crowd jumping.

But what really caught the eye were the cars that were doing both. *There's one!* A turquoise Peugeot 205, with the suede-headed owner in the driver's seat. He was revving the engine in first gear, pushing it as hard as it would go, whilst pulling back on the handbrake. Twenty or so other men leant on the bonnet with their considerable full weight, stopping the car from actually moving off. The engine pushed the car forward. The men held it back. The Peugeot's tyres squealed and popped like piglets being thrown on to a fire. Towers of acrid white smoke, from the tyres, from the labouring engine, soared and billowed into the freezing night air, until the car was invisible, lost in crowd and cloud.

'Burn-out,' said Debbie, nonchalantly, next to me. She and her friends Louise and Tori had come down for the evening. The girls watched with glittering, experienced eyes as the tyres of the little 205 whined and smoked amidst the cheering rabble. Burn-out. 'Sometimes, they do it til they burst 'em,' said Louise, but the driver stopped short and the screeching ceased. The pack moved on.

We were standing next to Debbie's black XR2.

'Someone's got money to burn,' commented Debbie, lighting a fag. 'Those tyres'll cost. Mine cost,' she confided. 'Well, they would have done, if I'd paid for them.'

Louise and Tori giggled and shivered a little. They didn't possess a coat or a pair of tights between the three of them. They didn't care. Debbie, Louise and Tori were excited.

'We're here most Fridays, but it's never like this,' bubbled Tori, who was unemployed but had the look (and the skirt) of a girl that could get what she wanted.

'No, it's not,' agreed Louise (blonde, hot pants, 'key accounts administrator'). 'There's normally only three or four cars.'

'Yeah, but tonight, I've seen about five of my exes here,' laughed Debbie (scrapey pony-tail, high boots, nurse). 'Which is a bit worrying. *And,*' said Debbie, thoughtfully, 'the father of my child's somewhere around . . .'

Today's children of the suburbs know their motors. Not for them the faded glamour of a classic car, nor the economy of a little runabout, nor the prestige of a revered make (they rate Nissan over Jaguar). They judge their cars as everyone in their late teens and early twenties judges anything at all: does it make you tingle? Is it sexy? Thrilling? Fashionable? Does it play the right music?

They know from their parents that they need transport to get anywhere, and they know from their peers that it has to be the right kind. They were brought up in the Britain that's bypassed and superstored and multiplexed, and they were bred on sports-wear and designer logos – checking for the Nike swoosh, the Adidas three stripes, the horse and rider of Ralph Lauren Polo, the code letters that say it all: CK, D&G, DKNY. Plus, they were fed on house music – bangin' choons, happy hardcore, jungle, speed garage – with its easy companionship and mild anti-establishment attitudes. They mixed everything up, and they came up with their own rules, their own way of talking the talk, if not walking the walk. After all, why walk, when you can gun the accelerator?

The suburbs' almost-adults like cars: fast ones, hot ones, bright ones, loud ones, customised ones, the right ones. And these jumped-up kid brothers of the eighties boy-racers, these naughty daughters of the Wash-The-Car troopers – you see them everywhere. They're not extreme, they're commonplace. Every weekend, in small towns across the country, in Brighton, Hull, in Cheltenham, Aberdeen, Southend, Northampton, groups of young petrol-heads meet up in car parks or bus stations or along sea fronts. Mostly, it's car parks, because then they can't get arrested for speeding (car parks are private property). Necessarily, it's out of town: cities are too crammed, the roads too twisty, too peopled, with no room to manoeuvre. The car kids meet up in an informal way: there's no tickets, no alcohol, no food. No entertainment other than the cars, and the occasional flash of flesh (mooning through a side window is a popular way to make your point). There's just the cars, and the people. This is a car cruise.

I'd been told that approximately 5,000 people across the country go car-cruising at the weekend. And the figure can double in summer. Certainly there's enough to support umpteen magazines on the subject (*Max Power, Fast Car, Performance Ford, Performance VW*) and to have made one or two specialist shops (such as Xtreme, in Harlow) very rich indeed. There's also enough people involved to get the police worried; someone was killed in Brighton at a car cruise when a burn-out span out of control and ploughed into the crowd.

I'd had a look at the most popular car cruisers' magazine, *Max Power*. *Max Power* features readers and their customised cars, and it's a quick read for those of us who aren't whipped into a frenzy by lines like 'Rockford Fosgate EPX-2, 2x Rockford Fosgate RFA-412 crossovers', or 'slide throttle linkage, machined cam followers, solid lifters', or, indeed, by 'You're better off with a beer than a woman. You usually get great head out of a beer.' Still, after flicking through, I'd been intrigued enough to want to experience a car cruise for myself. So I'd trundled up the M1 in my trusty, uncustomised Peugeot, parked around the corner and walked over to stand in a freezing Northampton car park, to see what all the fuss was about.

After a couple of hours' mooching, I still didn't quite know. I could appreciate the atmosphere; the spontaneous gathering of a lot of people, their palpable excitement, the burn-outs, the bursts of music, the spark of rebellion – *no one asked us to come! the police don't want us here! this is happening without your consent!* – but I didn't really understand the cars. Why a Ford Escort and not a Ford Fiesta? Some of the writers from *Max Power* had turned up, so I thought I'd follow them for a while, for enlightenment. I caught up with one, called Proby, who was bounding about the car park, squirly hair ajiggle, checking cars, taking down owners' names and addresses for possible future magazine articles.

I watched Proby for a while, trying to spot what was special about the cars he chose. What seemed strange to me was the number of cars he snubbed. This was a car park, after all, and there were all sorts of vehicles available for admiration. I spotted a nicely kept Mercedes, only a few years old. It was roundly ignored, no doubt to the relief of its owners, had they been around to see the crowd. But so too was an open-top Jeep, parked up especially for the occasion. Its driver, late twenties, baseball cap, sat proud and lonely, wondering at the swarm of youth that goggled before an XR3, that gathered around a Corrado, looking, not touching, respectful, yearning, then poured past other irrelevant vehicles to another car. No one came to see his Jeep.

I asked Proby why he picked the cars he did. The clamour of engines, burn-outs, bass-bins the size of wheely-bins meant he had to shout. Proby bellowed about 'tuning, styling and ICE' (tuning: what was under the bonnet; styling: the bodywork; ICE: In Car Entertainment, what your mum would call the cassette deck), but I didn't really feel any the wiser. So Proby pointed out a car for me. He used the same phrase as Dave. 'That,' said Proby, 'is our readers' idea of sex.'

It was another Ford Escort, less wild-looking than the pink number, but with the same lowered sills and bumpers, the same big wheels. Under the bonnet, the engine sparkled.

'Se-ex,' repeated Proby. I looked again. Somehow, I remained in control.

I wandered off through the crowds to find Dave. Dave was wearing jeans and a baggy jumper with a huge D&G logo on the front. Dave was twenty-four. He told me that he used to work in an office, but he told his boss to stuff it.

'Why?' I asked, and Dave explained that *Max Power* had phoned him up and asked if he wanted his car – a Vauxhall Nova – to be featured in the magazine. They'd seen it at a cruise and taken his number. Dave couldn't believe his luck, couldn't believe that the mighty *Max Power* – his favourite magazine – wanted to write an article about him and his car. The photograph and interview were set up for mid-week. But at the last minute Dave found out that his boss wouldn't give him the time off: 'So I walked.'

'He puts his car before everything,' whispered Dave's girl-friend, a pale and beautiful blonde, sitting in Dave's car to keep warm. 'And he loves *Max Power*.'

I went to talk to another *Max Power* star. Ces, a panel fitter, a sleepy-eyed lunk of a man with hands like pink dustpans, was standing by *his* Ford RS 2000, which was silver. He had a *Max* issue open on the car's back shelf, open to page 52: the page that showed him and his RS. The headline read 'The Real Thing!' Ces told me that the work on the car had cost him £15,000, 'so far'. He'd done a lot of it himself, so the bill was relatively cheap. Although, he had fitted 18-inch wheels, and they'd been too big, they'd crucified the bodywork, so he'd had to downgrade to 17-inchers. Ces had had another car before, an Alfa, which he'd sold once he'd finished doing it up. 'But you never make the money back,' he said. He said he didn't mind though, he just liked having a project.

There were other car nuts about, lounging on their perfected dream machines, but I soon tired of talking specifications. Actually, I soon realised that I couldn't talk specifications, that once we'd gone past changing the air filter I was pretty much lost. So I went and found Debbie and Tori.

Debbie was in a mood. She said that the *Max Power* photographer kept trying to shoot up her skirt. 'If I wanted to show that pervert my knickers I would do,' she huffed.

Tori shrugged. 'I don't mind,' she said. 'I'll do anything.' Her eyes flicked around the car park.

'What's more important, the man or the car?' I wondered.

'Well, if he's got a Lada or a Skoda, then no chance,' mused Debbie. 'If it's a little 1.1 Fiesta, then maybe.'

'Sometimes you look at the car and think, yeah, nice,' said Tori. 'But then you look at his face and it's, no way.'

How did you get into cars?

'We all got into them 'cos of boyfriends, really,' said Deb.

By half-past eleven, I was getting the hang of it. I reckoned I could spot a car cruiser's car at twenty paces. It was all about performance; the opposite of my good-looking yet lumbering Peugeot. Car cruisers took dinkmobiles like Renault 5s, Peugeot 205s, Vauxhall Novas and made them run like performance cars. They started with the exhaust system: derestricted it, changed the manifold, the air filter, put in a chip which controlled the fuel injection – essentially, just made the whole thing work more efficiently. Then they moved on to the engine itself, and performed open heart surgery: modified it until it accelerated like it was hell-fuelled, until they had the bionic car.

The car styling, too, originally came out of performance. You lowered your car because that lowered the centre of gravity, so the car cornered better. You widened it for the same reason. You smoothed all the angles for better aerodynamics. But now it's just a fashion thing. I'd been told that there were very few real car buffs, very few people who could afford to spend the money and the man-hours tuning the engine so it ran like a rally car. And even if you could afford to beef up the engine, you then had to muster the hoik in the insurance premium. (Ces had told me he paid £2,000 a year.) Most people I talked to had jobs, but not jobs that paid that much.

Because of this, most of the cruisers were just into 'the lifestyle'. All they wanted was their car to look and sound good. They weren't that bothered about tuning, just styling. Eighteen-inch wheels, big bore exhausts, tinted windows, graphics (there's a car out there with *The Dog's Bollocks, Hello Pussy* written on the side), sideskirts and bumpers the same colour as the body. The styling says bad-ass, though the car's a pussycat, in the same way that too-big trousers say hardcore, though you work in marketing. The other aspects of a car cruiser's car – the colour and the music, the ICE – really were just fashion. There was no reason for them, other than they frightened other people, which is surely the only good reason for fashion, full-stop.

It was nearly midnight. The cruise was still going strong. Now that the pubs had shut, more cars were turning up, hustling into the pay-and-display playground, jumping for some fun. The air was thick with burning rubber and blistering music. The crowd had swelled to over 300. Young people and cars . . . I wondered if they'd still love their motors once they'd used them for commuting for twenty years. I decided that they would. That old car romance would still tickle.

I started chatting to Sandra, who had come from Milton Keynes with Ian, her boyfriend, and his Rover Vanden Plas. She was telling me that when she was pregnant with her little boy, Hayden, Ian asked her if she would help him put the engine back into the car. 'I got stuck underneath!' laughed Sandra. 'I couldn't get out because my stomach was too big!' I could see Hayden, asleep on the back seat. He didn't look too squished.

Sandra was talking, comparing how much time Ian spent

with Hayden as opposed to the Rover, when, suddenly, I felt the
night change. Some of the lads had begun to drive out of the car
park, out of the enclosed, private space, and they were belting
their cars down the short road, screeching round the roundabout, accelerating, racing, showing off. They tore past punter
drivers, undertook them, weaved past, waved as they did so.
Everyone in the car park started to pour on to the pavement, to
have a look at the speeding rebels.

Three policemen, the ones in the squad car, walked out into
the road and began to note down registrations. They did this
very obviously, standing on the roundabout so they could be
seen, warning the drivers with their presence. But they didn't
stop anyone. How could they? Because this was what it was all
about, all the burn-outs, the engine-popping, the revving, the
tyre-spinning. This was it, the buzz, the kick! The air hummed
with reckless possibility, sizzled with Friday night fire. An
orange motor with *Mad For It* on its side hurtled past, flicking
the finger. People cheered. The blue 205 followed. A girl
dropped her top and pressed her breasts against the window.
More cheering.

The police moved the squad car across the road, blocking it.
And a strange thing happened.

Dave started it. I saw him.

'Wankers,' he shouted at the police. 'Fucking wankers.'

From nowhere, from the depths of the earth, came a low
growl which swelled and grumbled into the air like smoke from
a burn-out. It was the crowd! Then, in very slow motion, came
a movement towards the police – just one or two people – which
gradually turned into a full-scale march on the enemy. It took

about a minute-and-a-half. Ninety seconds and then three hundred people were shouting, heckling and striding *en masse* towards the squad car. They were a mob. They filled the road. Soon, they had surrounded the three officers, who stood in a circle with their backs to their wagon.

Still, there was a gap between the crowd and the law. No one was touching.

I went up to one of the policemen, to ask if he was nervous.

'Nah,' he said. 'Just had to stop them causing an accident.' He turned away casually to talk into his radio. But he tensed his shoulders as he did so.

'Oi!' shouted one lad in the crowd, pointing at the squad car. 'Your back light's out.' It was. 'You've got fourteen days to sort that out, mate,' said the joker. Everyone laughed. But the atmosphere was eerie now, teetering between good humour and itchy nastiness. All it would take, I thought, is one punchy nutter, or one trigger-happy policeman, and the whole thing will go off.

But then someone pulled a burn-out in the car park, and, with a weird sense of relief, everyone turned and left the police, left them in the middle of the road, ambled back to take a look, shambled back to naughtiness, left the really bad stuff behind, as the reinforcements arrived: four policemen in riot gear, with shields and hats and sticks like steel piping.

I went over to see Debbie, Louise and Tori. They were sharing a cigarette, unaffected by the strange almost-riot. Tori looked at the other two and me and shrugged her shoulders.

'Come on,' she said. 'Let's find some willy. That's why we're here.'

3

how to ruin a nice walk

Stirling Golf Club is known within the UK's golfing community for two reasons. First: SGC boasts the 1997 British
Amateur Ladies Champion, Miss Alison Rose, amongst its
members. Second: in 1998, the club was offered a £24,000
Lottery grant to improve and extend its clubhouse, on the con-
dition that its 150 lady members were given the same access to
the new facilities as the men. At its AGM, Stirling Golf Club
voted, by 92 to 62, to turn down the cash. It could not be bribed
into giving women equal treatment.

The members' misgivings were understandable. After all,
the club television had always been in the Men's Lounge.
Moving it into a unisex area would undoubtably lead to

disagreements over which programmes to watch. Heavyweight political discussion followed by raunchy guns-and-girls movie and the football highlights? Or Delia Smith? Also: although the existing ladies' locker room would be expanded with the extension, could the club really promise that its proposed facilities would treat its lady members in exactly the same manner as its men? Easy enough to put pot pourri in the men's lockers, but what about urinals in the ladies? Ho ho, only joking . . . Here's another. Did you hear the one about the woman whose husband had a heart attack on the links? She rushed to his side, leaving her car in the main car park, which she was not allowed to do, as a woman, under club rules. After her husband's recovery, she was sent a letter from the golf club. *Circumstances not withstanding*, it read, *we would like to remind you not to park in the main car park*. Boom, boom. (That last tale wasn't a joke. It actually happened, but not at Stirling: at Little Aston Golf Club in Staffordshire.)

'Stirling's not as bad as some. My husband Philip – he's professional – was playing down south, and there were some women on the balcony of the clubhouse having a drink, watching the golf, you know. The eighteenth hole was right outside the clubhouse. The women are watching the men play, and one of the men swears when he's playing his last shot. The women complained about his audible foul language. So the club banned all women from drinking on the balcony.'

I was having an orange juice in Stirling's main (mixed) lounge with Miss Alison Rose and Mrs Elaine Allison. It was Elaine who told the story. She was Stirling's current Ladies Champion;

a position she had held on eight different occasions. It was Miss Alison Rose who was considered the better golfer, however. Alison had just returned from America where she had been playing in the Curtis Cup; a team competition between amateur golfers from Britain and the United States. Last year, the British won, and Alison had scored the maximum amount of points, only the second woman ever to do so. This year, though, the British had been beaten.

Both women were in their late twenties, with the clear, pink complexion of those who spent a lot of time in the open air. 'All because of golf,' said Elaine.

Alison worked in a bank, and Elaine was 'a cake decorator!' She laughed with her hand over her mouth. 'I'm meant to say speciality icing artiste, or something. I'm a housewife really.' Elaine was open-faced, with a dark pony-tail and the nervous, chatty air of someone who talked to fill in silences; Alison was quiet, self-contained, short-haired, boyish.

Elaine said that she wasn't a feminist. 'Sometimes I go for a round with three men and I'm not allowed to go for a drink with them afterwards, you know, because they're in the men-only lounge. I play with it, putting my foot on the edge of the carpet . . . Like I say, Stirling's not as bad as some. The men say 'last bastions' . . . I don't want us to be equal with men, because I don't want to be a man. I just want things to be fair. I'm happy playing as a woman.'

Alison said nothing; she 'wasn't bothered'. She said that golf had given her a good life these past twelve years: she'd travelled all over the world, made some good friends, enjoyed herself. She supposed she could turn professional – some of last year's

Curtis team had – but she wasn't sure if she wanted to. She wasn't sure what her next move would be, really. There didn't seem to be too much left for her to achieve.

Mr Walter McArthur, club secretary, a tall, silver-haired, dynamic man, came up to the table. He said that he and some of the men were to play at St Andrews the next weekend.

'One of the last bastions of male chauvinism, St Andrews,' he winked. 'No ladies allowed at all in the club. No ladies toilet, you see. They haven't the facilities . . . What's wrong with that, eh?' asked Walter, though none of us had commented.

We all smiled, politely; 'Nothing,' said Elaine.

'Only winding you up,' grinned Walter. 'Only winding you up.'

Stirling's not as bad as some. For a start, Miss Alison Rose was made an Honorary Member, in acknowledgement of her successes. And, when the present captain, Mr Ronnie Crawford, was installed, a few months after the money-snubbing AGM, one of the very first things he did was to put the Lottery proposition back before Stirling's members. He made sure of a huge turn-out and this time, the motion was voted through. Now SGC has a spanking new clubhouse, with equal access rights to both men and women. There're now two mixed lounges and a junior member's room, where the television lives.

'There was all the fuss in the press about refusing the lottery money. But when we put it back to the vote, with a full attendance from members, and the result was reversed, we never heard a peep from the papers. They only want to report bad news,' Ronnie told me.

Ronnie didn't mind, really. He was used to the press; he knew how it worked. In younger years, he'd been a football referee – he'd reffed some internationals, England v. Iceland – and there'd been a newsworthy incident that had occurred at one of his matches. He'd had the tabloids on the phone all the next day, until he called them back and said, 'Right, I'm prepared to go on record with the full story. But not until two years from now.' They never bothered him again.

Ronnie was talking to me at the entrance to Stirling's main lounge. Behind and around him, club members scuttled hither and yon, from bar to car park, from locker room to links, in various states of excitement and concern. Well, the women were. 'Has somebody moved the box of name tags?' asked one bustly-bottomed lady. 'Got em!' boomed another, waving a packet of paper hankies like an enemy scalp. 'Here I am, reporting for action,' said a third, saluting Ronnie so briskly that her bust wobbled like a waterbed.

Stirling Golf Club was all of a jitter. For this week, the club was playing host ('and hostess, to be equal', quipped a passing gentleman at Ronnie, who just raised an eyebrow) to the 1998 Ladies' British Open Amateur Stroke Play Championships. Today and tomorrow were warm-up days; the competition was to take place on the Wednesday, Thursday and Friday. It was the first time that Stirling had ever had the Ladies Stroke Play competition on its links and as a club it was very excited. The ladies locker room was manned (womanned – oh, whatever) with at least two stout helpers at all hours; the Ladies Golf Union had set up in a Portakabin at the back of the clubhouse; the caterers were worried that there wouldn't be enough soup and sandwiches. Already, some of the golfers had arrived: straight-backed girls from South Africa, Italy, Argentina, Spain, as well as from Davenport, Nottingham, Ormskirk. Most of them looked younger than Alison and Elaine: there were separate trophies for the Under-18 and Under-23 winners.

'Where are they all staying?' I asked Walter McArthur, as he rushed past.

'Some are in hotels, some in B&Bs. Some of our members are looking after players and they are being generously remunerated for doing so,' nodded Walter, as though I was accusing him of holding back funds. 'Very generously remunerated.'

Well, good. It must be nice for the competitors to stay with a family that understands golf. I don't, really. I like golf's visors and slacks and logos: what other sport boasts sponsors that make its athletes walk round in hats labelled Ping? (Perhaps other firms could be named after golfing noises too, so golfers could sport shirts with Swish on them, jumpers called Thwack and half-mast trousers emblazoned with Oof My Lumbago.) I like golf's amble through landscaped, bogus countryside, too. But a game takes too long if you're not Tiger Woods. Golf palls when you take at least twelve shots per hole. Especially when you have to keep rushing about collecting grass and soil and using them to repair the divots you've carved into the links, in the manner of someone fag-burning the carpet and filling it with chewing gum and fluff. And I certainly don't agree with those Golf-Is-Like-Life philosophers: golf is like life if you're a bored squirrel. Except even squirrels would have to be stupendously stuck for amusement before they'd enliven the process of burying a nut in the ground by first thwacking it as far away as possible.

But still, Stirling Golf Course looked very beautiful in the light of the strange, Scottish, half-sun-half-storm weather. There were mountains – the Fintry Hills – purplish in the distance. Figures, in twos and threes and singles, were flecked across the links, dotted amongst the bright grass curves. I saw a girl flick up her ball from the green with her club and catch it in one unthinking, graceful movement.

In general though, the competitors had started to get to me: a lot of them were of the type of girl that had got to me when I was young. Clean-haired, sporting, no make-up, no nonsense, a born prefect who pushed her jumper sleeves to her elbows and had no time for wimps and who drove (cars, golf) like a man. The kind of efficient, intimidating young lady that makes me trip over my tongue and fall off my shoes.

Maybe all young lady golfers are like that; certainly when I had wandered over to the Ladies Golf Union in the registration Portakabin a little earlier, I'd been confronted with Golf Girl at her most responsible and sniffy: 'I'm sorry,' she clipped, 'but I just haven't the time to answer any questions. You should have been told to make an official appointment. I've got all this (she ruffled a pile of papers on her desk) to process before tomorrow so if you don't mind . . .' Golf Girl broke off. Her face bloomed in a smile that was aimed past my right elbow. 'Oh hell-*oh*, Alison,' she twittered, as Alison Rose entered the Portakabin. 'How nice to see you, so sorry about the Curtis, have you recovered?'

I looked at Golf Girl, at her polo shirt with LGU

embroidered crest, at her solid hips in pleat-fronted trousers rammed tightly into her chair. I looked at her little shiny eyes, and her little shiny teeth, and her little shiny earrings, and I really wanted to shove a golf club head-first up between her little shiny buttocks. Alison said quietly, in my ear: 'She's just a wee bit harassed, and a bit full of it. If you were to come back again, I'm sure she'd have time to talk to you.'

Alison looked like a Golf Girl but she was not. I thought: That's why you're so good at the game; and why I'm so bad. You have the patience and grace to put up with frustration and jobsworth officialdom; I just scrunch up my face and whinge like a diamond-jumpered baby.

I went for a walk around the fairways. Stirling Golf Club does not own its land: it rents it from the Crown, and its lease runs out in 2000. The Crown will no doubt lease it again to the club: although SGC was established in 1869, there has been golf played here for 400 years. King James played golf, and it subsequently became so popular with his countrymen that their leaders became worried: Scotland's young men were spending far too much time playing poncey golf and not enough at manly archery practice.

Originally, Stirling's greens were woodland, but the trees were cut down to build the town, and the cleared space was used for archery, and then golf. Actually, over the past forty years, more trees have been brought in; for a while there, Stirling Golf Club could have been mistaken for an airstrip. Now, as I tramped the length of its borders, along one of its two public rights of way, nodding at dog-walkers, raising a hand to the frantic ground-workers, pulling faces at the golfers, I thought it seemed pretty idyllic: its trees were mature and clustered, its hillocks were smooth, plucked.

I'd come to Stirling because my life thus far had been resolutely un-golf, and I thought it was about time it changed. I wanted to go golf. I was over thirty. I owned several V-neck pullovers. And it's quite the done thing these days. There are now so many golf clubs springing up in the south-east of England that the government has expressed concern. From 1602 until 1989, there were only 1,350 golf clubs built in England; between 1989 and 1997, 515 more sprung up, whilst the number of registered (English) amateurs rose from around 600,000 to well over a million. There are now over 2,500 golf clubs spread across Britain and golf has become just as much of a threat to the Green Belt as housing developers. But it wasn't just because of this that I was interested, and it wasn't just because of the V-necks either: it was because golf is a game that runs through Middle Britain like life-blood. No: like heroin in life-blood. Golf is the self-made man's drug of choice. Golf – a game so confounding, so contrary, so climate-ignoring that if it came as a suggestion from his wife, he would dismiss it as the airy-fairy notion of a typical bloody woman – golf is a grown man's ticket to oblivion. Most men of a certain age like to have a reason to avoid their family. They want to zone out. They want their own space, away from work and house and duty, they want social time with other men. Some achieve this by going to the pub, some from golf. Some men – like my dad – want the space without the chaps: these loners go for drives, or perfect the art of mind-blanking in front of the telly.

My dad has never been a clubby man, and in Wilmslow, a solo woman, married or not, was not readily accepted as a GC member even as recently as the late eighties (I remember a recently widowed mother of a friend applying to join the Bramhall Golf Club in 1987; she was refused, with the implication that 'her type' was not wanted), so as a family, we did not go golf. I did once, however, serve as a waitress in a local golf club's Christmas dinner. It was quite an eye-opener for a fourteen-year-old.

The assembled club had looked prissy enough, in their dark suits and long skirts. But they'd barely finished the starters (prawn cocktail, melon-and-a-cherry or a glass of orange juice) before things got lively. Chairs pushed back, men leaning round and across their partners in order to make their point to other men, quiet women becoming glassier and giddier and suddenly speaking REALLY LOUDLY before bursting into tears and rushing to the toilets, bolder women laughing and fluttering their mascara, hoisting their cleavage on to their sideplates.

By coffee, my cheeks were dyed pink from having to manoeuvre between clumps of half-embracing, half-throttling bodies to get to the table, and from the lazily salacious comments about whether I was serving cream, which to my utter mortification, I was. But if my face was warm, on the teeny, rainbow-lit dancefloor, things were hotting up to chilli con carne temperatures. There was much squeezing of behinds, from women as well as men: big clomps of golfer's bum squidged between hand-lotioned fingers, carved by Coty's Pink Shimmer nails. The men looked like huge, drunk, bottom-bothered bears. Their heads kept bumping downwards. Their eyes kept sliding sideways. I remember that one of them tried to say something. His dancing partner (his wife? or not?) put her hand over his mouth. 'Don't,' she breathed. 'Don't . . . speak.' She said this with such wildly wrought significance that I stopped in the middle of clearing the plates. God, how dramatic! It was just like the pictures. Except everyone was the same age as my parents.

I had hoped that Stirling Golf Club would provide as gripping an evening's entertainment, but Alison and Elaine had told me that it wasn't much of a club for the social life. Apparently, in Edinburgh they're always having dos; but Stirling was quieter, 'a bit cliquey', according to Elaine. I'd also hoped that, given Stirling's new pro-woman stance, and as I was visiting during the Ladies Amateur Championships, that I might get to have a game, or at least a couple of holes. Perhaps I could be the wild card entrant. But Walter McArthur had divested me of that little dream: 'There'll be no room for anyone, not even members, who isn't competing this week. We're terribly stretched, and we have to make sacrifices.'

So, as I walked around the greens, I felt a little blue. I'd turned up to go golf, in Pringle and brown slacks and lace-ups; all keyed up, looking the part. Yet I wasn't allowed to gain the experience. I was still a golfing virgin: no club-ball-hole action for me. Oh well. I supposed I could observe the technique of champions at close hand. And at least I was getting some fresh air.

It took me the better part of an hour to walk right around the golf course; I wiggled in and out of the fairways, worried about being felled by low flying balls. There was a covered wooden bench on the far side – ancient graffiti read: *Magazine, XTC, Kirsty, Stevie, Free The Weed* – and a Scotloo just by it, in case any ladies were caught short. (Why Scotloo? Why not Portaloo? Or why not Engaloo? Or – ho-ho – Vindaloo?) (Sorry.)

As I dondered back towards the clubhouse, along the road, I passed a skateboard park and, then, oh joy: a crazy golf course. I felt cheered instantly. If I couldn't have a crack at the real thing, then crazy golf it was! I could show those so-called champions, those capable, snooty Golf Girls a thing or two! Well: at least I could show the toddlers who were pushing their ball about on the loop-the-loop hole a thing or two. Out of the way, Tiger cubs! Make room for the new . . . I couldn't think of any famous women golfers. I couldn't picture a single one in my mind, apart from the wafty blonde one who 'trained' with Nick Faldo and whose stroke play was so impressive that he upped and left his wife.

Still, not to worry. Make room anyhow! I paid my two pounds, collected my 'iron' and strode purposefully to hole number 1. A simple hump lay between the tee and the hole. I squatted down, narrowed my eyes, pointed my club towards the three-inch high hillock, stroked my chin. I noticed that the toddlers and their father were looking at me strangely. 'Amateurs,' I said loudly, to indicate that my game was professional and therefore superior to that of the losers on the main course, set the ball in a dip in the concrete and had a crack. Fore!

Well, five. Hole in five. Not bad. Would have been three, except for the tricksy slope on the putting green. I marked my score sheet and set off for the next hole, just two steps away.

Number 2 was level playing, but with three barriers jutting out into the fairway to create a zigzag effect. Clearly, there were two ways to play this: either dodge through, which would take at least three shots, unless you were lucky with the bounce off the walls; or dare to chip. I dared. I set my feet shoulder-width apart, waggled my bum in coolly professional manner, and . . . oh dear. *She's skewed it wild, Brian, or Murray, or whoever commentates on golf. She'll be disappointed with that shot.* The ball soared to head height and plopped over the other side of the crazy golf park. Toddlers' Dad started giving me the evils, even though his little family were way out of range.

Where's a caddy when you need one? I tramped over to the ball, and tried to chip it back again for practice. Toddlers' Dad was not having this.

'Just watch yoursel' wi' that ball,' he cried, as it soared again. I don't know what he was bothered about: this chip wasn't even up to his knees. Mind you, I suppose that was about as high as his children's brains.

'Sorry,' I muttered. It took me seven tappety shots just to get the ball back on to the right fairway. Hole in ruddy eleven. Toddlers' Dad had put me right off my stroke.

Still, by the time I'd sunk it, he'd left. The whole course was mine. I was the Fair Mistress of the Fairways! Queen of the Green! So I challenged myself to a game of Pitch and Putt; far better sport on a crazy golf course than on the boring grassy version. What you do is go round the course as usual, except instead of playing for the hole you tee off from, you pick a hole four ahead, and play for that instead. It gives you an opportunity to pitch, to chip, to slice, to really let fly. Open your shoulders, follow through, birdie in the mouth of a concrete frog from a tricksy distance of a good ten feet . . .

Well, that was soon over. Toddlers' Dad had only disappeared to complain at the pay hut, the miserable twerp, and the attendant came out to tell me off. What's the problem, git-face? Can't handle a real woman in full-flowing, athletic action? Used to wimp-oh girlies who step aside, who leave the course free for the men on a Saturday, who make the sandwiches and then retire to compare lapel pins? Huh?

'Sorry, Mr Parky,' I said, meekly, and handed my iron back. I stomped off towards the real golf club, feeling exactly as I had done in my encounter with Golf Girl: narked off, to use the Latin.

Back in the clubhouse, I calmed down, and decided to check out the new locker rooms. In the ladies, I met Mrs Eleanor Walters, Ladies Captain, who was friendly and lit up with news.

'Have you heard the latest?' she trilled, excitedly. 'No? Well, a lady from South Africa has broken her foot and had to go to the hospital.'

I received her tidings with the appropriate mix of interest, concern and delight. Apparently, the South African Ladies team captain had just slipped – skidded on a slope by a putting green – and was now hobbling about in plaster. I went out to see if I could spot her. Instead, I saw Walter McArthur, chatting to a chum.

'Well, Walter, some of these more mature ladies can be a little hefty round the flanks. If they land with their full weight . . .'

Ooh, miaow, Humpty. It always amazes me how the fattest of men feel within their rights to comment on any female who dares to have a figure fuller than Audrey Hepburn. The speaker's stomach was suffocating his knees. If he slipped and landed with his full weight, they'd need another Lottery rebuilding donation, sharpish. Either that or they'd have to fill the hole with water and call themselves the Stirling Golf and Synchronised Swimming Club.

I couldn't spot the injured South African captain, so I went back into the ladies lockers, where there was some dispute as to who was 'on'. Two volunteers were required for the lockers, and they changed every two hours. The rota had been fixed for a while, but there'd been a little mix-up and now there were three ladies who had arrived for just two locker spots. Locker duties, in case you were wondering, included sitting behind a table flicking through last Sunday's papers; reading out the horoscopes to your fellow locker lady; helping the foreign competitors by showing them the lockers, clearly visible on every wall; occasional jump-up to run out and get a missing essential, e.g. paper tissues, hand towels, bin-bags.

The problem of locker duty over-subscription was a little difficult to solve, as the ladies involved were of the type for whom hanging about doing nothing was a disgrace on a par with going to evensong with your skirt tucked into your knickers.

'Can I make myself useful in any other areas?' said one, graciously, and was ushered out to help with the caddying rotas.

The two remaining settled back and told me golf tales: 'Most people work 9 to 5, I work 7.30 to 1.30, so I can fit in my golf.

And on a Tuesday I don't work at all, so I can play early and have a game of bowls in the afternoon'; 'We've just come back from Gleneagles. We were helping out at the championship. They're to hold it in France next year, but they'll not get the volunteers. We'll have to go over and sort things out'; 'Did you hear about Mrs Concannon? Well, she went to the doctor, with her hips, and he said, do you do any exercise? And she said, I play golf. And the doctor replied, golf's not exercise!'

They both fell about at that one – 'as if a four-mile walk three times a week isn't exercise!'. These were ladies who would not take kindly to being asked their years, ladies of an age where you were not-so-secretly proud to be active. One told me she used to play tennis and ski until she had an accident and shattered her leg. She decided to take up golf and 'I've never regretted it.'

I said: 'Have you made a lot of friends?'

She said: 'I'm a grand one for mucking in.'

In the bar, the gents were opining. It was 2.30 p.m. They were on the pints, sitting in a semicircle at the large picture windows along the left hand side of the bar. The eighteenth hole was in full, close-up view and they were watching a young lady finish off a practice round.

'Swing . . .'

'She's trying to change her swing now . . .'

'Needs a caddy . . .'

'Horrible chipper off the back of that bunker . . .'

'She's had a terrible round . . .'

The exchange took several minutes; the men didn't chatter

like the lady members. A comment was followed by many seconds of ruminative silence, until another fellow felt moved to speech. The atmosphere was far less active than that in the ladies locker room, although, to the untrained eye, both groups were doing the same thing: sitting about, talking.

Walter McArthur, one of the few men in the club with the bustling air of a lady member, joined me for a quick bite to eat. He munched through a cold chicken sandwich and said: 'We get all sorts of people in Stirling Golf Club. Teachers, surgeons, eye surgeons, lawyers, chemists, um, the unemployed . . .' Unemployed eye surgeons and lawyers, presumably. He told me that the more distinguished of the male golfers – the elders of the club – had an informal group they called the USSR.

'It stands,' said Walter, 'for Unemployed Superannuated Sick and Retired. Sometimes they joke and say the R is for Retarded. They meet most mornings in the lounge, for a coffee and to put the world to rights.'

He pointed out Robin Commons, twice Stirling's President, and a member of USSR, whose family had been involved with the Golf Club for three generations. Robin had grown up in a house that faced the golf course; one of his earliest memories had been squeezing through the fence to get on the greens. I'd met him earlier. He had been flustered and distracted: he'd mislaid his house keys. The rest of the USSR had milked his discomfort for jokes with the ponderous doggedness of sitcom writers.

'Well, now, Robin. You'd forget your head if it wasn't sewn on . . .'

'Are you sure the wife hasn't given them to her fancy man?'

'Thanks for the keys, Robin, I only took what I could sell
on . . .'

After lunch, back in the foyer, I gazed at the rows of presidential pictures. There was Robin, twice, black and white in
1960–61, then later, 69–70, full colour; and his father, 1937–38,
and grandfather, 1913–14, both monochrome. On the opposite
wall was the wooden plaque of champions – ladies included
since 1946.

On a polished table opposite the foyer entrance was the
Suggestions Book, kept by one McArthur, W. (Hon. Sec.).
Members' suggestions were written on the left page of the open
book, with Walter's response on the right. Every proposal was
dealt with precisely, promptly, fairly, according to regulations.
For instance: *I suggest that a supply of towels be available for visiting parties*, was one. *The committee considered your suggestion
but found no support*, answered Walter. In reply to the childish
scrawl: *Why should the gentlemen have their own lounge as well as
the use of the main lounge when the juniors have nothing?*, Walter
had written: *This is not a suggestion*. To: *I suggest that the bunkers
on all fairways be topped up at least 2 inches with sand and sieved
with a 2 mm mesh to remove large stones*, Walter pointed out,
kindly: *No signature*.

The gentle murmur of voices washed through from the main
lounge. Even at its most frantic, Stirling Golf Club had an air of
order and propriety. In the car park, the cars were parked in designated places; on the notice-boards, the rotas were marked for
all to see. There was a framed letter from the Queen in the
foyer; opposite, there were the original architects' plans. If ever
a member were to feel unsure of where he or she fitted in, if

they felt, perhaps, that their understanding of their place in the world was skewed, or slipping, that they were losing their grip as to who they were and what they were supposed to do, then Stirling Golf Club could give them the answer. It knew the ropes. It had a job for you to do, whether or not you still had a real, paid job. The Club gave you rules, procedure, rosters, registers; familiar, unchanging tenets. Same old jokes, same old crew, same old, same old. Golf as life. Last bastions.

4

mr and mrs

It was a long drive back down south from Stirling. And, as it always does on long drives, my mind wandered. Away it meandered from the upliftingness of our beauteous British scenery (which stopped being beauteous just below Carlisle, i.e. the scenic bits were all Scottish), to slip and slide towards matters more prosaic: namely, sex.

I'd been disappointed by the lack of lascivious after-hours activity at Stirling Golf Club. I'd thought that that was half the point. It had certainly seemed to be when I'd been a waitress at that dinner all those years ago. After all, if you were to judge by reputation – okay then, by top-shelf magazines – then aside from cars and golf, sex would appear to be the suburbs' most popular pastime. Look at all those nice, well-stuffed readers' wives, every one photographed across a nice, well-stuffed sofa in a nice, well-stuffed sitting-room. On second thoughts, don't. They're not always a pretty sight. Some of those sofa covers . . .

Sex in the city, in contrast, is rubbish. Watch the TV or read the papers and you soon conclude that the only people having city sex are prostitutes, thirty-somethings desperate to get hitched and fat-bellied civic dignitaries who chase posh babes around drinks parties. No one has time to get frisky in cities. They're far too busy doing other, livelier, groovier city things, like trying to flag down a taxi on a rainy Friday night.

Suburban sex, though, is hot stuff. It's the real deal. It's coitus uninterruptus, coitus fantasticus. It's the bored housewife welcoming in the horny-handed handyman to satisfy her needs – after he's tackled the bathroom grouting. It's the alter-native-to-Tupperware Ann Summers accessories party that gets a bit out of hand. (Actually, one of my school-friends' mothers went to such an evening. An invite was pushed through her door. *Marital Aids Party* it read. Unfortunately, she didn't have her specs on and thought it said 'Martial Arts Party'. She turned up dressed in a tracksuit, expecting to learn self-defence. True story.)

But most of all, suburban sex is wife-swapping. Swinging. Casual sex with someone neither a stranger (you know where they bought their suite) nor a person you know well (you don't know what they like to get up to on it). Come on and party with the free-and-easy out-of-towners. Toss your car-keys in a bowl, grab a handful of peanuts and soon you'll be grabbing a hand-ful of your next-door neighbour's spouse. Just make sure that everyone's adult about it. You don't want recriminations or you'll not have anyone to share the school run.

Despite my suburban upbringing, I've never tried wife-swapping. I never had a wife to swap. I still don't; and I can't borrow the wife of any of my male friends either, because, as yet, very few of them have managed to persuade a woman to exchange the spoils of her independence (car, career, flat, bubble baths as and when) for a Sony PlayStation and the entire works of New Order, stored alphabetically. And the few men I know that are married just can't believe their luck; they're certainly not going to transfer any contractual swapping option to someone who might be tempted to actually use it: 'Look, Ric, I swapped Liz for this lovely ickle puppy-wuppy, and a cake!'

A mother of a friend (not the Martial Arts one) did tell me that she had once been to 'one of those parties', but she said that she hadn't quite noticed at the time. She'd gone to a do with her husband, and during the course of the evening another woman had dropped a set of keys in front of him, tossed her head and turned away. The husband picked up the keys, tapped the woman on the shoulder and said, politely: 'Excuse me, I think you dropped these.' It wasn't until later, said my friend's mother, that they'd realised.

'And we thought we were so sophisticated,' she said. 'We'd lived in London in our time, and the party was in Borehamwood.'

You see? Not London. *Borehamwood*. I heard of other stories: all sorts of high jinks in a Radlett health club. Plus fables of golf club holes-in-more-than-one: I was told that 'on the pool table, she was never satisfied', which I'm sure is a line from Bobby

Goldsboro's 'The First Time'; and a cautionary tale about a double-couple holiday. Mr Smith fancied Mrs Jones, and, during the holiday, persuaded a reluctant Mrs Smith to get off with Mr Jones so that Mr Smith could get on, guilt-free, with fulfilling his Mrs Jones fantasies. Unfortunately, Mrs Smith and Mr Jones liked each other rather better than anyone had expected, and when they got back from holiday, they eloped. Which served Mr Smith right, and, quite possibly, liberated Mrs Jones. At least she could file her Gloria Gaynor record under Z, if she wanted.

I mused on these instances as I motored down the M6, and I thought: I missed out. All those years in Wilmslow, popping an artery in excitement over Peter Purves and Bonnie Langford appearing as Buttons and Cinderella in the Rex Theatre pantomime, when I could have been popping out of my capacious snorkel parka and learning the far more thrilling ropes (whips, shackles) of swinging. Who knows? Swinging could have been going on all around me. I thought back to my tennis club years, and to when I was a waitress, to see if I could recall any nonchalant pooling of car-keys in the butter-dish, or overly sweaty doubles matches. But I couldn't. Mind you, I was hugely self-absorbed when I was younger: there could have been an orgy involving the whole of our street, including family pets, all going at it hammer-and-fondue-set in our kitchen, and as long as I could still get to the chocolate spread, I don't think I'd have noticed.

I was also very innocent when I lived in Wilmslow. Once, one of my schoolteachers called me and my friend Debbie into his room and showed us pictures from *The Joy Of Sex*. Debbie and I were about fourteen. What did we do? We giggled behind our hands and ran out, of course. And never thought anything more of it.

When I got back to London, I set about remedying my naïvety. But how was I, a virtuous, innocent city-dweller, going to locate the suburban kinkdom of wife-swapping? Easy. The Internet. Mecca to pervs the world over. Well, Mecca to pervs with enough money to afford a computer, and, frankly, those were the ones I was after. I wanted those wife-swappers who saw their hobby as a recreation equivalent to collecting Victorian dollies, those who liked their leisure divertissements centrally-heated and within reach of a fringed cushion. Those who don't care what the neighbours think don't call it wife-swapping. They call it getting lucky. Or unreasonable behaviour.

I logged on – which, for the Internet-unfamiliar, meant I moved the arrow thing to the symbol marked 'Browse the Internet' and clicked the mouse twice. Then I typed in the word 'Swingers' in the Search space, and pressed Return. (I thought that 'Swappers' might get me Ye Olde Keith Chegwin Fan Club.) Anyway, the Internet gave me *thousands* of possibilities. The very first one was called UK Swingers, and it proved a most enlightening site, with teasing pictures (nearly all of sus-pendered women sprawled upon, yup, flowered sofas) and sample entries, which were nothing if not polite: 'Epsom. Close encounters wanted (of any kind). Ed, 49. Gabs, 48.' 'Swindon. Happily married couple. Educated, sophisticated, nudist club, regular private parties. John, 49. Jane, 42.' (*Sophisticated* nudist club? Replacing mixed volleyball with strip bridge?) Most of the advertisers were older than me, I noticed.

Another thing I noticed later is that if you ever use your computer to download dirty stuff – and I bet you've thought about it at least – then, for ages afterwards, these exceptionally embarrassing adverts and e-mails keep popping up whenever you use the Internet. By accessing one sex site, you become a target for erotic electronic junk mail: which, perhaps, is more fun than your everyday electronic junk mail, but you might want to think about this if you sit next to your boss. You might reckon you can hide your filthy habits by quick-clicking on to an innocent Home page and pretending you're looking into on-Web direct marketing; but if adverts for Wet Wild And Wanton suddenly scroll over your screen like Hugh Hefner's wallpaper, your superior is unlikely to believe you.

Anyhow, back to UK Swingers. I joined (£20 a year) and after a few furtive fumblings and unfulfilled flirtations (P. D. from Newcastle, you know who you are! You little tease, you), I struck up an acquaintance with three people: Micky, Janet and Jonathon.

Ex-police officer Micky and his wife Janet lived in Surbiton, with their two children. I met them on the other side of town from their small semi, in a large, bland, 'country' pub. We had a couple of drinks to break the ice; they seemed a bit shy, especially Janet, whose voice never ventured above a whisper. Once we were all settled, they told me that they'd got involved in swinging because three years ago they'd seen a BBC2 programme about it. Afterwards they'd had a bit of a chat. You see, they'd been married for fifteen years, and neither of them had slept with anyone else. What, thought Micky and Janet, if we're doing it wrong? (Don't tell me you've never wondered similarly.) They decided, bravely, and loin-girdlingly, that they were going to find out.

How, though? Because neither of them wanted to have an affair, they decided that they would join what they called 'a swinging circle'. But, unlike circles of the knitting or baby-sitting variety, swinging circles don't advertise in local libraries. Micky and Janet went through all sorts of difficulties trying to worm their way inside, so to speak. They tried contact mags, *Loot*, the back of *Exchange & Mart* (really) . . . Eventually, through a strange chain letter arrangement (they had to send £1 to every contact) they met their first couple. Unfortunately, Micky and Janet didn't much like them – she was nice, but he was an 'ac-tor type' who insisted on discussing his sexual fantasies very loudly in the middle of the pub – anyhow, they thought they'd have a bash. But once they'd gone back to the other couple's home, Mr Ac-tor seemed more interested in the telly than he was in Janet. No matter how – or what – she tried, her loud-mouthed thespian couldn't rise to the occasion. His performance was a flop. He dried, he corpsed, he crumpled under the spotlight. Still, he obeyed the first rule of show business: he left his audience wanting a lot more.

Despite this disappointment Micky and Janet persevered, racking up an enormous phone bill leaving voice-mail messages. (What did you say? 'Well, we got, um, specific after a while. We got sick of time-wasters.') It sounded as though this quiet pair became quite assertive; after several dismal encounters, they decided that in order to save feelings and, more importantly, time, they would have sex with a couple as soon as possible after meeting them and become friends later. 'Otherwise, you're left in the embarrassing position of having to ditch some new friends who want to know why you don't want to see them any more, when you got on well before the sex,' explained Micky, evenly.

As a rule, sadly, the men were 'crap! Either small, or limp, some both'. The women were fine, though Micky did have one fright when a lady became 'emotionally disturbed' when her man and Janet left the room to get down to business. The woman jumped up and followed them, then curled up in the corner of their room, watching them, muttering to herself. After that, Micky and Janet tried to interest their real, long-term friends in swapping: 'We dropped it into conversation,' whispered Janet. 'I said, "We met some people the other day who went to swinging parties . . ."' But their friends were horrified, so that was the end of that. 'To outsiders,' admitted Micky, 'Janet and I would be the last people to be interested in this.'

I looked at them, neat in their zipped-up fleeces, scrubbed and washed and ready for . . . what? walking the dog? nipping to the post office? a shared pizza before *Friends*?; and I thought, you're right.

Micky and Janet have been wife-and-husband-swappers for over a year now. And this is what they have learnt. That, whilst they're not about to join the Kama Sutra Dream Team, they *have* been doing it right all this time; that such kinky joys as home videoing, three-in-a-bed, orgies ('highly overrated, sheer exhibitionism. We just stood at the door and watched ten people writhe about on a double bed') were not as scorchio as they'd expected; that swinging – well, the organisation of such – is very time-consuming. All that sifting out of unsuitables, at letter and e-mail stage, then the lengthy chats over the phone, arranging meetings in the pub, or in motels like Travel Lodges, which could be expensive. Some liaisons involved cross-country drives, which also cost. And then there was the over-night baby-sitting to consider . . .

I said: 'It sounds as hard as organising a tennis round robin.' Micky said: 'Harder. We've had to cut back. It kept taking up too much of our everyday life. We had the loft extension to get on with.'

Still, Micky and Janet had given me heart; there they were, sipping bottled lagers in a Surbiton hostelry, two reasonably attractive, well-adjusted suburbanites not much older than me who had swapped and survived. I was a little disappointed that they hadn't managed to persuade their real, local friends to join in, that they couldn't get me in on an intimate, random, who'll-be-sleeping-in-my-bed car-key party, but still. They were living proof of my suburbia = sex theory. And by the time they'd finished their tale, I'd had more than a couple of vodka and tonics, and considered making a move on them. But I thought better of it. Both Micky and Janet had been careful to make it clear that they were only interested in couples, and I hadn't had much luck with persuading my boyfriend that to swing was truly, to live: 'Do we have to?' he'd asked, when I'd suggested it, and I had to say, no we didn't. We live in a city. If we want any extra-marital sexual kicks we'll press up against people in the queue for the crack dealer. Like everyone else does.

Next up was Jonathon, who lived in Chester. I met him in Covent Garden when he was down in London on business. Jonathon, a droopy-jowled, ponderous 42-year-old, described himself as 'an average bloke, not a stud'. He and his wife Clare had slept in separate beds, in separate rooms, for the past four years. At thirty-nine, Jonathon had had a mid-life crisis: he was made redundant from his job as an accountant; but 'I refused to believe that life ended at forty,' said Jonathon, bashfully, 'so I took the plunge.' Meaning: he visited a massage parlour. The experience was, he reported, 'not as embarrassing as I'd feared'.

Over a couple of years, Jonathon worked his way through about twenty women from contact magazines, plus a couple of men, 'to see if I'd like it' (he didn't). Six months after his redundancy, he started doing temporary accountancy work: in the office, when he had time on his hands and a computer to play with, Jonathon sorted out all his contact ladies – their addresses, phone numbers, those statistics deemed vital – into a handy spreadsheet.

'You see, the spreadsheet would help when I got a new contact magazine,' explained Jonathon, gravely. 'To check if any numbers overlapped.'

'Mmm,' I nodded.

'Actually,' said Jonathon, 'I believe that my, em, encounters' (he paused a little before the word) 'may have helped me with the numerous job interviews I was attending at the time.'

'In what way?' I asked, thinking, Jonathon, you can't have shown prospective employers your lovely spreadsheet, you just can't.

'Well, I'm never very comfortable with strangers, you see,' said Jonathon, 'and I feel that because I was meeting all these new people in what very easily could have become awkward situations . . . Um, it was good practice.'

I had a sudden image of Jonathon trying out his interview technique during his 'encounters'; of him laid out on an eiderdown intoning to a surprised lady-friend, 'I feel that I could bring both enthusiasm and experience to this particular position of lying on my back being energetically serviced by a stranger. I am good within a team and have strong motivation skills. You'll know I am excited about the way our shared project is progressing if my little legs start pumping like chubby pistons and I begin to whinny.'

After a few months of interviews, Jonathon landed a 'well-paid senior financial position'. And now, he's joined one of those legendary swinging circles. Only he called it a ring. His various contact magazine experiences had led him to meet men with similar interests, and now most of his sexual shenanigans involved couples 'where the wife is looking for multiple partners'. Sometimes, the sessions were filmed.

'You know,' said Jonathon, thoughtfully, 'I'm a shy person, but in the group sessions I tend to be the one to take off my clothes first, to break the ice. Also, I've had sex with older or less attractive women when the others have backed out – partly because I am happy to do so, but mainly because they're usually just ordinary, friendly people, like me.'

'Why don't you involve your ordinary, friendly wife?' I asked.

'Because I selfishly believe that it is my life,' said Jonathon, a little huffily. 'And she doesn't join in with other interests I have, like jazz music.'

Micky and Janet and Jonathon had all been ordinary, friendly people. They hadn't looked like sexual dynamos. I wondered if, under particular circumstances, they transformed, like those ancient film secretaries who took off their specs, let down their hair and turned into Brigitte Bardot. Perhaps they removed their fleeces and became Edwina Currie. I tried to imagine them in the very specific situations they had told me about, but it was difficult. Then I tried to imagine myself in those situations, and that was impossible. Everything became too corny: like a ludicrous slapstick French 'comedy', or worse, like a rubbish porn film.

I once wrote a lengthy feature on porn. I made a couple of discoveries. The first was that a lot of porn is ridiculous, nothing to do with any sex you've experienced (sample scene: man in nothing but zigzag-striped jumper, woman smiling seductively with penis in her *ear*). The second was that you lose your shockability much more quickly than you'd imagine. At first, you cover your eyes at the prospect of step-by-lovin'-step, medically-approved sexual health videos (especially at those, actually: would you want to see jolly hockey-sticks Clare Rayner ram a condom on to a dildo? No). But after a couple of days, you find yourself doing the hoovering and letting neighbours in for cups of tea whilst the telly is blaring the orgy scene from Anal Academy.

I didn't particularly like investigating porn: I didn't want ordinary, friendly Micky, Janet and Jonathon to be filed in my mind alongside it. But, try as I might, I couldn't imagine their encounters as anything other than a combination of seedy and cheesy. My mind kept merging their escapades with films like *Maximum Perversion*, with Micky becoming the pizza delivery boy and Janet the . . . you don't want to know. Well, you might, but it's illegal. So I decided that I had to get to a wife-swapping party myself. Then a real-life sex-in-suburbia experience could supplant my mental clichés, which, by now, were flipping between *Carry On Up Your Next-Door Neighbour* and *Debbie Does Dorking*.

It took a bit of Internet flimflam, but eventually I was asked by a man called James (43, 'in computers') to one of his irregular house parties. He and his wife lived in High Wycombe, and they invited me as an extra female to a soirée of 'around twelve to fifteen, mostly couples. There might be one or two unaccompanied men,' said James, 'but we know them. It's all people we know well, or those who've been recommended by friends'.

It sounded like a cross between a dinner party (was I to be fixed up with one of the rogue male spares?) and the old boy network. Still, James had been reassuring over the phone. I'd explained that I was a writer, without 'wife', and, thus far, inexperienced in the joys of swinging. None of which presented a problem to James; plus, he'd been willing to answer some specific questions. Such as: where within the house does the swinging actually take place? How does it start? When does it finish? Do you *have* to join in?

James said: 'It's my job, as host, to make people comfortable, and I can say that we have a reputation for running "no pressure" parties. For instance, sometimes, it may be one of the lady's time of the month, or she may not want to play for some other reason. She is welcome to stay and chat anyway.'

I said: 'Who would she chat to? Wouldn't everyone else be otherwise occupied?'

'Well, for instance, she might be sitting next to a couple who are playing together, where the man is receiving, ah, oral. He could still have a conversation with the lady.'

I thought: Not if it's being done right, he couldn't. I also thought: Would the lady, meaning me, actually want to have a conversation under such circumstances? I began to feel nervous. I quashed my worries by thinking about how all sex can seem strange if you think about it for long enough; and about how numerous conversations could be enlivened by a spot of simultaneous, yet unrelated, activity, e.g. by drinking a lot.

James told me that people 'played' all over the house – 'we are a little cramped for space, however' – and that for the first hour or so of his parties, there was very little to distinguish them from your regular Chablis and Twiglets affair. After that, his wife, Carol, might make a move on somebody – 'she's quite a character, Carol' – or James himself might put on a video, presumably not of last week's missed *Coronation Street* episodes, but you can never tell what turns people on.

After I'd spoken to James a couple of times, I felt: fluttery, intrigued and in a flap about what to wear. Just how you should feel about going to a party. The outfit I eventually settled upon was a knee-length skirt and snug jumper; giving, I thought, a professional yet fun-loving image, à la post-Spice Geri Halliwell. I bought a bottle of white wine, made sure my mobile phone was close to hand (safety precaution in case of real perverts), and set off. It was seven o'clock on a Saturday night.

I was one of the first to arrive, which had been my intention. I wanted to see how the evening developed and I didn't want to walk into a roomful of strangers, all of whom knew each other well, or were making athletic efforts to do so.

James and Carol's house was small and semi-d, in a leafy, neatly yarded street lined with parked cars. I parked up and rang the bell. Carol answered the door. Mid forties, dark, shoulder-length curly hair, big friendly smile . . . see-through blouse, lacy black all-in-one (cut thong-style to reveal homely buttocks), stockings and suspenders. Ever get the feeling that you're over-dressed? I thrust the bottle of wine at her, faintly panicked.

'How lovely of you,' Carol soothed. She kissed me on the cheek. 'You must be Miranda. Do come in. Shall I take your coat? It's a lovely colour. Would you like a drink? Follow me.'

James was in the kitchen, at the back, fixing drinks. He seemed a good ten years older than Carol, in collarless shirt and pleated-front trousers, with side-parted, slightly greying hair. He had the look of a young David Attenborough. This unnerved me quite a bit, as the only other person I know who resembles Our Nation's Most Illustrious Naturalist is my dad. Uh-oh. Pervier and pervier.

James also kissed me on the cheek, then gave me a glass of white wine and ushered me into the small, brightly lit sitting-room, where there were bowls of crisps and nibbles set out upon the glass coffee-table and a man displayed on the (non-flowered) black leather settee. Comfortingly, this man, too, was conventionally attired, in slacks and a polo shirt. Less comfortingly, he had a pony-tail. This was Mike, said James. Mike stood up and kissed me on the cheek. Hello, Mike.

'Nice to meet you Miranda. Have you come far?'

'From London.'

'Bad traffic?'

It's strange when you anticipate weirdness and are confronted with deadening normality. How reassuring! How disappointing! I'd been promised an orgy and ended up at a convivial committee meeting. Still, it was early yet.

We spent the first ten minutes talking about holidays, discussing delayed flights and unpredictable weather. I sipped my wine, minded my Ps and Qs and felt exactly as though I was house-visiting some friends of my parents. It was just that one of them had forgotten to put on her skirt. Then it was revealed that Mike was an artist, so we all had a bit of a chat about that. James and Carol said they found it difficult to make it into London for exhibitions, though they'd liked what they'd read about one of the Turner Prize nominees: 'The lady who makes those rather intriguing feminine sculptures. *Vagina dentata* ha-ha-ha,' said James.

'Cathy de Monchaux,' I said.

Mike looked miffed.

Carol said: 'Mike's work is rather more traditional, isn't it, Mike?'

Mike looked even more miffed. Hurriedly, Carol added: 'Not that your art is conventional in any way. Just that it tends to be figure studies, of the whole rather than part of the human body, doesn't it? Now, is everyone all right for drinks?'

The doorbell went, and Carol disappeared. Mike grumbled something and stomped off to the toilet. I was left with James, who moved over to sit next to me on the sofa.

James was concerned that I felt relaxed. I said I was fine (actually, I felt relieved that some other guests had arrived as I'd started to worry that the party was just for four). He offered me some crisps and burbled on for quite a while about the swinging scene in general; how it had taken him and Carol a few years to set up their present easy set-up, with people – friends – who knew each other well and 'liked to enjoy one another and watch each other enjoying themselves'. I realised that it wasn't just James's hair-do that was like David Attenborough. It was his breathy bedside speaking manner. James spoke neutrally, but with a slightly fanatical undertone; he reminded me of somone who had gone through years of intense therapy after a nervous breakdown, or a born-again feng shui-ist. I felt as though he wanted to *convert* me to swinging, for my own good.

He rattled on for a good fifteen minutes about clubs that he and Carol had visited, about other, unsatisfactory encounters. On and on he talked. I became distracted. Where were Carol and Mike? And the other people who'd arrived? I began to study the black-and-white photograph positioned above the black mantelpiece: what was it exactly? To be specific, what part of the body? It took a little while for me to realise that it was the curve of a woman's lower back and her bottom. The photo was a moody affair, an Athenarotica number. The title would have been folded round the back. I imagined it was called 'Sensual World', or 'Intimate Desire', or 'Bodily Functions', or something.

'. . . bringing over these vibrators from America. What's unusual about this type is that they're not for internal use. Yet they've been described as the Rolls Royce of vibrators. Have you ever used one?'

James paused. Clearly, I was meant to respond. But I didn't have anything to say *vis* US stimulatory hardware; and I was disconcerted to note that during his monologue James had turned towards me and moved rather closer, so that his knee was touching my upper thigh. I felt like you do when you're fourteen and a boy you don't fancy suddenly clamps his arm round your shoulder: you don't want to be impolite, but you certainly don't want him to leave it there.

So, you casually wriggle out of his grip. I jumped up and said: 'I think I'd like another drink.'

In the kitchen, thankfully, were Carol and Mike, plus two other couples who had arrived together. I was happy to see that the two new women, whilst briefly skirted, were rather more warmly wrapped than Carol. Dressed to pull, in minis and little low-necked tops, they looked as though they were off to a nightclub. One of the women, a big girl with a big laugh, gave me a smile.

'You after a tipple?'

'Did you say *tip*ple?' said Mike, and everyone laughed.

The conversation had died down when I came in, which made me nervous. I scanned about for the white wine. Everyone seemed to be leaning casually against cupboards and the table, in usual gossip-in-kitchen party mode. But when I looked at Carol, who was leaning back chummily against one of the new men, I noticed that he had his hand down her shirt and was busily locating her tipple like nobody's business. I glanced at James, but he didn't seem to have noticed.

The doorbell rang again.

'I'll get it,' sang James and bounded down the hallway.

'Shall we go back through to the lounge?' said Carol, making shooing movements with her hands.

In all, there were thirteen of us and it was quite a squish in the sitting-room. Everyone was a good deal older than me: I still felt as though I was chatting to my parents' friends. There was no background music. At one point, James came round with some warmed-up pieces of pizza. I had a long talk with Sue, who had been the PA for a company director until she was featured in the *News of the World*. She'd been at a swinging club in central London with her boyfriend of the time, and they'd got chatting to a nervous-looking couple who said they were new to the scene. So Sue's boyfriend took the girl on to the dancefloor, and Sue spent quite some time talking to the man, 'with a little kissing and cuddling'. They exchanged phone numbers. But it was a set-up. Sue was followed home, photographed; and the photo – along with her name, address and where she worked – was printed in the next edition. A double page spread.

'I was quoted extensively,' grinned Sue. 'Extensively.'

Sue lost her job. But she didn't seem to care: 'I needed a change anyway,' she declared. 'I want to put something back into the community. Look after old people. Or children. Or maybe animals. Or all of them together!'

Sue had been making me laugh, so that I had forgotten to keep an eye on the general party action; but now I checked, I noticed that the lounge was less full than it had been. It was ten o'clock. James had been in a few minutes earlier and put on a porn video. Most of the guests had made a few fruity comments as a result: the atmosphere was of a polite post-wedding party – a bit naughty, a little giddy, but no swearing and cigarette-smoking in the kitchen only. Next to me on the sofa, a couple was watching the porn with a blankness I found disturbing. Briefly, I thought of Fred and Rosemary West. I wondered where the rest of the party had gone.

I went into the kitchen, where I met Kev, an earnest, boyish dentist (of all things); one of the rogue males. Like Sue and James before him, he seemed keen to talk about swinging. In fact, other than the brief art and holidays discussion at the beginning of the evening, wife-swapping had been the sum total of conversation topics. Kev told me that he held parties too, but he preferred to come to other people's. He said that he found being the host a little trying: one time, he was 'playing' with one of his lady guests when he was forced to stop for a couple of minutes, in order to say goodbye to a couple of others. When he returned, he found that his position had been taken up by another man.

'Which I thought was a bit much,' murmured Kev.

I said: 'Mmm.'

'Anyway,' he continued. 'I live in a flat and my downstairs neighbours complained, so I've had to stop holding parties.'

'What did they complain about?'

'Oh, the noise. They said the lavatory flushing kept them awake. They're an elderly couple. And they also said the last orgasm was at half-past one in the morning!'

'What? So they could hear everything?'

'Apparently.' Kev sniggered softly. He took a step forward and put his hands on my waist.

I said: 'Where's the toilet?'

The bathroom was spotless, pink and black with ornate taps. On a side table, next to the bath, was a piece of sculpture: a black female torso from belly button to upper thigh. She was bending forward, her behind in the air, legs apart. The sculpture was a little anatomical for my taste.

I decided to see what was going on in the other rooms. Where was everyone? I pushed open the door of the front bedroom. And found out.

I was reminded of house parties when I was a teenager, when if you wanted to get off with someone, you went into a bedroom where there were umpteen other snogging couples and tried to find a space on the floor. Except that then, the lights were always off. This room was lit like the soft furnishings section of a department store. I looked a little harder. Actually, there weren't quite as many people as I'd first thought. There was Sue, and Mike, and two or three others. Sue popped her head up, laughed to see me, and waved.

'Come on in!' she said.

But I didn't. Really, I couldn't. I spotted James in there, and I flapped a hand at him and called: 'Thank you for having me!' (ha!). Then I went down the stairs and made my own way out.

5

keeping up appearances

Of course, no wife-swapping party would be complete without accompanying curtain-twitching. The reason why Kev had been so nonchalant about his complaining neighbours is that he knew that curtain-twitching – the original Neighbourhood Watch – is as much a staple of suburban life as driving, or golfing, or swinging. Has that car been on that particular drive before? Who's that arriving at number 7 at this time of night? Have you seen the state of Mr Brown's dinner suit, the one that Mrs Brown has just thrown out of their bedroom window, along with the rest of his wardrobe . . . oh look, and Mr Brown himself?

And, before you get the wrong impression, such queries are

not just idle nosiness: curtain-twitching has a regulatory aspect, a sense of standards set, of rules made to remain unbroken, of norms and tenets prescribed and upheld. Curtain-twitching referees the eternal suburban game of 'keeping up appearances'. After all, without the curtain twitchers' steady stream of unbiased reports and league tables, there is no way you would know just how you're faring *vis-à-vis* the Joneses.

Unless, that is, you lived in North Staffordshire or South Cheshire. For this particular area of Britain has its own particular monitor of propriety and success: the locally-based, locally-biased *Style* magazine. I think it was in Knutsford motorway services that I first came across *Style*. It was bracketed separately, away from the higgledy pan-national *hoi polloi*, the *Bella*s and *Best*s, the *She*s, the *Woman*s, the *Now!*s and *OK!*s and *More!*s. *Style* stood alone, in glory, in its own special see-through plastic rack. On its cover was a picture of a nicely-dressed young lady (polo-neck, leather gloves) standing next to a Land Rover, above the line NORTH STAFFORDSHIRE BANK EXECUTIVE DRIVES UP INTEREST IN OFF-ROADING. Underneath, in smaller letters, it read *Win! A Jacuzzi Bath Worth £1,800* – which referred to a competition on the inside of the magazine, and wasn't a sly comment on the state of the North Staffordshire Bank Executive's personal hygiene after all that strenuous four-wheel-driving.

A quick flick through revealed that *Style* magazine is a light 'n' glossy mix of property, fashion, cars, socialising, holidays, food 'n' drink, 'n' local charity endeavours. Its articles have titles like *It's Curtains For Drab Drapes!*, *Executive Features!*, *A Glass Act!* and *Viva Majorca!*. Its social pages, Style Review, show men in dinner suits and ladies in satin tents brandishing donation cheques the size of doormats: headlines include *Rotary To Rescue* and *Rotary Club's Ladies' Night*; *Golfers Raise £2,000 Through Pro-Am Event* and *Pro-Am Event Raises £2,340 For Charity*. *Style*'s opening pages are covered in houses – designer properties, barn conversions, country residences, 'delightful', 'detached', 'deceptively spacious' three- and four- and five-bedroomed (three *en suite*) houses; plus their interiors: fitted kitchens, luxury bathrooms, prestige bedrooms, executive dog kennels. *Style* covers everything in which a curtain-twitcher is interested, and is available throughout North Staffordshire and South Cheshire at just £1.50 every month.

Style is popular, with a certain type of person.

'We were told,' confided David Smith, whose company publishes *Style*, 'by a local carpenter, that he sees *Style* on the bedside table of every bedroom he works on. He specialises in fitted wardrobes.' David was pleased with this. 'Well, fitted wardrobes. It's just who we're aiming for.'

Like most magazines, *Style* knows its market.

'Our readers,' announced David, 'are people with a bit of money, who like to live a quality life. But who aren't the old-fashioned hunting and shooting set. Not the rah-rahs.'

Style reaches its market via its sharply-angled feminine approach: it aims at the ladies in order to get to the gents. *Style* targets the wife of the well-off businessman, who, these days, may well have a business herself. In fact, there's been several *Style* articles about successful ladies, including an image consultant, a feng shui expert, a violinist, and a horse-breeder-come-fashion-shop-proprietor. Featured gentlemen include a professional golfer and a self-made millionaire. *Style*, explained David, is not about those born to money, but those who've worked long and hard to earn it. And would like their neighbours to glimpse some of the spoils of ditto in a local, glossy magazine.

Before *Style* was launched, there was market research done, to identify its catchment area. David was given a map that coloured the resulting locations. Then he himself drove around, checking the checkers' results. 'You see, some of the roads go off down one end,' tutted David; and those roads that do, do not get *Style*. But along the cuter of cul-de-sacs, the best of boulevards, the roads where every res is a des, *Style* plops through every letter-box, every month, without any resident paying a penny. In fact, most of *Style*'s circulation is made up from these hand-outs; the advertisers want to hit a certain audience, and David makes sure *Style* whacks them right between the peepers. He gives *Style* away to local heads of business, prominent people in Staffs society. He's chuffed to see *Style* in dentists' waiting rooms; delighted that *Style* is the coffee-table staple of regional banks and corporations.

There's a lot of local feedback on the magazine. People phone up and register their views. Generally, the property section meets with high approval, as does the cheque-waving Style Review, and the fashion. However, certain covers have caused unfavourable comment: notably those of September 1997 and March 1998. The first featured a local lady in lemon yellow day-suit (the readers thought her skirt too short); the other was of a chap in electric blue double-breasted, with black button-down shirt and hectic tie (reader verdict: looked like a gangster).

Style readers, along with all good curtain-twitchers, set great store by appearances: clothes, hair, grooming, *style*.

Style was set up by David's company, Smith Davis, with the local paper, the *Sentinel*, which is part of the Associated Newspapers group. Ultimately, then, it's owned by David, his partner, Pete Davis, and the Rothermeres. *Style* is a bit of a branch out for Smith Davis, who usually publish in-house cheer-em-ups, like *Towers Times* (for Alton Towers), *Portcullis* (for those employed by HM's Customs and Excise Department), *Wavelength* (P&O) and *Talkback* (JCB, for some reason), but it's proved remarkably successful.

'Oh yes, we're ever so pleased,' said David. 'In fact, we were thinking of inviting Lord Rothermere to our Christmas party. But he died.'

Style seemed to know what it was talking about when it came to appearances, so I thought I'd pay it a visit, watch and learn. It's produced in the small potteries town of Burslem, by a handful of Smith Davis's staff: despite *Style*'s female slant, all those who work on it are men. There had been a lady fashion editor, but she left and, when I visited, staff writer Paul Berra had taken over her job. Paul has been a journalist all his working life; he was twenty-six years – 'man and boy' – on the *Manchester Daily Express*. A modest, welcoming chap, with a small boy's smile, he wore a suit and shirt that didn't seem to me to trip the fashion light fantastic, but such things are all in the details these days.

When he writes about fashion, Paul calls himself Tanya Beaumont. As Tanya, he was a little worried about his special winter fashion pull-out. I was asked to give it a quick scan over; 'We need the feminine touch,' cried Tanya. Everything seemed okay to me; Tanya spoke in the same language as every other women's magazine I'd seen that month – 'key shapes', 'slouch chic', 'Soho-Boho' – and told the same auto-amnesia story. Forget short, think long! Forget skirts, think trews! Forget black, think white! (Or was it the other way about? I forget.)

'It looks fine,' I said.

'I've been checking up,' said Paul proudly. 'Most of my ideas come from reading the *Telegraph*'s fashion pages.'

We nipped over the road for a sandwich – 'there're quite a few places popping up round here now' – then Paul took me out on an assignment. We drove to the outskirts of Burslem, to the pretty garden estates of Brown Edge, where Paul interviewed thirty-year-old pipe fitter Jonathan Egan about his car, a new-to-you DeLorean.

'That's Jonathan with an A-N, not an O-N?' asked Paul. Paul's a great believer in the local paper doctrine that puts as many readers' names in the magazine as possible, and makes sure you spell them correctly. Jonathan lettered everything out, including Tracey, 'E-Y', his girlfriend's name. Then we went for a DeLorean drive.

We thundered round the little lanes, a rocket-fuelled tank sent to panic the sheep. When we stopped, the gull-wing doors flapped like a stretching giant. Paul and I had a good look round. The side windows didn't open. The back window had slatted blinds. The body was unfettered metal. The boot had room for an exercise book. The back lights were made from a seventies computer game. The silhouette was as wide and as flat as a steam-rolled boy racer. The DeLorean was strange, but terrific: massive, fantastic, utterly ridiculous.

But, as Paul admitted afterwards, it wasn't really what *Style* is about. Amazing as it was, the DeLorean was too macho, too curio for anything but the back pages. Not one for the ladies. And, as we know, *Style* is nothing if not conscious of its female appeal. So, to get a more representative Stylistic impression, I went with another journalist, Pete Davis, to his cover story.

Pete was to interview two Very Special Ladies. The VSLs were so deemed because of their attachment to two VSM: John Rudge and Brian Little, the managers of the two local football teams, Port Vale and Stoke City. The VSLs – Dellice Rudge and Heather Little – were to be interviewed in the Royal Doulton Visitor Centre, though no one told me why. Perhaps there would be a few spare pieces of commemorative porcelain lying about; neither of their husbands' teams are in the habit of winning much. Still, Stoke City had had higher hopes since ex-Premier manager Little had agreed to sign up with them a couple of months previously. And Port Vale are Robbie Williams' favourite team and he knows all about rising from the dead.

The Royal Doulton Visitor Centre was just down the road. Pete and I set off in high spirits. The weather was bright, Burslem was busy and sunny. It's not a flashy town by any means – the buildings are small and red brick, with, it seemed, every other one a pub – but the pavements were crowded with workers and schoolchildren, the traffic was heavy, life was being lived with vim and scant regard for the Green Cross Code. On the way down, Pete told me about the book he had written a few years back, about the miners' strike: 'It seems a long time ago now,' said Pete.

At the Visitor Centre, the Royal Doulton PR was already brandishing the teacups: white with elegant flower motif and golden trim. There was a matching teapot too, and free scones. The photographer, Matt, explained that Dellice – a long-established Staffs resident – would be pictured welcoming new girl Heather to the local area, over a cup of tea made from locally-produced chinaware. We were early, but Matt the photographer was already set up. Pete had his questions jotted down in his notebook. Everything was prepared.

The VSLs arrived separately, and in some slight confusion: a problem with directions; an over-heating in the unusually mild temperatures. They were both turned out smartly, one in blue, one in black and white, hair coiffed, lipstick straight, eyes bright, seemingly ready for their cover shots. Now if they wouldn't mind just leaning into the teapot and smiling towards Matt . . . Oh dear.

'Didn't they tell you I hate having my photograph taken?' barked one of the VSLs, suddenly. She didn't seem very happy. It was decided to finish the photographs later. A few questions, to be going on with?

But 'Why did you ask me that?' snapped the same VSL, when Pete asked her if she was interested in sport herself. And 'I'm not telling you!', when he wondered about her child's exams.

Things were becoming a little tense. Perhaps some tea? The Doulton PR hurried to assist: scones were proffered, sugar-lumps plopped. Pete changed tactic, he threw some wild questions: 'Do you keep fit?'; 'What kind of question is that?' hurled back the VSL. He lobbed easy ones: 'Do you like Staffordshire people?'.

The VSL would not be mollified. She just couldn't relax. She treated every enquiry as if it were a trick, as if it were live and dangerous and would flip without warning and bite her on the nose. Soon the other VSL grew irritated, and her mood, too, began to turn. Her expression switched from eager to glazed and she leant back in her chair. Occasionally she muttered, 'Well, I'm just a bit boring', and gave a high, brittle laugh.

Poor Pete. Poor VSLs. No one was happy. Somehow, the afternoon had turned strange. I started chatting with the Royal Doulton PR just so I wouldn't have to watch. She whisked me through a Doulton history, made me goggle at some prices, and told me that in the local area, there were thieves that specifically targetted Royal Doulton china.

'Oh, you can't have Royal Doulton on display,' piped up a VSL, who'd overheard. 'You have to keep it upstairs, in the bedroom, locked away in a cabinet. You can't trust people with Royal Doulton.'

Clearly not. Watch your friends like a hawk. Never leave a visitor alone with a figurine. Turn your back on the vicar to set out the shortbread and he'll have smuggled a shepherdess under his cassock.

From Royal Doulton safety procedures, talk turned to home decoration. Pete popped in a question. And suddenly, incredibly, the atmosphere changed, and the VSLs were away.

'I've just had my kitchen revamped,' said one, breathlessly.

'It was gas – double oven, gas hob. Well, I'm used to electric, it had to go. The cupboards needed moving, different handles, tiles . . . I'm going yellow and blue, with terracotta radiators . . .'

'I love all that planning,' cooed the other. 'It's the most exciting time. We might buy the plot next to ours. I would like to build another house, perhaps sell ours, or let it. I'd love to start again. I know now just where I went wrong – but it was my first project . . .'

'I'm into renovation. My first effort was a little sewing box I bought for £6 from a bric-à-brac place . . .'

'I bought a rocking chair, I thought I'd have a go at that. Stripping, re-upholstering . . .'

'. . . I cut a piece of paper, measured the pleats to get it right . . .'

'. . . I like old things – well we've had our suite thirty years!'

'. . . put it into one of those auctions and got £46! I was so proud!'

The VSLs paused, flushed, excited, bonding across bone china and over the thrills of *découpage*. Pete ventured another question: 'Do you know a lot about antiques, then?' The VSLs turned, surprised to see him there. One fixed him with a beady eye.

'Oh, I'm not into all those eras,' she sniffed, dismissively. 'I just buy things as and when.'

I thought about the interview as I drove away from Burslem, back on to the M6, and up to Wilmslow. (It was my mum's sixtieth birthday the next day, and I was invited to her afternoon party. In the garden, if fine. No men allowed.) I thought about the sudden, united passion of the VSLs, the light in their eyes when they talked about their homes, the words they used: project, planning, effort, proud. I remembered a TV programme I'd seen about cowboy builders, and a woman in it who'd had a dodgy bathroom extension: how upset she was, her chin out, tears brimming, saying, 'This is all I've got. This house, my family. He's ruined it.' And I remembered another programme, one of those *Changing Rooms*-type numbers, where a grown man – a bouncer! – had also burst into tears. But – innit luvly – his had been tears of joy: he'd been overcome by the sheer beauty of his redesigned kitchen. There's a thin line between love and hate, and it's a question of millimetres and a couple of misplaced rawl-plugs when it comes to home decoration.

Recently, as a sort of research – I was buying a flat for the first time – I spent a night in, watching as many of those 'invite a TV crew to rip out your furniture/lawn and replace it with luridly painted MDF/decking' programmes as I could. There were *loads*; I didn't move for the whole evening, and I haven't got cable. Each one was presented by a youngish, prettyish woman who kept bounding about from house to house (small pre-fabs owned by nuclear families on BBC1; gay couples' revamped townhouses on BBC2) exclaiming at the handiwork of a couple of ponce-o designers, one or two 'hunky' labourers and umpteen other bit players: paint-splashing neighbours, nerdy estate agents, secondary presenter sidekicks, shipped-in experts and consultants, amusing pets, etc. Mostly, there was a concept: an entire cul-de-sac of houses would need their gardens doing up; or there was only twenty-four hours and £2.50 available to turn a potting shed into a self-contained granny flat; or everything had to be 'environmentally sound'. Though what they did with the old, CFC-laden, asbestos-heavy, plastic-fantastic, unrecyclable fittings was never revealed.

The reason why there were so many of these programmes on the telly is that they are very popular (or, at least *Changing Rooms* is, and the rest are hoping to mop up any viewers who can't tell the difference between one Carol and the next). DIY is booming in Britain. There are those – e.g. T. Blair – who would put this down to a rabbitlike expansion of the middle class (and it would have to be rabbitlike, for, as is hammered into every Briton from birth to death, class is genetic); there are others who label such home improvements frenzy as a trend for 'nesting', as though you could go for a quick rummage in long grass and come home with a sideboard in your beak.

Judging by the VSLs, though, I'd say that the DIY boom is all down to passion. When they were talking about their homes, their faces lit up. They were aglow: with Planning Control, with Self-Determination, with A Long-Term Project, with Co-ordinating Upholstery, with Love. Their husbands, the football managers, might be important figures to outsiders, but within the home, the VSLs were queens. They envisioned, planned, designed, spent, commanded, shaped, governed. They ruled.

An Englishman's home is his castle, said someone, once; rightly enough, if said Englishman was one of those who were born to own Northumbria, or Kent, or swathes of Scotland. In those cases, a castle tends to be thrown in, along with a couple of crates of serfs. But for most Englishmen, and women, and those of Scotland, Wales and Ireland, their home is not a castle, but a combination of haven and hell. Hell, because their home is owned not by them, but by someone else – the council, the landlord, the bank – who charges obscene amounts to let them stay there. Haven, because they get to choose the curtains.

Under such circumstances, curtain-choosing – the area where you exercise the control – becomes life-defining, all-important. Visit any large John Lewis's, or out-of-town B&Q, or the Ideal Home Exhibition and you'll see how crucial interior decoration can become. The intensity of the discussions! The passion of the arguments! The vibrancy of the colour swabs!

Actually, I've been to the Ideal Home Exhibition a couple of times, and on both occasions I was thoroughly overwhelmed. It is a massive event. The last time I went, there were four full size, fully constructed five- and six-bedroomed homes in the centre of the hall – the Showhouse Village – and said village took up less than a tenth of the floor space.

The Village was very popular actually; everyone wanted a peek inside the showhomes, a nosy poke round someone else's cupboards, even if that someone was completely virtual. The queues to get into the houses stretched round corners and lasted for hours. And the queuers appeared to have prepared for their endurance wait by stocking up on body fat beforehand. These people were almost as big as the houses they were visiting. Their double chins swayed gently in the air-conditioning as they waited to wander through homes that they hoped would put theirs to shame. Once inside, they prodded tallboys with hot dog roll fingers; they pushed their vast bottoms into straining wicker chairs; they blew sighs from chubby cheeks to see the golden tapped bidets. They shuffled through the eco-friendly kitchen in the Conservation House from Bellway Homes;

trudged up the split staircase of the Badminton House from Crest Homes; waddled over the light wood floor of the World of Colour House Beautiful Home; made like well-built dancing sprites in the unique spaciousness of the Celebration House from Wimpey.

'Oh, we're just here to get ideas really,' said one woman when I asked her why she had come.

'And have you got any?'

'Well, I don't know if you spotted this in the downstairs lounge, but I liked the double curtain effect. And they've unusual radiators in the Conservation Home. But otherwise,' sniffed the lady, a touch disdainfully, 'not really, no.'

After the Show Village, the queuers and I visited the Furniture section and stood in line to wriggle in a leather arm-chair that gave an all-over body massage when you flicked the switch inside the armrest. Vibrating suites were definitely one of the more popular items at the Ideal Home: the others included travel-irons that ironed your clothes whilst they were still on the hanger; the *Encyclopedia Britannica* on CD Rom; rollers that gave your gloss paint a pseudo-wood finish, complete with knots; and wheely-bin covers – surely the modern-day equiva-lent of the doilies that were put round piano legs by prudish Victorian Dads.

'My husband'll kill me,' laughed one woman, showing me hers. It was a specially-shaped and laminated paper print of rustic autumn leaves, specifically designed to wrap around the wheely bin and cover its unseemly green hue. 'It cost £13.99,' said the woman. I thought that, at that price, her husband would be fully justified if he left the wheely bin as it was and just used it as a cover for his unseemly wife, but I didn't comment. For those of you who are interested, other bin-disguising designs included: spring flowers, summer flowers, funny cartoon frogs and dry stone wall.

The Ideal Home showed me that, as a nation, we are entirely capable of losing it over home interiors. It doesn't matter where you live, either. People who live in cities come over just as unnecessary as the VSLs: they merely flip over different things. Instead of obsessing over fitted wardrobes and flowered borders, they hit a certain age and want to talk postcodes and sea-grass matting. They rush to 'invest' in a leather bean-bag. (Warning to youngsters: twenty-eight is when it happens. Before then, social discourse requires only that you can discuss both adverts *and* the opposite sex without food falling out of your mouth. After twenty-eight, wherever you live, you've got to be sofa-bed-cognisant. It's a right drag.)

But, remember, DIYers, your own home is never enough. That's why the Ideal Homers spent all that time in the Show Village; that's the appeal of *OK!* and *Hello!* (look at the state of Cher's guest bedroom eiderdown!); that's why *Style* has become so successful, as well as all those interiors magazines; that's one of the fundamental tenets of curtain-twitching. The fatal attraction of housing, its promise of security and independence and expression of your own wonderful personality through innovative use of *faux*-mosaic tiling is not limited to your own humble abode. Other people's homes are just as enthralling. They're a glimpse into another world, a different life, one that looks better – more chic, more monied, more exciting, more serene – than yours. If only you had pine shutters and an

Arabian throw rug, then maybe you'd live like a building society advert too . . . The reason why the VSLs got so excited about their homes is that, like us, they think a nice home means a lovely life.

The next day, I sat in the back garden on borrowed plastic furniture with thirty-two of my mum's friends. Several were from the school where my mum teaches; some lived in Wilmslow; others were mothers of people I knew. We had a lovely time. We slurped at wine. We queued for the buffet. We jumped from our seats to collect dirty plates. We offered to wash up and make the coffee. We made Mum take the weight off her feet (she was a bit tipsy and kept rushing around clearing glasses and taking photos).

Conversation flowed. Divorces – 'I said, "Is that her? What a sight! Tight jeans that split her right in two, you know. You'd think he could do better than that"'; children – 'This new girlfriend, well, she's wonderful, according to him. She's much better than the old one, at least. You never got a peep out of her'; home improvements (of course) – 'He offered me a choice. Holiday or new kitchen. Well, what would you choose? Same as me. Holiday. But I got the kitchen too, heheh . . .'

The home improvements talk led to Sue, who's recently moved, telling me of her Terrible Patio Traumas. She'd employed an Irish workman, Patsy, who'd turned up at her door one day and told her he'd done the front paving at number 26. (He hadn't.) There were problems right from the start. She found him drawing dinosaurs in the hardening cement, with beer bottle tops as eyes. Then Sue pointed out that the edges of the patio weren't parallel. Patsy measured across and said they were. Sue argued that he needed to take two measurements to check that there was no widening or narrowing. Patsy disagreed. There was a row. Patsy left.

He came back, but things still weren't easy. It was his drinking. Sue may have encouraged this by buying him a bottle of Johnny Walkers (she felt guilty about the argument); whatever, it was six weeks since he'd finished and she was still finding cans in the bushes. And one time Patsy turned up at Sue's house at half-past eleven at night; stumbling across the front path from a taxi, tripping on the threshold, muddying the floor.

'I told them Race Hoss Road,' he slurred on the doorstep. Sue fetched a chair for him to sit on. She couldn't let him past the hall: Patsy was filthy. He would have ruined the carpet.

'It's Racecourse Road, Patsy,' she said, soothingly, 'but you don't live here.'

'Race Hoss Road! Race Hoss Road!' cried Patsy, triumphantly. 'I told em! Race Hoss Road!'

Sue and her son got Patsy into the car to take him home. He managed a few slurred directions. When they went round the King's Arms roundabout, he waved at the central grass. He'd taken a kip there at some point during his evening. It was all quite funny, said Sue, until they got to where he actually lived. Patsy's home was a caravan: no electric, no toilet, no heating, no nothing. Just scattered cans and a filthy sleeping bag laid out on the filthy floor.

Still, he'd parked it well. The caravan was on the most desirable road in Alderley Edge, parked bang next to property that cost hundreds of thousands, in the thick of the footballers, the stockbrokers, the businessmen, the higher echelons of curtain-twitchers. With his caravan, Patsy had landed on his tottering feet. He was smack in the middle of the *Style*-life lifestyle. Now, if he could just find the right interior designer . . .

6

my hot night in Cheshire's flesh pots

I was back in Wilmslow for a Saturday night. I couldn't remember the last time I'd been for a night out in Wilmslow. Whenever I went back to see my mum and dad, it took me a good half hour's drive into Manchester before I could relax enough to have a drink. Wilmslow's pubs, with their under-aged bubble-heads, their puffy-faced executives, their freeze-dried smiles, had lost their appeal some years ago. But I'd decided to see if anything had changed; whether that thing was me, or Wilmslow's drinking holes – which my mum insisted were 'quite the place to go out, these days'. I'd phoned my brother, who'd said he'd come along too.

As teenagers, of course, my brother and I spent our lives

trying to worm our way into pubs. I failed mostly because – even when I finally made eighteen – I looked about as grown-up as a Cabbage Patch Doll; Toby was barred due to his dangerous earring. The local pubs, in those days, were of one type. Swirly-carpeted, dark-timbered olde worlde snugs with *faux* tapestry seat covers and bum-fluffed men with their jacket sleeves rolled up to the elbow. They smelt of B&H and Aramis. The juke box – if there was one – was programmed to play Dire Straits 'Romeo and Juliet' non-stop from 7 p.m. to closing time. Except for 'Bat Out Of Hell' hour. Oh, adult pleasures! When I did get let in, I gave a friend the money to go to the bar. I drank Blue Bols-and-lemonade. It made your tongue turn purple.

Then, there were only pubs. There might have been wine bars, but no one I knew was about to drink wine. Boys drank pints of Boddingtons' or Robinsons'; girls drank the same, or, more usually, something more eye-catchingly ladylike: Pernod-and-black, Southern Comfort-and-lemonade, Bacardi-and-Coke, Malibu-and-pineapple, Martini-and-lemonade, Blue Bols-and-lemonade, Baileys-on-the-rocks, Archers-on-the-rocks, weird premixed drinks called Taboo and Mirage (Taboo-and-lemonade, Mirage-and-Coke). The pubs were heady with breath that hummed like a Boots perfume counter. The toilets were spattered with rainbow-hued sick. It made my head swim just to think about it.

Over the last few years, however, Wilmslow – at least, according to my mum – had undergone a bit of a renaissance. From being the place to shop, it had become *the* place to go out. There were quite a few restaurants – including Pizza Express and Café Rouge – which was a new thing: there used to just be

103

The Mandarin (Chinese) and Trevi's (Italian), both reserved for special occasions. And suddenly Wilmslow was littered with bars. Not pubs: bars.

A few years before, a couple of new pubs had appeared in disused buildings: The Blue Lamp in the old police station; Bank Square wine-bar in what used to be the Midland Bank. Now, said my mum, the whole of the town was bristling with scrub-boarded hostelries. Gilbert's Sports Shop was now The Nose bistro, the store next door to what-used-to-be-the-cinema had been magicked into Samuel Finney's pub, the huge derelict house by the Recreation Centre had become a two-floored drinking house called the Rectory . . . There was even a new place called Eskimo on Grove Street, which Mum thought had once been Charles Charnley's the Chemists. I wondered if I'd be able to remember all the changes, or if I'd find myself at the bar asking if they stocked the spray version of Sun-In.

It wasn't just restaurants and bars that Wilmslow boasted now. There were two newish nightclubs that came recommended. One was Kell's, out past the airport on the Altrincham roundabout, where Manchester United footballers were rumoured to shake a million pound leg; and the other was called Peruvia, closer in, in the Moat House Hotel, once the Valley Lodge.

Nightlife in suburbia is traditionally dire; if you're not one for wine-bars, nor wife-swapping, nor bridge clubs, nor fortnightly hoe-downs in the Leisure Centre, there's really nothing for you to do after 8 p.m. Other than sand down the skirting board. Or talk to the other half. No wonder DIY has taken off. So I was interested to see if the new leisure revolution (boozing in banks! sipping in sports shops! pickled in a chemists!) really had changed my local social scene. Would stilettos still be perma-glued to feminine feet? Would this season's longer length skirts make a showing (as I recalled, any fashion for dresses that stretched further than mid-thigh was always rejected by Wilmslow girls as impractical, i.e. you wouldn't pull in it). Would the local top lads still insist on drinking pints of bitter; or would lager, or perhaps even alcopops, have made a beverage impression? Would Toby's earring still be regarded as radical?

Toby arrived home, and we worked out a schedule. Eight thirty at the Rectory. Nine thirty: the Eskimo Bar on Grove Street. Kell's no later than 11.30, because it was busy Saturdays, then Peruvia after 1.30, when the crowds had calmed down. The pair of us dressed for battle: Toby in flash suit, me in slinko trousers. No trainers, no sportswear. Some things, we just knew, would never change.

The Rectory car park boasted a few choice motors – a flashy Lexus, several BMWs and a Mercedes SLK graced the gravel. We crunched past them towards the entrance. Shoulders back, gender forward: Toby strode like a sportsman, I minced like a model-stroke-actress. There was a bouncer outside the door, not tall, but built like a sideboard; two more, kitchen-dressers with earpieces, just inside the entrance. Each gave us the onceover more than once. I felt like a fraud.

The Rectory's décor was ye olde vibrante slap-dashe: wood beams hastily painted in turquoise and russet, industrial radia-tors given the scrunched-cloth-in-gloss effect. Some bricks were left exposed; there were black, twisted metal candlesticks; a few sofas, in hot colours; and big fireplaces, painted black and left empty. The floor was wooden boards. Downstairs, the front room was full; the back, getting there; but no one was allowed upstairs until later, according to the round-faced bargirl.

I asked her about the bouncers. She said: 'On Fridays and Saturdays we're open until one in the morning, so it's no trainers or jeans. And you're not allowed in after 10.30. But basically, if they don't like the look of you, you'll never get in anyway.' She smiled to say, you look fine, you see, you're in aren't you? We took our drinks and went to sit in the back room.

The music thumped cheerfully from speakers on high: disco classics, funky stuff, good time sing-songs. I was inordinately cheered to hear Shalimar's 'I Can Make You Feel Good'. (Shalimar was my favourite group when I was sixteen. They were a mediocre US disco trio whose sole fame claim was a flamboyant body-popping sequence on a seminal *Top Of The Pops* by Jeffry, who wore thin-lapelled suit jackets with nothing underneath. I thought he was fantastic.) I had a scan at the other clientele. They varied from pub-crawling groups of teenagers, through perkily-jacketed foursomes in their mid-thirties, a pack of celebrating twenty-something blokes, eating at a long table towards the back, and a solitary grey-haired man whose sartorials had matured sometime around 1983. He sported double-vented grey jacket, slip-on woven loafers, massala tan, lager stomach and a number 2 crop which gave way to a cloud of silver hair at the nape that he must have tied into a pony-tail on occasion. Peter Stringfellow, eat my thong!

A tall, slim lad came over. And, blimey, we knew him! It was

Alex – Toby and I used to baby-sit him and his sister Nicole. We had a chat about what he was up to, which was working for an insurance company and saving up to buy a camper van. Suddenly, Alex stuck his tongue out: he'd had it pierced. It didn't quite match with his neat appearance: his short hair, smart trousers, nice shirt.

He shrugged: 'They haven't even noticed at work. I got it done because you can't see it.'

I said: 'I bet you don't waggle your tongue at the bouncers here.'

Alex said it wasn't worth it. He'd once come for a drink in The Rectory and the bouncers had kicked off over the fact that Alex's polo shirt was untucked. Alex had explained that you're meant to wear it untucked; and the Liverpudlian bouncers had retorted that he should remember that he was in Wilmslow. Eventually, they let him in. But they made him sit behind a pillar.

Toby and I stayed for a time, chatting with Alex. But we had a schedule to keep to. We left at 9.25 precisely. Verdict on The Rectory: heavy. Though I thought that the décor could have won a *Changing Room* gong.

Off we gambolled to Eskimo, in the old shop. I was sure it hadn't ever been Charnley's the Chemists. What did it used to be? I wondered. Johnson's the Stationers? I didn't want to stand outside for too long checking, as the bouncers looked itchy. I remembered. Eskimo used to be a butcher's. We nodded at the knuckleheads and strode in, keeping our jokes about meat markets to ourselves.

Eskimo was a narrow, bright room, with stairs upstairs to the restaurant, and a long bar on the ground floor that had real live fish swimming inside it. I felt sorry for the fish. They were at the wrong level: forced to circulate forever with a crotch-eye view of proceedings, like Wee Willie Krankie. Still, the fish were the sort of detail that gave Eskimo its desired air, that of a groovy hairdressers, or the reception area for a design magazine. They gave it a wash of approximate modernity, the fish and the glass bricks and the block areas of matt paint. The fish said 'sharp, cutting edge, young, smart'; they said 'hard surfaces, loud music'; they said 'expensive beer, no trainers'; they said 'go home, Mum'.

Eskimo was full. We jostled to the bar. The girl behind it was the spit of Jo Guest, the *Loaded* babe, with a bob so blonde and skin so tanned she looked as though she was in negative. We watched as she served a young man whose eyes matched his pink Polo shirt. Jo mixed three liquids into a Martini glass, then set it alight. The glass was passed to the lad, and as he slurped his fire through a plastic straw, the bargirl poured in two more liquids: something beige and opaque from the left, something clear and blue from the right. The whole palaver had the air of an alcoholic chemistry experiment. You expected a grand finale, an explosion at least. I looked hard at his ears to see if they were steaming.

'What's that you're drinking?' I asked.

The young man paused, handed over a fiver, belched with airy gravitas and replied, without looking at me: 'Flamin' Lamborghini.'

We needed no further introduction. We ordered two each.

'Here's to the miracle of Italian engineering,' said Toby, and we hoovered them down. One, whoof; then two, bang. Suddenly, Toby's face melted. It visibly slackened. He stamped his feet and clapped his hands, once. He started laughing. So did I. I had no idea why he was, but it was my head that was doing it to me: it was bouncing gaily somewhere high above my body, a balloon atop a string. I felt hilarious. I felt marvellous. All cylinders firing, brain racing through first to fifth, heart going for burn-out. I slammed my hand on to the bar in glee. Looking about, I vaguely clocked that most of Eskimo's clientele seemed quite sober, smart in their couples and double-dates. Everyone had combed their hair before coming out. This made me giggle even more. I looked at Toby. When he turned to look at me, his eyes struggled to catch up with the movement. I supposed mine were doing the same. I tested myself, by shaking my head like a wet dog.

Something, someone caught my eye. Who was that? Over there! Look! Six-foot tall, make-up applied like anaglypta, dress the size of a hanky failing to cover a pair of thighs that could crack concrete. A drag queen! In Cheshire! Well, you could have tickled me purple with last year's feather boa. Things really had changed around these parts. I started to make my way over. I wanted to chat. I felt so happy that she'd make it, that she'd dressed herself up for a night out in Wilmslow. Who'd have thought that Cheshire would allow it? Perhaps she'd moved suburbwards to escape the competition – Manchester's Gay Village is peppered with trannies. Perhaps Wilmslow had progressed so far as to offer a lady-boy revue, perhaps in what was once Country Casuals. Perhaps she was going on to Kell's.

Unfortunately, when I actually got within a foot of her, I was forced to make a violent veer toilet-wards. Not because the Lamborghini was fighting back, but because I suddenly realised that my quarry wasn't a glamorous drag queen at all, but a rock hard, six-foot, who-you-looking-at woman. Uh-oh. Easy mistake to make.

I tottered back to Toby, at the end of the bar. He'd struck up conversation with a group from Stockport, a rental car company on their works night out. The manager was about twelve and very keen to be liked by his staff, so when one girl asked us if we wanted a drink – 'It's all on the tab, we're not paying a penny' – we agreed. Set fire to those ridiculous posemobiles and set 'em up, Jo!

Then I remembered that Nicole, Alex's sister, had told me she'd worked behind Eskimo's bar for a time. She'd explained about Flaming Lamborghinis (a mix of Baileys, Blue Caracao, Kahlua, Sambuca, Galliano) and had also recommended Test-Tube Babies, which consisted of Baileys, Grand Marnier and grenadine. When you poured them in together, the grenadine congealed into a blob, which looked 'dead like a foetus', as Nicole had explained. She'd meant dead as in 'really', as opposed to dead as in 'miscarriage'. I'd wondered at the time if James Bond would have seemed so debonair if he'd swapped his Martini for pickled IVF. But, at this particular moment, a Test-Tube Baby seemed like an excellent idea. Set 'em up again, Jo!

Ha! Things were going all car advert: hyper-speedy and then slam! into slo-mo. I unwrapped my tonsils from around my teeth to chat with two off-duty suits, Mike and Dom. We hadn't got much further than their printing firm's profits over the past few months when Dom started opening and shutting his mouth like a yodelling goldfish. He was having a funny turn.

'Posh Spice!' he finally shouted. 'Posh! Posh!'

Everyone wheeled to look, but no, it wasn't: just an unembarrassable young thing in black mini dress and dark flop fringe. She had square-framed specs on and, I noticed, black stiletto sandals. And now Non-Posh had reminded me, I conscientiously checked the footwear of every other woman I could see. I was cheered to see that the stiletto was still very much the dominant shoe; but, instead of the wipe-clean Dulux-bright court shoes of my past, today's Wilmslow stilettos were, mostly, strappy mules, and, mostly, of a hue known as the old brown, i.e. black.

There was a gold pair opposite, however, belonging to a girl who looked like she'd been born in them. She was dazzling. Her hair – long, straight, white-blond – hung like a curtain of spun barbed wire. You'd have been scared to run your hands through that without your gardening gloves. Her skin was crispy bacon, with a Crisp 'n Dry sheen. Her dress, appropriately enough, was a shred of golden Bacofoil. No extras: no straps, no pockets, not much in the way of skirt.

'Bloody hell,' said Dom, who'd noticed her too.

Goldie Girl would have been quite triumphant, were it not for her two mates – one blonde, one dark – who vied for the collective eye. Both were taller than Goldie, who was Kylie-sized, so both had more flesh to display. This they did with some style, in a black halter-neck and hot pants (the dark girl), and a strangely gladiatorial white and silver ensemble for the blonde, which recalled Frankie Howerd in *Up Pompeii*. All three girls were bronzed to the exact hue of Ronseal woodstain. They were Barbie Goes Hardwood. Three limited-edition handcrafted replicas of the well-loved little lady carved in polished lumber from the protected forests of Cambodia. Not Actual Size. I felt like applauding.

They didn't look that happy though, the Barbies. What they looked was ready. They were prepared, waiting for something that they knew was bound to happen. Unlike every other all-female party in Eskimo, they weren't chatting, screeching, laughing, falling off their heels with hysteria and grubby punchlines. No, the Barbies were silent, scanning the room, not looking at one another, each flipping her hair behind her shoulders, sipping at her drink. You could feel their anticipation, sensed that they were limbered up, primed, muscles stretched, minds concentrated; for any minute they would step into the ring in those sharp high heels for a fight with a quivering contender.

And here he is! Dom made his move. Towards little pint-pot Goldie. As he teetered over, she licked her teeth, looked down sweetly with spidered eyes, flicked them up again and gave him a 1,000-watt smile. Seconds out, round one. It didn't look much of a contest.

It was 11.15. We had to get to Kell's. But Toby didn't want to go. He'd been talking to the car rental girl and she'd said Kell's was rubbish – 'dead posey' – and that Peruvia was meant to be much better. And some of his old friends had said they'd be at Peruvia. So he just wanted to go straight there.

For some reason, I was set on Kell's. I had to go, I knew. But

I couldn't remember . . . oh yes. I'd said I'd see two friends there, Jim and Helen, so I did have to go. Toby and I decided to split up.

The taxi dropped him off at Peruvia. It was held in the Moat House Hotel, opposite Swampy's tunnels, out of Wilmslow, towards the airport and the M56. Kell's was further away, almost in Hale Barns, actually on the roundabout that fed you on to the motorway. Kell's was in the Four Seasons Hotel. The taxi sped on, along the dual carriageway, through the tunnel, under the airport.

It pulled up outside a modern, red brick, one storey building that could have been a town hall, or a police station, or a Methodist church. There was a green telephone box outside that said *Telefon* on its top. I paid the taxi and went in. No queue. Eight pounds entrance. One pound cloakroom. Through the double doors. And straight into a Prince video *circa* 1982.

Except that, this being Wilmslow, there were no black people. But the stage set was there: Kell's had two floors and a central golden staircase that split halfway up, à la Hollywood musical. The banister was made from tubular metal; there were lights on the verticals of the steps. Kell's was decorated in an Irish-stroke-Aztec theme: the Irishness of the phonebox out-side was developed on the interior with sporadically positioned Celtic symbol details; the Aztec was a huge fake-stone head with big eyes and curly tongue that dominated the staircase. The eyes were red and kept flashing. In fact, the whole club blazed with light: no darkened snogging corners, no mystery, no quick glimpse of someone that could be the most gorgeous person you've seen in all your life but now you've lost them in the gloom and the crowd. The ground floor had a tiny, sunken, floodlit dancefloor, with lean-on-me bars around it for close-up viewing, that were thronging with people doing just that. Upstairs, other men and several bouncers hung over the top balconies, scanning the dancefloor. The dancers were nearly all female. White trousers flashed like lightning. My eyes began to bleed.

I found Jim and Helen, on the top floor near the DJ booth. They were in good moods, especially Jim, who'd been to the bar and found that pints weren't allowed. Half-pints only. Jim thought this was funny. And he'd been to the toilet and reported that all the blokes in there were slapping each other on the back, giving each other pep talks so they could get out there and face the women. This also made him laugh. Jim was a teacher at that time, so he had a finely tuned appreciation of young people's suffering. Helen, a doctor, was working in psychiatry. She declined to comment on what she made of Kell's.

On the table next to Jim and Helen were two girls. Blondes: one in mini skirt and mini top, made from a reflective material, like the stripe on the back of a policeman's luminous jacket; the other in gold-trimmed bustier and shiny trousers. They'd come gift-wrapped. I went over to chat. Their names were Nicky and Denise, and they liked coming to Kell's 'sometimes' because 'it was a giggle' and because, on occasion, 'there's basketball stars and footballers'. Nicky had seen Ryan Giggs once. Nicky and Denise were doing their A levels but they weren't sure what they would be doing after that. They looked at me politely, not curious, not hostile, just blank and well-brought-up. I had a brief, violent flashback: a yawing wrench of memory that slammed me straight into a school disco at the age of seventeen? eighteen? when every single girl had come dressed as her mother, in sophisto-slapper backless number and *diamanté* accessories. It couldn't have been that bad, surely? Surely? I slunk back to our table.

There were a lot more girls than men in Kell's, and most of the girls were drinking from fist-filling bottles of alcopops: Hooch, Metz, V2, Moscow Mule. The men were too, except for three lads near us, in tucked-in shirts, smart trousers, wet gel, who had a bottle of champagne between them. After some consultation with one another, they sat down on the table along from Nicky and Denise, but the girls – though they didn't actually ignore them – just didn't register that they were there. The lads kept stealing glances. One of them went to the bar to get two extra champagne glasses, but, just as they were about to pour, Nicky and Denise got up and walked over to the staircase. The boys went back to their champagne in silence. One put the empty glasses on the floor. You could see them adding up the cost in their heads.

Copping off can be a desperate business. It's so formulaic, when you're young, or you think it is. The roles are prescribed. The conversation is scripted. The evening is timetabled. You know that you should follow the recipe – champagne and sweet-talk, like in the films, moving swiftly through to dry-grind dancing and alfresco grope, then home – but then you find that you can't do the sweet-talk and champagne is expensive, so it's Asti or alcopops and long, awkward pauses. And soon, the evening isn't going to plan, it's sliding away from you, it's slipped from its established moorings and you can't find anything, not a word, to say to this person, this far-away being who's supposed to be the prize, the point of all this boring, excruciating agony. And into the pauses crawls a terrible worry that the opposite sex is fundamentally flawed, deeply warped, and you will never have a proper conversation with someone you actually fancy. So – you get off with each other just to fill the roaring silence. Or you don't. You walk away to your mates and shrug a bit, because you knew that she was a dog, or he was hanging, or wasn't interested, or, anyway, wasn't anywhere near good enough to pass your mates' standards, and you couldn't stand to be the centre of the post-party grief.

I was sinking; I needed another drink. To get in the spirit, I ordered a bottle each of Metz, V2 and Moscow Mule. I couldn't face Hooch, even for research purposes. Metz was meths and sugar, V2 was Martini, with sugar, and Moscow Mule was vodka and ginger and sugar. Moscow Mule it was then. Jim, Helen and I decided to make a move towards the dancefloor, to work off some of our collective saccharine rush.

The dancefloor was getting full and, if not exactly steamy, slightly tepid, mildly moist. There were some amazing get-ups out there. I'd forgotten just how much people dress up to go out in the suburbs. In most city clubs, people try to dress as down-beat as possible. They want to look nonchalant, not-trying, as though they've got no money (but a trust fund of style) and they don't want to cop off (but they can't help but be irresistible). Here, though, there were outfits that would make Donatella Versace look like a bin-lady; Caprice, a nun. An all-in-one turquoise lycra catsuit was our favourite, though a white crocheted knee-length cardy with white bra and knicks was definitely worthy of note (and, possibly, coat). The men, though, were disappointing. Each one wore a bright, single-colour shirt (pink, yellow, turquoise; Ralph Lauren Polo, Yves St Laurent) ironed, usually untucked, top button undone. Dark, loose-fit trousers; laced-up, stout-soled shoes. Still, as there was only a handful who were dancing, they didn't distract too much from the female fashion entertainment.

'That was "Lifted" from the unbeatable Lighthouse Family,' boomed the DJ, across the club. 'And now here's some sisters to tell you about *their* family . . .'

'We Are Family' by Sister Sledge came booming out. The girls on the dancefloor cheered a little and then boogied sedately on, mouthing the words to one another, smiling, shimmying carefully from side to side. They looked young enough, and their clothes were painstakingly wanton; but they moved like your teetotal aunty. Not a one was really going for it, letting rip, losing it, jumping or stomping or making an idiot of themselves. No one was swept along by the music, taken over, full to bursting. That might have mussed their hair, or worse: no one likes a sweaty armpit. The girls carried soberly on with their pedestrian ballet, expending minimal energy, smiling and swaying and keeping their dresses nice. They were having a bit of a giggle, a teeny sliver of a good time. It was Almost Dancing. It was Stepford Clubbing. I wanted to scream.

Instead, Helen and I went and threw ourselves around like maniacs for a while, but you can't really go mental to a Radio 2 staple. When we got back to Jim, he was having an argument. He'd dropped his drink, and some of it had splashed on a thirty-something Born-Blonde woman in checked skirt and jacket.

'You're a silly bugger, aren't yer?' she snarled, stiffly brushing away non-existent droplets of Moscow Mule. We refrained from mentioning that her outfit was made from lino, which was known to wipe-clean. But then Jim started laughing. It didn't go down well.

'It's not funny,' spat Lino, and we agreed that, no, it wasn't, but then neither was wearing an outfit made from floor covering, which wasn't even shagpile, and was she aware that the big, big sale at Allied Carpets was starting Monday and perhaps she could afford enough of a roll this time for a skirt that would actually cover her enormo arse, and then we made a run for the door. Off to Peruvia!

We stumbled out to the car park and found a taxi. It took some time. 'I've been watching the floor show,' said the taxi driver. I asked him where it was. I thought perhaps we'd missed a room at the club.

'Didn't you see them?' he asked. 'The couple, at it in that car? Silver BMW 3 series. They were bonking. You could see his little white arse go up and down. In the summer, you know, they do it on the grass.'

He dropped us off. Twelve pounds to get in this time. But after the fear and the clothing of Kell's, Peruvia was a shot of pure, sweet, hallelujah adrenalin. We were greeted by Toby, and a waterfall of sweat. The walls were pouring, the ceiling rained, the floor was ankle-deep in the salty flushing of a week's pent-up pheromones. I sploshed to the bar.

Peruvia was in a room that was long and low and darkish, so you couldn't see all the way to the back. The dancefloor was small, and halfway along, but apart from the strobes there was nothing to differentiate it from the rest of the club: people were dancing any- where, between chairs, around tables, on top of chairs, under tables. Peruvia was one of those clubs where if you were upright, you were moving. Everyone was dancing. Everyone. If you stood still, if no part of your body was acknowledging the fact that the air was filled with music, rent with beats, then you looked wrong. (You looked, in fact, like an undercover copper.) One or two people had found seats, around the side tables, and a few were leaning against pillars, looking like they'd just finished a work-out with Madonna, but otherwise, Peruvia was a non-stop danceathon. An exercise class, with added booze and cigs and unsuitable footwear. And a shower during, instead of afterwards.

It made me smile. There wasn't much point in doing any- thing else: talking was near impossible for a start. So I went for a quick tour around the club. Like Kell's, there were far more girls than boys; and they were girls and boys, most of them. I was by far the oldest and scruffiest there. In fact, apart from Helen, I was the only female in trousers. The girls were all turned out à la Posh: in black or white versions of a short-skirt- and-have-you-met-my-bra theme. Some girls wore see-through T-shirts over their bra; some had shirts unbuttoned to the navel, so you could see they were wearing a bra; some had thought, Sod it, and just worn the bra. Everywhere I looked there were spaghetti straps and little skirts and high heels and slinky expressions, topped with smooth hair and square-framed glasses. Everyone was wearing glasses. Peruvia was packed with Misses Magoos. I asked one girl where she got her specs from. She was from Sheffield. (Sheffield! And she'd travelled to

Wilmslow for her night out!) She told me that they weren't real, that they were just clear. Her eyesight was perfect. The specs were a fashion statement. I asked a few other girls, and they all gave the same kind of answer. I thought of all the years I spent at their age, refusing to wear my glasses, squinting across night-clubs, trying to make out which door was the Ladies, which table held my friends.

The other new Wilmslovian trend, apart from the feminine sartorial switch from Bucks Fizz to Posh Spice, was the intro-duction of gay men. I spotted a good twenty of them: and those were the obvious contenders, muscle boys in skin-tight T-shirts and skinhead haircuts, vogueing with the fervour of Duracell rabbits, as though they really were working out with Madonna. Well. This was a genuine revolution in attitude. No way would you have seen a gay bloke south of Withington, even ten years ago. Not unless he had a particular death wish, a specific desire to be pummelled into pavement jam at the blunt hands of ten or so Cheshire-bred dunderheads who called themselves real men. My drag queen mirage had turned out to be a premonition. I picked up a card, a flyer for another night. It read, breathlessly:

Equvino Nightclub is based at the Moat House Hotel, in the plush upmarket surroundings of Wilmslow near Manchester Airport, and is home to one of the most flamboyant and pres-tigious Saturday nights in the North known as Peruvia. Dress Policy. This unique night is aimed at a cultured crowd who come to enjoy themselves and dress with a sense of occasion, catering for straights, gays, whatever gender. If you feel this is not for you, then don't come!

I cheered. I couldn't help myself. No one bothered anyway, what with all the whooping and yelps of joy that were going on. The Peruvia crowd were a happy bunch, a good-time crew that crowed in glee and smiled at each other and danced without embarrassment and started bellowing conversations with people they didn't know. In short, Peruvia was not only 'flamboyant and prestigious', it was a good night out. And it was ten minutes from the 'plush upmarket surroundings' of my mum and dad's kitchen. I felt strangely proud. It had taken ten years for House music to make it down the M56 from Manchester to arrive at Wilmslow, and it had had to dress up to get over the county line – but, finally, it had made it.

I went back to talk to Toby, who was grinning like a loon. Jim and Helen were dancing by the door, where it was cooler. They, too, were smiling. Toby introduced me to a man of about fifty, who was the father of one of his friends. Toby screeched in my ear: 'He's the two hundred and twenty-seventh most wealthy man in Britain.'

When I asked him if it was true, the man said: 'Yes. And I made it all from toilet roll.'

My evening was complete. I felt deliriously upbeat, thoroughly cheerful, sweaty and benign and content with the world in the way that you are when you're enjoying yourself and you can see that everyone else around you is too. Toby said: 'If Wilmslow had had a club like this when I was growing up, I wouldn't have had to leave.' He was drunk and lying, but I knew what he meant.

7

Sunday driving

S unday morning. Waking up after a night's light-to-medium
roistering can be difficult at the best of times, but waking up
in your parents' house when your soul is panicking, your heart
is dehydrated and the devil has been sick in your head is something close to purgatory. Oh, you have been very bad. And oh,
how you will suffer for it.

I awoke with The Fear at about 6 a.m. Six o'clock is The
Fear's happy hour, its chosen moment, its prime time. The Fear
always strikes then, in that lonely stretch before the sober world
awakes, long before you've had your recommended eight hours,
years before you can make it out from under the pillow without
your vital organs collapsing in on themselves and drowning in

a lagoon of bile. The Fear cooks itself up during those short, sweat-drenched minutes of sleep between going to bed in a drunken stupor and waking up in a stupid funk. The Fear is when your heart races, and you twitch with self-loathing. You panic about everything: what you said/did/kissed the night before; about your appalling job/lovelife/personality and the impossible feat of making it any better; about how you're wasting your life on witless drunks and one of them is you; and how you're wasting it on empty evenings that do nothing except add frown-lines to your brow and take away hours, days, decades of your brief existence. The Fear is when the corners of your mind start to curl and unpeel, like a stamp from an envelope.

I poked one arm out of the duvet and fumbled at the floor, to find the glass of water that I'd left there just three hours before. When I drank, the water threaded down through my body like a silver snake, which then died a sad and terrible death in the acid of the bile lagoon. There was nothing more I could do. I certainly couldn't get up and fill the glass again. Carefully, I slotted my head back under the pillow and waited for the panic to wear itself out.

My mum and dad got up a couple of hours later. I could hear them pottering around, clattering crockery in the kitchen, listening to the radio, the splash of washing up; then stomping upstairs to the bathroom, back down to the back door, into the garage, the garden, the extension, on with the hoover, shout at the cats, back up the stairs, the creak of the ironing board opening on the landing, the crackle of the radio . . . There was nothing for it: I had to get up. The noises were getting louder, more impatient. They were saying: 'It's a lovely morning and we don't get to see you much these days.' They were insistent, morally certain: 'It's nearly dinnertime,' they said, 'and we know you got in late, but you could make a bit of an effort.' The noises were getting annoyed.

I heard Toby's door squeak open, and I knew my time was up. I let him go downstairs, gave it five more minutes and then oozed from under the duvet, slithered across the floor to my clothes and slip-slopped downstairs to the kitchen.

My parents were hovering around the kitchen table, doing their 'let us parent you' bit: wanting to pass teaspoons, locate cereal packets, check that we were able to butter our own toast. Parents never get over you growing up, do they? They try really hard to treat you as an adult, dutifully asking about your life, your friends, your opinions, but you know that they're constantly restraining themselves from grabbing you in a headlock just to see if you've washed behind your ears. Mum looked as though any minute she'd make a lunge for Toby's nose with a bit of kitchen paper and grip on like a vice until he blew. I made a slow move towards the kettle.

But after Sunday lunch – which started straight after breakfast – Toby and I perked up, fuelled by the sugar rush from the glasses of lemonade and the jelly with tinned mandarins in it, fortified by two different types of pizza (my mum gave up on Sunday roast when there was just her and Daddy left). Afterwards, I was left feeling heady, hysterical, happy enough. My dad leant back in his chair and made a few harrumphing noises. I knew what was coming next. The Sunday Drive.

It was okay by me. After last night's merrymaking, after all my little trips thus far, I'd realised that what I'd taken as established suburban dogma – from telly, from newspapers, from sitcoms, from commentators – was actually wonkier than anyone cared to admit. The central tenets of a semi-detached existence had turned out rougher, showier (driving), more pointless yet life-affirming (golf), politer, more twisted (wife-swapping), more fundamental (DIY), and more fun (showing out) than I'd ever been led to believe. The cliché had warped. The sharp, bright snapshot of Middle Britain was oozing at the edges.

Perhaps a return to my past might reveal more. A rerun of my own out-of-town life . . . no, far too frightening an idea. A reconsideration of the things I once took as read, that would do. I mean, I'd already started by staying local last night. I decided to make the most of my brief home visit. I would take the givens of my pre-adult history and hold them up to contemporary light to see if such principles still held up, if they still even existed. And, as those givens had been donated to me by my parents, I was happy for the moment to go along with whatever they wanted to do. Anyhow, I was far too hungover to make a break for it.

The Sunday Drive was a regular event in my parents' household. When Toby and I were very young, we would be driven to adventure playgrounds or to improving museums: usually the Lowry one in Salford, as it was next door to Dad's work so he had a valid escape clause if we were really brattish. When we were older and had better things to do, like homework – listening to records and hitting each other – my mum and dad would still drive off on a Sunday, together, or separately. Their trips were one of two types: either they visited new building developments (they spent a whole year of weekends checking out the joys of Castlefield and Salford Quays), or it was a jaunt to an antique fair. Although that was just my dad: Mum hated his taste for elderly gewgaws and tomes, and still does.

Today's drive promised to be a combination: an exciting tour around not one but two construction sites, plus fayre of crumbly artefacts. It had been decreed that we would drop Toby off at the station, and then motor up towards Bolton, past the new superstore being built at Dumplington, on to the spanking Bolton Wanderers Reebok Stadium, and then to somewhere called Last Drop Village, which, as far as I could make out from my dad's vague description, would contain cups of tea and Victorian books.

So, off we set. My dad drove. He has a new car which he bought after his last one was written off in an unfortunate incident with a plain clothes police vehicle in a north Manchester car park. It's a long story. The car he has now is a Fiesta; and he drives it as well as he drives all other cars; that is, as well as can be expected under the circumstances, that is, not very well at all.

After dropping Toby at Macclesfield station, we tootled dreamily along the motorway towards Stockport, and then along another motorway towards Preston, and then another towards who knows where. Soon, all three of us were cocooned in that strange state of limbo that is motorway driving, that detachment that comes when you travel long distances without actually being engaged with any of the detail of those distances. You skim through, you glide by, you gaze vacantly at the flashing monitor of your windscreen, at the flicking white lines, the pulsing uprights of the central reservation. You sing along to the radio. The road stretches, before and behind. You're neither here, nor there: you've left your immediate problems and you haven't quite reached all the ones that await you elsewhere. You're portable and transported.

Because Dad was driving, I should have been on red alert, ready to warn him of potential dangers, like oncoming service stations about to lurch into the fast lane. But my hangover had mutated into brain-death, and my mind could find no reason to involve itself with anything whatsoever. I settled into gentle jelly-headedness, aided by my dad's choice of tape: Jazz Moods, a noodly selection of elevator tunes. The motorways drifted by. M56. M63. Soon there'd be the M62. Then the M61. Turn-offs for Runcorn, Warrington, Liverpool, Wigan, Preston, Blackburn, Blackpool . . .

Then, all of a sudden, we'd arrived. 'There it is,' said Mum, stretching over Daddy, pointing to the right. And it was: a vast, pillared, beige-slabbed, *Brideshead Revisited* manor house with a lofty green glass dome, a front foyer the size of a Hollywood ballroom and two wings that stretched out to the left and right like curved streets of overgrown mews houses. There it was: Buckingham Palace, but with a bigger garden. We drove and stared. The palace grounds filled the area between two motorway turn-offs; it took a few minutes to drive past their full length. They weren't quite finished. You could see that the earth in front of the house was churned and speckled with diggers. Little men in hard hats scampered between unlit, unpainted, Victorian-style road-lamps that marched alongside the motorway and swept across the mud towards the foyer.

Weedy, regularly-spaced saplings pointed feebly towards the sky; sculpted pathways meandered through man-made mounds; single chunks of pale stone chugged towards the manor house on creaking lorry trailers. Welcome, world, to Dumplington Hall.

Actually, the palace was named the Trafford Centre, and it was due to open in a few months as Britain's penultimate all-shops-under-the-same-roof out-of-town shopping-centre. (The government had granted planning permission for just one more; the even bigger Bluewater, in Kent.) But the Trafford Centre was right near Dumplington, and my mum had christened it Dumplington Hall from the outset. We turned off at Junction 3, drove past a sports centre and turned right on a roundabout to cruise past Dumplington Hall's rear. It was truly huge, like a Vegas hotel, on all the wrong scale to the few surrounding buildings. An Asda, an out-of-town superstore in its own right, cowered in the manor's shadow on the other side of the road. It didn't look big enough to be Dumper's garden shed.

A sign announced that Selfridges was due to make its northern home within Dumplington portals; another, that Peel Holdings were the proud lords of the manor; still another, that there were plenty of job opportunity vacancies going on the Dumplington estate – parking attendant, shop assistant, floor sweeper, game keeper, car jacker, etc.

Mum said: 'They're worried that when there's a football match on at Old Trafford, the whole motorway will be blocked solid, once this is open. They reckon that people will come from all over the north-west.'

Dad tried to drive in to get a closer look, but there was a

gateman – an acned youth in overalls who grunted in a manner that indicated that Chez Dumpers was not yet ready for the viewing public – so we turned around and drove off. I decided to try and get a closer look later on in the week. For the moment, though, we would continue: to the next destination on our grand Sunday Drive. The Reebok Stadium. The brand new Bolton Wanderers football ground.

Reebok had paid for it, hence the name. Now you have to say, Bolton versus Sheffield United at Reebok, like you'd say Sheffield versus Bolton at Bramall Lane. If sponsorship carries on, things could get confusing: Arsenal versus Manchester United at Nike, Man U versus Arsenal at Adidas; and then, after a while, because only the big firms will be able to afford to pay for new arenas, stadiums will be called Nike Air Max Trainers, or Adidas Poppa Pants to differentiate them from the others, like the Nike Deputy Dawg Hat or the Adidas String Vest. You'd have to watch from the Reinforced Crotch End or the Breathable Armpit Stand. Well, maybe not. I know nothing about football.

Don't get me wrong: I like watching football well enough, but all that 'I've supported Wrexham since I was foetus' one-up-manship – I just don't get it. How come, as you grow up and learn about the world, you're allowed to change your mind about anything and everything – food, clothes, music, politics, leisure options, preferred sexual partner – other than the football team you support? That choice is made at nine years old and it is an irrevocable one. You can never go back. You can never say, 'I was wrong about supporting Stockport County, they're rubbish, but then I was only nine, eh?' You're not allowed to.

Call me a progressive, but there's not many opinions that I had at nine years old that I'd stick by today. That's because I was nine, and I thought that Abba were the epitome of musical prowess, that Nadia Comaneci had the best life of anyone in the world and that there was a horrible monster that lived in the wardrobe that would only stay put if I didn't touch the carpet with my bare feet. I also thought that a nutritious diet consisted entirely of Frosties without milk and lime green icepops. I supported Chelsea when I was nine. So, I suppose I could have waded into a football discussion with 'I'm a Chelsea supporter and if you hold your nose when you eat exploding spacedust sherbet, right, then your eyes will pop out and fall on the floor' but I think people would think I was odd. Although maybe that kind of insight does constitute conversation for a Chelsea fan, I don't know. It probably would do if I said it over a mobile phone.

Anyhow, we drove to the Reebok. Very impressive in a modern tube structure and wavy canopy way. Actually, it looked utterly incongruous, as had Dumplington Hall, looming as it did over crumbly terraces and knackered social housing, a spaceship that had crash-landed in a very surprised and very ordinary north-west town. It was the only thing you could see that shouted, 'MONEY, INVESTMENT, ADVERTISING OPPORTUNITIES, CORPORATE WORLD.' Everything else whispered, 'making do'. It wasn't Bolton's fault, nor the Reebok's, it's just that both of them were surprised to see each other.

There were, my dad confessed, reasons apart from novelty aesthetics as to why he wanted me to see Dumpers and Reebok.

He had worked on them himself. Well, he'd helped out. Dad is an aeronautical engineer, but he also runs a small firm – employees: himself, my mum (secretary) – that helps architects in the design of big buildings. What he does is check that the buildings won't collapse when the wind blows, by making scale models on our kitchen table and then taking them to work to put in a wind-machine so he can work out the stresses and forces.

So, at Dumpers Hall, Dad had told the architects to increase the thickness of the green glass of the dome, or it would come crashing around the heads of the paying punters as soon as the breeze got up above brisk ('They weren't very happy about it,' he grinned. 'It cost them a lot of money.'); and at Reebok, he'd tested the roof of a sports centre that was to be built by the side of the stadium, to see that it would stay on, generally. That test had taken a little longer than it should have, because he'd left the garage door open and one of the cats had got in and fallen asleep on the model Reebok mini-turf. She'd damaged one of the stands. The Toe End, I believe. Still, the real-life roof looked mighty solid; and now the architects were assured that it was reinforced to a standard that could support Catzilla, so no harm done.

After that little gawp, we set off again, to our final Sunday Drive destination: Last Drop Village. It wasn't far. It was sign-posted with those brown heritage signs, the ones that seem to have sprouted all over the place over the last few years. They have a little picture on one side, of a flower, or a king's head, or a carousel, or a choo-choo train, and they point enigmatically to a turning, usually off a motorway. They point to: Birdworld, Frontierland, The Roman Experience. They point to places that don't really exist, or at least they didn't exist five years ago. They point to the Visitor Centres of Great Britain. They point to Britainland. Or possibly: Walesworld, The Scotch Experience and Englandland.

I'd been a bit obsessed with Visitor Centres ever since I read a publicity leaflet from the British Tourist Board that listed the Visitor Centre Top Ten. I'd thought: I wonder what a Visitor Centre actually is? I mean, I'd been to the Royal Doulton one with the VSLs, but I'd never got to look around. I wasn't sure how it had qualified for such a status. So I'd read the Top Ten, and, honestly, when I'd finished I was none the wiser. I read through the rest of the Tourist Board bumph. There was no Visitor Centre explanation anywhere; though other Top Tens indicated what they weren't. I can tell you that Visitor Centres are not leisure parks; nor piers, steam railways, wildlife attractions; nor museums and galleries, historic houses and monuments; nor attractions charging admission. They're not cathedrals or churches either, though I expect you (and, one would hope, God) knew that. What Visitor Centres are, is new: 1996 was the first year to list the Top Ten. Certainly, they weren't around when I used to harass my mum about doing something other than going to the swimming baths. Packing me off to the local Visitor Centre for the afternoon had not been a leisure option.

I'd read and reread the VC Top Ten on many occasions since. Straight in at Numero Uno was Cadbury World, in Birmingham; then came the Old Blacksmith's Shop, Gretna

Green; followed by a near tie between the Giant's Causeway Visitor Centre, Bushmills, and Gatwick Skyview. All boasted well over 350,000 visits per year (Cadbury World got 532,629 in 1996). This meant that despite the fact that I had only ever been to one Visitor Centre in the whole of my life, and that was by mistake, everyone else in Britain was busy visiting them like nobody's business. Well: they were a lot more popular than the steam railways.

And they were so varied, so all-encompassing. It seemed that you could turn anywhere, anything, anybody into a Visitor Centre. There was a Visitor Centre for Chester (Number 6). So you could have a VC for an entire city, as well as one for a horsebrass shop on the Scotland–England border. Lower down the list came the World of Beatrix Potter, the Rob Roy Centre and the Wedgewood Visitor Centres. So, that was children's authors (deceased), legendary Scottish heroes (ditto) and special occasion cake plates covered then.

Last Drop Village had not been listed, but it did have brown signposts, so I asked my dad if it was a Visitor Centre. Disappointingly, he said he thought not.

'Last Drop is a sort of village,' he said, brightly. 'But – it is for visitors, I suppose. And, I suppose, it isn't really a village. Not really. Um. You know.'

I didn't. And I still thought Last Drop Village might be a Visitor Centre: my dad's not known for his observational qualities, and if Birmingham International Airport (Number 7) could have one in its name, I didn't see why Last Drop couldn't.

We drove out to the edge of Bolton, away from the Reebok, and up through a Barrett housing estate on the far perimeter. A small hill stretched out above the estate; at the top was a cluster of seemingly elderly farm-buildings, surrounded by a moat of concrete parking space. We parked up. This was it. Last Drop Village.

It was 4.45 p.m. We got out of the car into the wind and wet, struggled towards a gap between the old cabins, tottered into a small square. I looked about. It was a strange sight. The buildings were unmistakably ancient (timbered, eighteenth century), but, equally obviously, were as genuine as a Wild West set. Once barns, they were now ye olde bakery, ditto bookshoppe, comely maidens' hair salon. They'd been renovated and restored, then put to contemporary irrelevant use: haylofts, chicken houses, cow sheds turned into craft shops with local sculpture, an ice-cream parlour, a tea shop; even a health and leisure club, and an 86-room hotel plus conference facilities. All set around a cobble-and-concrete square, with fake stocks and central wooden signpost pointing to shops that stood all of twenty yards away. The Last Drop was a 'unique concept', according to the brochure displayed in one of the shop windows, under a pink-and-silver bow blu-tacked to the glass. Not all that unique: just Legoland, with older bricks.

We were too late for the Sunday afternoon junk sale, sorry, 'Antique Collectors' Fayre', to Dad's mild chagrin. But we hadn't missed the Snooker Special, due in a couple of weeks, which promised to be 'an evening to remember with Former World Champion, Snooker Star, Dennis Taylor, which includes a 4-course dinner, served in a relaxed and friendly atmosphere, £21.50'. The list of forthcoming Last Drop attractions was posted in a glass box on the outside wall of the craft shop. As well as Dennis, there was a Murder Dinner, a Caribbean Evening, a Ho-Down and a Bavarian Beer Keller Night; all due to take place at the Last Drop Village, though whereabouts, exactly, was not made clear. I supposed that the Village in these cases didn't actually mean the Village, but the Hotel. Actually, the small print under 'Last Drop' said *Village And Hotel, Restaurant And Conference Centre*. Clearly, the Last Drop was up for anything. No doubt it would dress up as a Visitor Centre if I asked it nicely.

We went for a cup of tea in a low-beamed café. We could have been anywhere in England – there were the scones, the tea-cakes, the gonky teenage waitress, the standard stainless steel teapot that pours your tea all over the saucer – except that we weren't; we were in a specially constructed craft village, an open-to-the-elements mini Arndale Centre with nothing that you wanted to buy. At least in a Disney World Genuine English Pubbe, you can get Mickey Mouse ears. And at least Disney World's big, with skyscraper rides and hamburgers the size of Texas and grounds so huge there's trains to take you across them. You could walk around the Last Drop in the time it takes to whistle 'Scarborough Fair'. One verse. Anyway, the Last Drop wasn't even an efficient craft centre: the shops were shut, and it wasn't yet 5 p.m.

In fact, the place was spectacular only in the paucity of its ambitions: it was a playcentre for idiot north-west daytrippers, who couldn't work their way around real-life old places, such as Buxton, or Castleton, or Chester; nor around real-life theme parks, like the Granada Studios tour, where you get to walk down Coronation Street. They settled for Last Drop, like babies settle for rusks and milk. Except babies can plead ignorance: they've yet to taste curry. Or pepper vodka.

Still – my mum and dad seemed happy. They weren't exactly beaming, but it was clear they were pleased to find a clean, pleasant place for a cup of tea, that we hadn't had to pull over at a Little Chef on the way home. They murmured half-finished comfort sentences at each other and at me: 'Shall I . . .?'; 'Would you . . .?'; '. . . warm enough?'; 'It's nice to . . .'; '. . . yes, isn't it?'

There were two young girls on the next table; the only other customers in the tea shop. They were under twenty, but dressed like forty-year olds – with handbags that toned with their shoes – and they were wondering loudly with each other as to whether trouser-suits were suitable attire for a wedding reception. I slurped my tea and thought about Sunday Driving. I thought: I'm going to have to motor a lot further tomorrow.

8

a big day out

Mrs Dorothy May Pickering lives in a semi-detached house on the outskirts of Barrow-in-Furness, in Cumbria. Her house has a garage and a gate and gardens front and back, and everyone says that the gardens are beautifully kept. Mrs Dorothy May Pickering has lived in her house for the past forty-three years. Her husband, Mr Edward 'Ted' Pickering, died there, on 19 May, 1972. He had a heart attack.

The friends of Mrs Dorothy May Pickering call her May Pick. Acquaintances call her Mrs Pickering. I call her Granny. She calls me Jennifer (my mum's name), or Nell (her [dead] sister's), or, occasionally, Miranda. She refers to herself as Granny, or sometimes Mummy, when she thinks I am my mum. When she talks about her own mother to me, she calls her Granny, or Mummy, but never Great-Granny. Other conversational conventions include dismissing everyone under eighty as a boy or a girl, as in 'the girl who does the vac-ing' (the cleaner, who's in her forties), or 'the boy who does my roses' (the gardener, who's retired), or 'that boy whose daughter got married to the doctor, you *do* know, with the two little boys who were badly behaved that time with Granny in Ulverston' (nope, got me there).

Granny and I talk about many things. The weather, my brother, 'What kind of silly job is it that you do anyway?', the fact that she doesn't want a wheelchair.

'I don't want one of those,' Granny says.

I say: 'But when we go out for a walk, you just have to sit and wait in the car. I could push you. Or Toby could. We'd take turns.'

'I've not got the space for it,' sniffs Granny. 'It'd have to be left in the porch and everyone would see it. It'd be pinched. You'd never get it in the car. I couldn't work a folding-up one by myself. It'd be too dear, especially if it was one that folded up. Who would push it? You're not here much. I don't want to be a burden.'

Granny doesn't have a wheelchair, but she has two chair lifts. One murmurs her up the first part of the stairs; then she has to haul herself off it to hoik and bundle on to the next one, which transports her, in stately slo-mo, right to the top. If you stand on the landing and watch her ascend, you're reminded of the opening credits in *Camberwick Green*, where a puppet would appear very slowly from within a musical box. The puppet would only speak to the camera when it was fully emerged, facing stoically forward and holding steady on its wooden feet.

I've been on the double chairlift myself, when Granny was in the kitchen playing Russian dolls with the tupperware. The slow progress of the chairs means you have time to get a good look at all the crockery and knick-knacks displayed on the hall mantel: a green jug, a George VI coronation mug, a gold-edged flowery plate. Granny doesn't think that the cleaner knows they're there: 'That girl only dusts what she sees in front of her,' she huffs, though everything looks hospital standard to me.

The truth is, Granny's eyesight has failed so much that the cleaning girl could start farming cress on the dining-room carpet and Granny wouldn't know. Granny uses a plastic guide so that she can find where to put her pen to sign cheques; she positions the telly close enough to her nose for Kilroy to lean out and kiss it (and don't think she hasn't thought of that); she peers at big print books through a magnifying glass with built-in high-wattage bulb. She gives my mum bank statements to read out aloud. But Granny's hearing's not what it was either, so this ends up in argument, with mother and daughter (grandmother and mother) screaming figures at each other like sparring city tradesmen, except the amounts are hardly much to shout about: 'Twenty-four pounds twenty-three pee.' 'Eighty-four pounds! Well, I've hardly had the heater on this winter so I've not used the gas for that kind of money.' 'TWENTY-FOUR POUNDS TWENTY-THREE PEE!' 'NO NEED TO SHOUT I HEARD YOU THE FIRST TIME!' Etc.

Granny's bodywork is past its best: eyes, ears, knees, hips, hands, fingers, feet, seizing up, wearing out, softening then freezing into all the wrong shapes. But her engine ticks over fine. She's not daft. Not yet. She knows what she wants and what she doesn't. She wants Jennifer to stop working so hard. She wants me to get married. She wants *Emmerdale* to return to how it was before it had all those silly new characters going on with one another. And she doesn't want a wheelchair.

Well, she has a point. She's got to ninety-six without one. She has friends that take her out: Iris, who drives her to Asda; Audrey, who takes her to church, and who arranges her special altar flowers (May pays for them on the Sunday closest to Teddy's death); the ladies from the Inner Wheel, who ferry Mrs Pickering to their speaker lunches. When her friends come round, Granny makes sure she's sitting on the chair in the hall (coat on, hat on, bag on knee, stick in hand) a good ten minutes before they arrive. She doesn't want to make them wait whilst she gets herself to the front door.

I arrived within half an hour of the appointed time. I'd phoned Granny when I set off, and said I'd be there to have a cup of tea before taking her out for a pub lunch.

The doorbell made an impatient, tuneful, farting noise. It took Granny quite some minutes to answer it. But I could hear her voice from the moment I rang, talking me and herself through, telling me that she was coming, just getting herself out of the chair, now where's her stick, ooof, just a tick until she's steady.

She's shrunk in the last few years, and widened, and she was still a bit bent over from sitting down, so her skirt hung like a wonky lamp-shade, lower at the front than at the back. As she made her way back to the lounge, I glimpsed architectural undergarments: thermals, stockings, petticoats, bandages, as complicated and structured as scaffolding. Covered buttons, snap suspenders, nappy pins, in beigey, pinky fleshtones. Medically coloured.

Granny's house is big: kitchen, front room, back room, two bedrooms, a box room and a bathroom. But it's collapsed into itself, like a Tardis in reverse: she lives in just the sitting-room, with occasional visits to the kitchen, the bathroom and her bed. Everything's within reach of her green chair with the lacey arm-rest covers: the phone, the TV remote, the magnifying glass, the address book, the radio, her glasses case, her hearing aid, the coasters for hot mugs, the angle-poise with the bright bulb, the tapes of someone reading a newspaper that she's sent every fortnight by 'The Blind'. The clutter seemed to be even closer than the last time I visited. Maybe the objects shuffle inwards when Granny nods off during *Coronation Street*.

She eased herself down into her chair, queen of her court of bric-à-brac. I went into the kitchen to make the tea. She shouted directions.

'Can you find the biscuit tin? It's the square one near the butter dish. The lid's a bit stiff, you'll have to wiggle it, but watch your fingers. Use the bread knife to cut the fruit loaf – be careful, it's ever so sharp.'

It's a cliché that old people become childlike; that as your age increases, your common sense dwindles to toddler standard, and so others treat you accordingly: 'Now, Nana, is it wise to leave Tiddles in charge of paying the milkman? And do we need to spend a penny before we go?'. But what no one admits is that the infanticised pensioner still insists on treating younger people as babies, because that's how they appear to an elderly person. The generation gap means that everyone approaches everyone else as though they're yet to learn their two times table, as though they're just not adult enough to know what's going on. It's a kindergarten out there.

My gran – who makes a pot of tea with all the pace and dexterity of a sleep-deprived four-year-old – hollered instructions at me as though I were only just out of knitted booties.

'Watch yourself with the kettle, remember it's boiling water. Can you manage that tea-tray?'

No, it's fighting back. Aaargh. Revenge of the floral-printed tin.

'What's that?'

'Nothing, Granny. Here I am. Now, are you comfy, sat like that? Do you want me to move your chair a bit?'

I put the tray on the coffee table, on top of the *Past Pleasures* brochure, next to the minutes of the previous month's Inner Wheel meeting. Granny is a long-standing member (twice president) of the Barrow-in-Furness district Inner Wheel; and the Inner Wheel, if you didn't know, is the ladies branch of the Rotary Club. Only wives of Rotarians can become Inner Wheelies. And only high rank professionals, upright pillars of local society (male) are invited to become Rotarians. Rotarians are like Masons, but without the secrecy or the saucy apron-flaunting. They're left with the boring bits: the barbeques for a dialysis machine, the bonfires for a new church roof, the dances in a dicky bow to flatter local dignitaries.

My Granpa was Barrow's chief postmaster and made a

perfect Rotarian, being, as I recall, a decent man given to rule-keeping and politeness. And Granny, who gave up work when she married, was ideal for Inner Wheel: born to wear a smart hat and marshal a tombola barrel.

Most of the ladies of the Inner Wheel are past the middle of middle age. This is because their Rotarian husbands are subject to a lower age limit. You can't join the Rotary Club if you are under forty years old; there's the Round Table for you whippersnapper whip-rounders. Actually, secretly, Granny thinks that 'the standards aren't so high' for the Round Table: 'Well, you could say of their members that it's quantity before quality, you know. Sometimes they drink too much and they're too young for it. They get a bit rowdy.' It should be noted that Round Table membership does not lead to automatic Rotarianship, come your fortieth. Similarly, Round Table wives can join the Ladies Circle, but this does not, necessarily, mean they will qualify for Inner Wheel. So, you can't afford to let the elastic of your respectability knickers lose its ping in later years. Not if you want to be a Wheelie.

The ladies of the Barrow Inner Wheel (District 19) meet once a month over lunch. There's a speaker at each meeting. Apart from that, there's all the palaver of a club (proposing, seconding, apologies, subscriptions, any other business); plus, the good causes: '£50 to the parson's son who's raising money to fund his heroin addiction, sorry, his voluntary work abroad'. Every year, there's a national Inner Wheel Conference, where all the ladies of all the UK branches put on their hats and descend upon the nicer hotels of Blackpool to pass comment on the finger buffet and whether the foyer mirrors are smeary.

Granny used to go to Conference, but she can't now. Not without a wheelchair and we all know what she thinks about them.

Granny told me about last month's Barrow Inner Wheel meeting. It didn't sound much fun. She'd been cold and the food hadn't been satisfactory.

'We thought it very moderate,' she pronounced. 'No taste to it, and the main course would have fitted under your dessert spoon.'

The speaker – a woman who made screen prints – hadn't been up to much, either.

'I didn't care for her, going on about how much her paint and paper were worth. Well, what do I want to know about that for? But it was a nice journey there and back and it was nice to see everyone,' Granny conceded. 'And it makes a change.'

It makes a change. Granny's life has moved in on her. It's solidified around her, it locks her to the spot. She's lost the careless fluidity of a life lived in and out of the place she calls home. She doesn't nip to the postbox, pop round a neighbours, dash from the garden to the lounge to answer the phone. When Granny says 'it made a change', what she means is, 'I went out of the house'.

She makes the most of a change when it happens. She enjoys herself, looks on the bright side ('it was a nice journey'). Toby had told me about my mum taking Granny to Bolton recently, to see Toby perform in a play. In the play, he'd had to kill a baby. We'd been worried that Granny might be upset by this, but she'd insisted that she'd be fine – 'I like that *Inspector Morse*, don't I?' – and, in the end, she hadn't quite been able to make out which one Toby was anyway. But she had been

144

introduced to someone out of *Last of the Summer Wine*, who was also performing. Granny told him that she watched him every Sunday and then, when he'd moved away about two feet, said, loudly: 'He makes all that money and you wouldn't think it. Not with what he's got on.' She repeated that to me now. 'Well, really,' she said.

'Still, it made a change,' I said.

'A nice change,' she agreed.

We had lunch in The Ferryman, by the docks. Park the car outside the door, run round the side to let Granny out, help her on to her stick, into the pub, slowly, slowly, robot-rocking across sticky carpet, around chairs and tables and stools and children to the family dining area, hat off, coat off, settle her in, oof, dash back to the car, drive it round the corner, park it, back to the pub, what would she like to drink? to eat? does she want the toilet? order the food, pay for it, wait for it, wait for it, eat it – 'Mine's lovely, is yours lovely?' 'Lovely' – run out, to the car, start it, bring it round, on with the coat and the hat and the bag, up on the stick, across to the door, stopping now and then – 'What's that say?' 'It says that this is a children-friendly establishment.' 'It's a whattie?' – then wobbling outside, flinching a little under the drizzle, round the car and carefully, painfully, happily, heavily down into the passenger seat. 'It's ever so posh, your car.' And off.

Granny told me about the time when she'd been at a lunch with some of her ladies and she'd tried to eat the pattern off the plate.

'I'd thought I still had some veg left. I had to ask the lady

next to me: "Am I chasing my peas, or scraping at the glaze?"
Oh dear.' Granny often says oh dear, when she laughs.

We decided to take a drive to the sea. Barrow is a bleak place,
though I never realised it when I was younger. The seaside, at
Walney, is a long, wind-thrashed, oil-speckled, pebbled stretch,
with no pier, no donkeys, no ice-cream; no shops, amusements,
neon, no nothing. Well – there're a couple of concrete sea-
breaks that point yearningly towards Ireland; an immobile
home caravan park, some cracked and pebble-dashed terraced
houses; and, away in the distance, there's Sellafield.

The sea is grey and vicious: when the wind's up, it can take
your breath away, crashing down on to the breaks, rearing up
with a roar, grabbing for your hair and clothes, grimly wild.
There's not much activity on or in the water, except for dogs
being walked. When the tide's out, sand stretches away from
the pebbles, and the dogs go bananas, as dogs will, pelting along
the beach, then back to their owners, in and out of the foam. It
must be fantastic to be a dog. You get such single-minded, all-
encompassing happiness from such teeny things: you jump for
joy at stickstickstickstick or otherdogotherdogotherdog or you
bark, again and again, at waves that never, ever stop rolling in,
just for you to bark at. Dogs love nothing more than doing the
same mind-killing activity over and over. We should train them
to work in call centres.

There were a few about today, rushing around, yapping
daftly at the wind. I parked the car in a mini car park that faced
towards the sea. Granny didn't want to get out, but she was
most insistent that I took the air, so I wandered down to some
rock pools to try and catch limpets. As usual, I was useless at

it – I can never kick them off first time, and they're always
locked by the second attempt – so I collected a few *That's Life*
stones (warped by the spooky Sellafield sea into don't-show-
your-mother shapes) and mooched back. Granny was asleep,
snoring tunefully. I woke her up, and we set off for the real
event of the day. A Visit To That New Foreign Shop. Granny
had been going on about it for a good few weeks.

'Everyone says that the cut flowers there are very good
value,' said Granny. 'Is it a German shop, Jennifer?'

I said I didn't know and that I was Miranda.

'You do know where it is, though, don't you? You're not
taking me to Asda first?'

Where we were going was Aldi, a supermarket that specialises in its own, cheaper versions of big-name brands.
Granny loves big stores: Kendals, John Lewis, Asda; anywhere
she's left free to make her own progress and to peer and prod at
the produce. She told me that the Inner Wheel had had an
after-hours visit arranged with Debenhams and that they'd
wanted her to go, but she hadn't, because she thought she'd be
an inconvenience. 'Well, they told me afterwards that I didn't
miss anything,' she sniffed delightedly. 'It wasn't a patch on
M&S.'

One of the reasons Granny likes supermarkets is that she can
lean on a trolley to help her walk. Another is that there's always
people in supermarkets, children with young mothers, nice lads
who fill the shelves, other elderly folk. She does like to talk to
people, my gran. First things first, though. The cut flowers.
They were cellophane-wrapped and in a plastic bucket, just to
the left as you went in. Not many bunches left, either. Only

£1.69. Sweet peas, chrysanths, pinks; a bunch went straight into the trolley. Granny seemed very pleased: 'Everyone says they're good value,' she said again.

Granny wanted a few bits and bobs: jelly, Nescafé, Coffeemate, cereal, some biscuits. We staggered along the aisle at the pace of creeping rheumatism, radars scanning for bargains, speedos set to trundle. Granny kept stopping and pointing at stuff.

'What're these, Jennifer?' jabbing her finger at prepackaged strawberries. 'Do we want them? Are they biscuits?'

Like the owl-eyed forger in *The Great Escape*, it's only when you take Granny out of her own environment that you realise just how blind she is. So I played the James Garner role, stuck close by, steered her around obstacles, such as other people. We had a bit of a laugh; I held out a tin or two, and she made a few wild guesses: 'Butter beans? Sponge pudding?'. It reminded me of when I worked the till in Woolworths; the manager discovered that I was short-sighted and stood back by the make-up stand, holding out a product. I had to say what it was. I said, a book; but then he made me read out the title and I just couldn't, I had no idea, I couldn't make out a word, I'd only said a book because I'd looked at Louisa behind the record counter and she'd mouthed 'book' to me. So, after that, I was made to wear my specs, so that I could spot the kids on the Pick 'n' Nick. What a humiliated little grub I was, in National Health specs, Woolies overall, regulation American tan tights and low-heeled blue or black court shoes. Didn't they know that my friends would come in? Maybe even someone I fancied? In the US I could have sued

the manager for negligent traumatisation of my tender adolescent feelings.

Still, Granny seemed quite happy to bump about without
seeing; she had her specs on, but they don't make much difference any more. Everything was a nice surprise when she got up
close: a stand of washing powder, the meat freezer, a small child
in another trolley. 'How much are you?' she grinned at him, and
his mother smiled back. I kept up a running commentary for
her as we creaked and tottered along.

'Here's the coffee Granny; now you wanted some didn't you,
but they've not got Nescafé, so will their own brand be all right?
Have a look at it, or they've got a bigger jar, and there's hot cross
buns on special offer, nice warmed through with a bit of butter,
then flambéed in gin, what do you think?'

Aldi wasn't quite right for Granny's needs, seeing as she had
her favoured brands and she liked to stick to them. She wasn't
going to swap her Nescafé for an unknown, untested coffee;
nor her Special K, which she calls her K Flakes, for some Aldi
attempt. We selected a couple of jellies – strawberry, orange –
and an Aldi version of Coffeemate to try, and decided to press
on, to Asda.

Barrow's Asda is shopping nirvana for Granny. Ever since it
opened, she has never found a shop she likes as much. It is a
good supermarket, as supermarkets go: high ceilings, well laid
out, always lots of tills open. Not Dumpers to look at from the
outside, but clean, simple, spacious. Just the ticket. And for
Granny, it's like a drop-in social club. Almost as soon as we'd
manoeuvred ourselves inside, Granny met someone she knew.
Well, someone she knew met her.

A nicely-dressed lady in her late sixties came over for a chat. 'Hello, Mrs Pickering, how nice to see you.' It was A Girl From Church, as Granny told me in a stage whisper. I didn't catch the Girl's name, but she, too, was with her grand-daughter, a lanky-limbed teenager who stared with blank disinterest. The Girl and Granny chatted about why they were in Asda (doctors' waiting-room talk: 'Oh I'm just in for my cereal', 'Oh well, it's my teacakes, you see'), then a bit about church, and then Granny made a grab for the Girl's shopping.

'These look lovely buns,' she trumpeted, squishing down hard with clawed thumbs to check the freshness. 'Are those toffee bits?'

'They're nuts and raisins,' said the Girl. 'There's ones with chocolate chips in too. On offer, four for 70p, by the bakery counter.'

That was all my gran needed to hear. The Girl From Church was discarded with a wave and an airy comment about the visiting bishop, and Granny set her teeth with a click. We were off for some toffee-studded buns.

'The lady said they were nuts and raisins,' I said, so she wouldn't be disappointed, but Granny ignored me, hurtling northwards in a lurching manner towards the garden furniture. Her gait was determined, but wayward. I caught up and steered her over to the west – Tea Coffee Cereals – whipping a jar of Nescafé off the shelf as we careened past at an appreciably faster pace than we'd managed in Aldi's. I felt we were becoming out of control. Granny was going at quite a rate. She had the wind in her sails – well, her skirts – and once up to speed, she was difficult to divert from her course. I kept running around the front of the trolley and giving it a sharp push to the left, so that Granny skidded regally out to the right but still kept coming, forging ahead, rocking from side to side, trolley shoved resolutely forward, like a demented wind-up toy.

'There's your K Flakes!' I yelped, but there was barely time to toss them in the trolley before I had to pelt round the front again. An almighty shove and we made a 90-degree turn to proceed down the central alley east to west, swerving round a woman who'd been foolish enough to make a move for the Jaffa Cakes within feet of Granny's front wheels.

The central alley was wide and emptyish, and Granny picked up speed, until she was barrelling over the shiny tiles like Mother Hubbard On Ice. I could see the bakery aisle coming up on the right. There was no time to slow her. She would hit it too fast. She'd never make the turn.

'GRANNY!' I bellowed. 'SHALL WE ASK THIS NICE MAN?'

Instantly, with a noise like a long vehicle run amok in a forest, Granny dug in her grip-fast heels, yanked back on the trolley, set her skirt sails to reverse, and screeched and skidded to a halt, sending the Nescafé jar crashing against the front of the wire and permanently skid-marking the floor. When I caught up with her, her eyes were wild, and her stays were still creaking in the tailwind. I grabbed hold of a bewildered shelf-stacker and pulled him close to Granny. She peered at him with interest, through steamed-up lenses.

'Well now,' she said, quite calmly, 'could you possibly direct us to the bakery counter? We fancy those buns with the toffee bits in them.'

'Nuts and raisins,' I muttered, as though anyone was listening.

The shelf-stacker rose to the occasion. He offered to walk Granny there. They pitched off together, Granny back down to a more manageable rolling speed, the shelf-stacker bending down to get an exact description of the wayward cakey goods. I leant against a pillar and breathed a heavy sigh of relief. Soon, I'd get her home.

The evening was spent pleasantly in a chatter of gossip and the clatter of little jobs that needed doing: I changed a light bulb in the box room; put the bins out; tried to unstick the gate. I heard all about the neighbours. Mad Vonnie down the road who won't throw away cardboard boxes and keeps newspapers all over the place, and who had a house fire and was lucky to get out alive: 'She's a terrible housekeeper. Her garden's an awful mess. But I'd not fall out with her for the world,' said Granny. 'She's had a rotten life.' The young couple that Granny worried about because 'the boy' had been made redundant from Vickers: 'I haven't seen them since before Christmas, except just to say hello to in the garden, but everyone's got so much to do these days haven't they?' And, much the most excitingly, the family of the 'Lady of the Lake' man who'd been accused of murdering his wife years ago and dumping her in Coniston. Granny gave a sigh and said, disappointedly: 'I've never heard a squeak out of them. Still,' she admitted, more brightly, 'everyone says they built a lovely conservatory out back.'

She wore herself out about half past nine, and fell asleep, propped upright on the cushions of her favourite green chair.

The carriage clock on the mantelpiece ticked quietly on. I watched a murder-mystery for a while. I had a strong urge to go out – for a walk, a drink, a drive – but I knew she'd worry terribly if I just disappeared, and if I asked she wouldn't let me. So I sat, looking at the telly, through *News At Ten* and a documentary about a child killer, and the clock ticked and the seagulls cawed in the distance and Granny made a few huffling noises like a dreaming kitten, and then she woke up and wondered who I was for a minute, and we both decided it was time to go to bed.

9

the marble palace of concrete dreams

In the morning, I lay looking at the light that streamed silver through the curtains. I lay like that because I was unable to move: the bedclothes – pink brushed-nylon sheets, flower-dotted pillow cases, blanket upon blanket topped with small quilt and candlewick bedspread, bottomed with plastic fitted sheet that crackled like a crisp packet – had worked their way around me until I was wrapped like a mummy, noosed and trussed. I wriggled in a disco-Houdini manner until I managed to fall out of bed and on to the floor, sweating and trailing lengths of pastel sheets and blankets. It must have sounded like I was having athletic sex with the wardrobe. But, of course, Granny was oblivious to the racket and looked mighty surprised when I came downstairs, flushed and ready for breakfast.

'Oh, I didn't hear you get up,' she said, and immediately, before I'd even located the kettle, launched into a busy monologue about what she was doing today and what time her lift was arriving and when was I leaving and she didn't trust me with the burglar alarm and would I be all right driving back by myself and why was I going and where was John and why wasn't he with me and why hadn't he phoned?

John is my boyfriend. My Granny first met him a couple of Christmasses ago, and this is what happened. John and I arrived at my mum and dad's house, early evening. Granny was already there, installed in her seat, six inches from the telly. Mum went straight into a high state of fluster: whisking John's coat from his shoulders, shoving him on to the sofa, forcing a glass of Sainsbury's lager into one hand and a sideplate with cake in to the other. Her frenzy panicked the cat, which puked, quietly but decidedly, on to the sofa and on to John. Disaster. The puke really stank. Double disaster. Mum moved into overdrive. John was hurtled from the room, swabbed down with bleach, his clothes thrown straight into the washer; the sofa was attacked with vim and Vim; the cat committed hara-kiri; you can imagine it. Anyhow, finally John returned to the lounge, reeking of Dettol and Domestos, and sat down again, a little gingerly. Once he was settled, Granny leaned over and said, loudly: 'Well, John, I EXPECT YOU FEEL BETTER NOW YOU DON'T SMELL OF PUSSY.' Honestly. She did.

So, when she asked about him, I said I wasn't surprised that he hadn't phoned – I wasn't, I was surprised he ever talked to me again after that little episode – and that I would be fine by myself and anyway I would be going back to Mum and Dad's later. Granny said 'Mmm': she'd moved on, to what she was going to wear for today's Inner Wheel lunch. I went upstairs to help her choose her outfit. She favoured a navy suit, or a purpley checked jacket with co-ordinating skirt. Both jackets had small food stains on them that Granny, fastidious and hygiene-obsessed, could not see, but I surreptitiously sponged them clean when she went to find a hat.

It took her a good three-quarters of an hour to sort herself out, but she didn't need my help, and when she coasted electrically downstairs half an hour before she was due to be picked up, in suit with matching shoes, feet together, hat plonked firmly on her curls, she looked very smart. She said: 'The others don't wear hats but they like me to wear one. They say I always do.' She showed me her Past President's ribbons, which hung on a chain around her neck. We chatted for a bit, and had a cup of tea, and then she huffed and hoiked herself out of her easy chair and rocked slowly into the hall, to sit heavily down on the chair by the door, so she'd be ready for when President Brenda knocked, and I kissed her and set off for Dumplington Hall.

I stopped on the way and spent some time on the phone persuading the nice PR girl at Dumplington Hall – sorry, the Trafford Centre – that I deserved a guided tour of the estate and manor house, unfinished as they were. I did tell her that I didn't usually write about shopping centres, and that I wasn't sure whether my usual employer, the *Observer*, would be interested in Dumpers, wonderful as it was, but still, she seemed pleased to hear from me and invited me round that same day.

The Peugeot coped admirably with the drive. I'd been worried that its recent long distance hammering would have knocked something vital out of kilter (any journey further than south to north London usually resulted in me shelling out cash for some minor tweak) but no, it started up quite happily and rumbled stoically along in the slow lane. The journey only took a couple of hours.

'Marvellous motorway links,' I said to Kate the nice PR, over a cup of coffee and a digestive. She agreed, and told me that soon Manchester would have its own ringroad, the M60, formed by connecting several motorways into one. The M60, hoped Kate, would funnel even more drivers around the city before flinging them wide-eyed and open-pursed towards the purchasers' paradise of Dumplington Hall. She didn't put it quite like that, though; she showed me a wall map, with coloured catchment areas and a dotted line to show where the M60 would be.

'Nine point six per cent of the population of Great Britain, a total of 5.35 million people, will be living within a 45-minute drive of the Trafford Centre when it's completed,' trilled Kate. 'Motorway links are clearly important, but we're also offering to invest in public transport connections. We anticipate that forty per cent of Trafford Centre visitors will arrive by public transport: tram, train or bus.'

We were in one of several two-storey Portakabins to the side and rear of Dumpers. Our cabin had a room that boasted an architect's model of the estate, and Kate walked around it and talked me through what was going to happen where. The foyer area of Dumpers Hall was to be a dining extravaganza, a smorgasbord of snack outlets, with different areas corresponding to different cuisine; the wings were reserved for shopping: 'our flagship stores are Selfridges – which will be the only Selfridges outside London – also Debenhams, BHS, Boots, C&A'; and round the back, on the upper level, there would be twenty cinema screens. 'We're investigating the possibility of a bowling alley, also,' said Kate.

Amusement arcade? Penny slot machines, shoot-em-up video screens, glue-sniffing teenagers bunking off school?

'No.'

Kate, who was young and enthusiastic, told me the story of Dumplington Hall. Once upon a time, a very rich man called John Whittaker was driving past Trafford on the M63. He noticed that there was a vast area of unused land by the motorway, the scrubby sort of field where kids play Chuck the Dog-Turd and War. He thought: 'Bet I could make some money out of that.' Actually, according to Kate, he thought: 'What a fine situation for an out-of-town shopping emporium of an exceptionally high quality.' John Whittaker was chairman of Peel Holdings PLC, a development company, so he got Peel to buy the land – which luckily hadn't been designated as green field, but as UDA, an 'urban development area'; still, it took some legal wrangling – and set about turning it into Dumpers. It was a massive investment, an enormo-project. £660 million in building costs; 1,068,000 square feet of retail space; 291,925 square feet of catering and leisure; 10,000 parking spaces. A year and a half in the construction. Ten years in the planning, development and design. There'd been a lot of research.

'We've been to visit the Metro Centre, Lakeside, Meadowhall,' said Kate, naming other out-of-town shopping malls in the Newcastle, Thames Estuary and Sheffield areas. 'Well, there was nothing about them,' sniffed Kate. 'Well, no, Meadowhall was okay, but if you've ever been to Lakeside, you'll know that there's just not the quality.'

Quality. The Dumplington watchword. Everything had to be the best for Dumpers Hall. Marble was imported from Italy for the floors; Peel and Bovis had undertaken to make 'best endeavours' to get all materials and labour from the local area, but marble-wise, the north-west was found wanting. Similarly, the local trees were not considered up to scratch, so special, half-grown ones were brought over from Germany. For if Dumpers' requirements could not be satisfied nearby, then the world would be scoured – not only for raw materials, but for ideas, influences, specialities. The heads of the company even dutifully trekked all the way to Las Vegas. For research purposes. Don't laugh.

What ideas did they get from there? Are they going to have a roller-coaster running all the way around the shopping centre? Will there be high-kicking lesbian chorus girls and house-trained white tigers on hand to entertain worn-out consumers? What about baccarat games? Barbra Streisand? Buckets of drugs? Are you sure there won't be any slot machines?

'They weren't all that impressed with Las Vegas, actually,' sniffed Kate. 'They only liked one thing. The ceiling in Caesar's Palace. Apparently, it's like the sky, it changes into night and day.'

So, Dumpers' foyer-stroke-dining-area, the Orient, was to

have a similar, though much larger, ceiling. During the day, the magic ceiling would be blue, with moving clouds; at night, more than 2,000 stars would come out.

'The constellations will be in exactly the right positions,' enthused Kate. 'So there's an educational element.'

We went downstairs to an ante-room, to put on wellies and hard hats. Three middle-aged men were changing out of theirs; they'd just been on a visitors' ground tour themselves and seemed very happy with it. Except that one of them had a false leg, and he'd got his foot stuck for just a second – nearly left his welly behind and dunked his plastic toe in the mud. He was laughing about it now, sitting on the changing bench, waggling his good toes at us.

We drove to Dumpers in Kate's car, along the Victorian lampposted way.

'They've painted some of the lampposts already,' noted Kate. 'They only went up last week. Every time I come out here, I'm amazed at how much more has been done.'

We parked, and picked our way across the mud to the foyer. The wings stretched out on either side of us like the columned cloisters at the Vatican's St Peter's Square. ('It's all designed in a classical style,' said Kate, 'because it's a long-term investment. We're thinking of the future, we don't want it to date.') Dumpers Hall was vast, enormous, so much bigger than I'd expected, a lowering, towering monument to . . . well, to just how much money can buy, and how fast it can stick it all together.

At the top of the foyer entrance, above the Corinthian

columns, across the classical balustrade, were a few figures: women in togas brandishing significant objects – bits of wood, a pot, some scales. It looked as though the electricity had gone down, but they were still determined to cook tea.

'I think they're meant to represent something to do with Trafford,' said Kate.

'So we can assume that the bits of wood they're clutching aren't the imported German variety, then?'

But Kate hadn't heard, she was striding forth gamely, tramping over planks and slabs and through gloop to the Dumplington interior. I followed, and we both stopped in the centre of the foyer. We looked up to where the magic sky would glow blue, then starry. But the ceiling was yet to arrive, so all we could see was your regular north-west type of sky: grey, rain-bloated, dull.

Kate waved her arms about as she told me what would be what and where. There would be a huge boat that would seem to crash through from the front entrance into the foyer's centre, and centrally, a paved space that could be used for fashion shows, dinner dances, concerts, film premieres. ('We're hoping!' said Kate.) A vast video screen would hang down opposite the boat, showing the various attractions that could be found in other areas of Dumplington's vast manor. There'd be a fountain, too, and all around, an array of today's highest quality eating outlets, including – and Kate lowered her voice as she told me – a Rainforest Cafe. She seemed very excited about this, her eyes snapping as she warned me not to breathe a word to anyone about this hotter-than-a-sauna news. The Rainforest Cafe, if you don't know, is an American invention, an eco-friendly hamburger joint where, every twenty minutes, there's a pretend tropical storm to remind you that you shouldn't be sitting in a hamburger joint stuffing your face with intensively-farmed meat, you should be out there saving vast swathes of tropical forest from being turned into intensive cattle-rearing territory to provide meat for hamburger joints. At least, that's how I understand it. It's a kinky eating experience. I wondered if Kate was a Catholic.

We proceeded on, to the upstairs restaurant area. This was themed, according to the countries of the world of food: France, Italy, the USA, China – and that seemed to be your lot, food-country-wise. Strangely, France had been warped into New Orleans. Kate said: 'We paid to send a local artist to New Orleans to see the jazz.' The local artist had returned, and used his new-found knowledge to help distress the walls of the Frenchy eating area into authentic New Orleans-style shabbiness, and to paint a jolly mural of people playing jazz. Over in the Chinatown space, there was an arch, just like the one in Manchester, but the Dumpers Chinatown managed to cover a larger variety of cuisine. There was to be Japanese food round there, and Thai too.

We squelched through into the main shopping area: the long, two-storey wings. Here there were workmen, working: wielding bars, shifting slabs, talking into walkie-talkies, eyeing us with a combination of annoyance (we were walking on the Italian marble) and amusement (our hard hats were too big). Kate said that the two wings were to be slightly different from each other, to stop shoppers getting lost. So, Peel Avenue would be your regular stores – Boots, Top Shop, Miss

Selfridge; Regent Crescent would be more upmarket – designer boutiques like Selfridges, Tommy Hilfiger, Ralph Lauren; and the décor and architecture of each would also be different, again to help you keep your retail bearings. We compared and contrasted, and found that the Regent Crescent columns seemed slightly more stately than those on Peel Avenue. We checked the potential paintwork: 'One of the things we felt when we visited other shopping developments was that they were mostly too white, that they lacked colour,' said Kate. So, above the Regent Crescent first floor shops, someone had picked out the twirly bits in gold, and green, and red, to see which looked best.

Above the shops, too, there were hand-painted portraits of what looked to be dignatories, or gods, in decorative oval frames.

'Who are they?' I asked Kate.

Kate laughed, a bit. She said: 'Oh that's a little joke. The portraits will be of the chairmen and directors of Bovis and Peel, also the chief conceptual architect, the head of structural engineering . . . you know, the people at the top who helped realise the Trafford Centre project.'

Ah yes, of course: the far-sighted patrons. Those who had the vision. The saints of the shopping centre, the lofty-minded boardroom executives, whose valiant efforts and sheer determination had turned a dream into reality. They built this cathedral to commerce with their own bare hands – well, they paid for the workmen anyway – and all they wanted for their efforts was a hand-painted caricature and a high investment return. I supposed the other alternative would have been mounting their heads on stakes. I hoped that whoever the local Michelangelo was would do them justice.

We moved on: up more stairs to the cinema area. My feet were beginning to hurt. I said, rattily: 'Won't you be destroying central Manchester for a second time? I mean, it's all got to be rebuilt after the Arndale bomb, and now, even when it is, the Trafford Centre will have enticed all the shoppers away anyway.'

Kate looked a little hurt.

'Well, I like a variety of shopping experiences myself,' she said. 'I mean, sometimes I'll just nip to the shops round the corner, sometimes I'll go to Altrincham, sometimes into Manchester. We won't be competing with Manchester, because Manchester has arts and culture.'

She marched on, spouting about how, 'in fact', Peel were going to invest in Altrincham, in a leisure-stroke-retail-stroke-hotel manner, and how – now Peel had won the take-over battle for the Manchester Ship Canal Company – they also hoped to develop the whole of the shipping canal area, make it nice and pretty so that vacationers could take leisurely barge holidays that ended up at Dumplington Hall. Kate told me that now, Trafford locals were very pro-Dumpers: that, initially, perhaps, some had harboured hostile feelings, but when they realised how much was being invested and how many jobs created (7,000 when finished, with 3,000 in the construction stage) and how Peel were also applying to build a regional sports centre just nearby, perhaps including a nine-hole golf course (here, Kate hesitated before admitting that actually the sports centre would be funded both publicly and privately) – well, anyway, everyone just changed their minds. Now the North-West is rooting for Dumpers. Oh, and did she mention that it was likely that it would open between 10 a.m. and 8 p.m., so there wouldn't be a rush hour overlap; and that Peel was offering to pay for sales training for local people?

'We can't guarantee them a job afterwards, but we will fund their training,' said Kate.

How many have taken up the offer?

'Not that many so far. But we're going to take out radio advertising on Key 103.'

We were back out by the car now, and Kate said that she'd whizz me quickly round the rest of the site, so I could be sure of my bearings. We passed a small copse of trees. 'That's to be the site of the hotel,' said Kate. 'The idea is that the Trafford Centre is the stately home and the hotel will be like the stables.'

So Dumpers Hall was right, and a much better name than the Trafford Centre, too. Still, I thought it best not to mention this to Kate – she had moved on, anyhow, to how there was to be a Café Rouge in the New Orleans dining area – 'all my friends are very pleased'; and how the whole of the food foyer would, of course, stay open later than the retail area, as would the cinema; and had she mentioned Festival Village, the craft section at the end of Peel Avenue? Which would be set out like a real market, with stands and striped canopies, and would sell artsy bits and pieces, you know, earrings, antiques, candles, gifts.

It was hard not to get caught up with Kate's enthusiasm, and I couldn't find the heart to sneer at her too much. After all, she enjoyed her work – it was her first proper job since college, she told me – and she had given me a digestive. And anyway, my flabber had been more thoroughly gasted by Dumpers than I ever would have imagined possible. It wasn't just its massiveness and the rapidity of its erection – nothing new there, such qualities have always impressed the ladies – it was the sheer scale of investment in Dumpers, the mountain upon mountain of money that had been shovelled into the project, not just to make it, but to make it *classy*.

That was what made Dumpers different. Dumpers was a shopping centre built with as much care as an up-to-the-minute art gallery, or a new church, or an all-facilities sports centre, or a state-of-the-art city to replace the old one that was blown up by terrorists. A hypermarket crafted like the National Gallery's Sainsbury wing. Prince Charles would be pleased. All that cash, all that time, all that man-power, all that design-effort gone on gilding a building that might just as well have been a bolt-together warehouse.

I looked around with Dumper-friendly eyes. What endeavour! What daring! Surely, it was a good thing that I was witness to. After all, we're forever hearing about the ugliness of those corrugated iron blocks that circle British cities like an incroaching army, the metal box B&Qs, Homebases, Tescos, Sainsbury's. Not even their mothers would call them good-looking. No, they're eyesores. So cheap, so trashily made. They will insist on being obvious about their money-making: they don't bother to disguise their cost-cutting in construction, they don't bother to dress up their true purpose. Or if they do, they don't do it with much style: just the odd flower-bed here, a fake town-clock there.

So, Dumpers was undoubtably the high water mark of British shopping centres. It was the best built, of the highest quality and there would be no more of its kind. In a strange way, it did remind me of Las Vegas. Not the high-rollin', low-down-dirty Vegas of Frank Sinatra and his Rat Pack, but the new, nineties, family-orientated Vegas, that had a crèche and a funfair and a McDonalds to keep the kids entertained whilst Mom and Pop got on with wagering the school fees. Dumpers, like today's Vegas, was clean and vice-free, wholesome, friendly, fun for all the family; safe as houses, if the houses were in a good area. It was reassuring. There was no danger.

Who wants to shop when you risk running a gauntlet of muggers, or stepping over the community-cared? Dumpers had removed shopping from all its contexts. It had taken fashion out of its natural, evolving, look-at-me environment – the city; it had collected gobbets of food from around the world and shoved them all together higgledy-piggledy, away from the culture that had created the recipes; it had made going to see a film the same as eating a burger or as buying a pair of handcrafted earrings. It had smoothed off the corners, and made everything equal.

I thought of the Last Drop Village. The whole of it – teashop, conferencing facilities, local crafts and all – would be swamped by the foyer of Dumpers Hall. The Rainforest Cafe would drizzle all over the Last Drop. And I remembered the first time I'd been to a hypermarket: it was in France, in 1990, and I'd thought how weird it must be to have to drive right outside of a city to get your shopping done. And I also recalled a statistic: that out-of-town centres now account for over

25 per cent of British shopping space. Yet the first one – Newcastle's Metro Centre – was only built in 1986.

Like Las Vegas, like every out-of-town shopping centre, Dumpers had taken one, money-making activity (gambling, shopping) and got rid of the seedy side, the awkward, nasty bits that might make you stop and think what you're doing, or might make you not do it in the first place. No heavy bouncers on the door; no sad losers at the bar; no penniless fuck-ups waiting to bash you on the head for your winnings. No piss in the multi-storey lift; no *Big Issue* seller in the doorway; no long walk in the rain across the litter-strewn precinct to the cash-point. Everything was just good, clean, warm, dry, landscaped, lifestyle, easy-access, easy-excess fun fun fun.

10

the most average town in Britain

I met Keith in 1985. He was from Birmingham. He had a wedge haircut that tickled his eyes. He was good at darts and snooker. He lived on hot curries and beer. He stole full crates of Newcastle Brown and stacked them up in his room. Keith was an artist.

He's much the same today, except his fringe is shorter and his work is bought by Charles Saatchi, as opposed to by no one at all. Keith's art is 'difficult'; not the kind of thing that would look nice over the mantelpiece. It's made from debris that he finds knocking about, in skips, outside hospitals, against the walls of disused buildings. His work used to be fiddly: drawers filled with medical slides, postcards in racks, a pencil that he'd sharpened into one long continuous shaving and then rolled back together into a pencil shape. For some reason, though, these days Keith's art is bigger, clumsier, more obtuse: stacked benches and mattresses and bits of rusty metal and moldered doors and huge and broken plastic tubes. He says he's not sure why his stuff grew, he says he keeps trying to make smaller work, that people would at least consider as mantelpiece-friendly, but he can't help it, the work is big. And not much like art. Even if you could squeeze one of Keith's pieces in the space above your carriage clock, your friends might mistake it for dry rot.

I watched when the removal men came to his studio, to take the work that Saatchi had bought. They arrived in a lorry, marked Art. They went into Keith's studio and studied the work for a time. They packed it up. Then, bit by bit, with painstaking gentleness and concern, they manoeuvred the wrapped slabs of rotten wood, the swaddled knackered mattresses, out of the studio, down the twisted fire-escape, across the car park and into the lorry. It was as though the men had come to clear an abandoned house, a condemned place, except that instead of chucking all the old junk out into the backyard, they had decided to package it like aged china, very carefully, in individual pieces, in bubble-wrap. I couldn't read their expressions.

If you punch the stats, feed the computer, access the info (current trends, contemporary research, filled questionnaires, answered questions), and then process it correctly, it's not hard to pinpoint The Most Average Town In Britain. I'd asked a friendly marketing consultant, and he'd run the raw material through the designated programme. (The material was stuff about voting and shopping, work and age, choice of leisure pursuit and fave holiday destination; the programme was, um, the programme.) He'd run all the relevants through the specialised analyser and the answer it came up with was: Preston.

Now, before Mr Marketing had done that for me, someone had told me that The Most Average Town In Britain was Swindon; someone else said Gravesend; another, Northampton. So I was happy to get some hard facts at last. Preston was the winner. Preston had come out on top. Well, in the middle. Preston was our nation's Average, as normal as it comes. Preston was my destination.

I was keen to locate Averageville because I wanted to go there to see if it felt familiar. Wilmslow was clearly disqualified from such a title because of its obvious wealth and ditto taste; yet, when I had lived there, despite the shag-me cars and shagpile carpets, the predominant atmosphere had been one of cosy middlingness. That was the point. Most people had moved there because they'd made money, and made it in places that were far from bourgeois; thus, despite its racy exterior, Wilmslow was very proud to be suburban. It desired to be the norm; the bulky, comfy median around which clustered the moderate, the respectable, the best of all worlds. The houses were large, but unremarkable. The countryside was pretty, yet tame. No one ever did anything *extreme*. Some of the hairdos might have seemed a little OTT, but they still operated within accepted conventions: of gender, of fashion, of what was deemed suitable for your age and earning power. I never met an artist in Wilmslow.

But now I was due to meet one in Preston, and I was running late. A few weeks earlier, I'd mentioned to Keith that I was going to visit Preston, and he'd said that he had to go there too. The town's public art gallery, the Harris, had commissioned him to do some work. Of course, he couldn't just put some of his old stuff in there: the work had to be tailored for the gallery, in as much as Keith tailored anything. So Keith and I had decided to visit Preston together. We were to meet in the Harris coffee shop at two. I was looking forward to it; I hadn't seen Keith for a while and it's always good to see friends outside London, away from routine and from having to go back because it's work in the morning. Not that Keith was much of a nine-to-fiver, but you know. Often you have a better time with people when they and you are out of context.

Preston wasn't far from my mum and dad's; the drive there was quick, uneventful, fractious. The motorway was crowded. There was no time or space for dreamy remove, for soothing non-driving, for motorway cruising. I wished that I was aiming further north. Past the exit to my Granny's, above Penrith where it spews out the Lake District visitors, the M6 changes completely. From being a man-machine conveyor belt, it becomes as beautiful as a motorway can, slicing through mountains and climbing slowly towards Scotland, open and empty.

In the end, I arrived a little early, and drove around Preston for a time. The Most Average Town In Britain has an old centre, surrounded by multi-storeys and covered markets and business blocks, all built in the 1970s. You couldn't tell, but at the turn of the century, Preston had had status: it had been made rich through the textile industry, chic by its annual summer fair, when fancy London types travelled up to test their parasols against the north-west rain. Nowadays its claim to fame – other than being Average – is that a few years ago an ancient elk was winched out of Preston harbour, in an area called Poulton. You can view the Poulton Elk in all its dried-out, moth-eaten glory in the lowest floor of the Harris Museum.

The Harris Museum and Art Gallery itself is an imposing classical edifice that stands in Preston's centre, close to the law courts where Child A and Child B of the Jamie Bulger case were tried and found guilty. The Harris – 'a Greek Revival listed building', according to the Preston Essential Guide – was started in 1882 and finished in 1893. It belongs to an age when benevolent burghers of industry and commerce wanted to make their mark, to leave a monument that was more than just a statue, that would encourage lowly workers to improve themselves and would rubber-stamp their name on the guest list to heaven. The Harris was named after Edmund Harris, a local lawyer who in the 1870s bequeathed to the town the considerable remains of his family money – upwards of £300,000 – for 'good works'. As well as the Harris public art gallery and library, the money was used for an orphanage and a college.

The Harris is the most important-looking building in Preston. Its columns are straight and high. There is an imposing staircase up to the main entrance. Its balustrade, at the top of the building, is decorated in golden letters which read: ART LITERATURE SCIENCE. There's a paved square in front of the Harris, called the Flag Market, that hosts the annual town crier competition and the Historical Fayre. The town radiates out from around the Harris.

Its coffee shop was towards the back of the ground floor, swamped by the museum's massive dimensions. I sat down, and almost immediately, Keith turned up. He had an air of not being at one with his surroundings, which was usual – Keith, although confident, always appears a little lost – and he was scruffily dressed. 'How can you say such a thing!' he protested, when I commented. 'These trousers are new! And bottle green! An attractive colour which is probably fashionable!'

We went upstairs to meet the Harris curators. A man and a woman. They were young, earnest, quiet. They seemed as though they'd be more suited to outreach social work. They said, let's go for lunch. So we went for lunch, around the corner, in Brucciani's, a huge pastry and coffee establishment that first traded in the 1930s. There were pictures of long dead filmstars and ornate mirrors hanging on the glossed magnolia walls; the café was filled with tea-and-caking shoppers. We sat at a narrow table and Keith explained to the curators what he wanted to do for the Harris.

In the middle gallery, said Keith, he wanted to put some empty library shelves. Long, rusting, bookless, they would pro-vide a comment upon the declining state of Harris's admirable art-for-the-people and open-to-all educational aspirations; on the slow decline and imminent death of the British public library. Or so I assumed. Keith can explain his work, but doesn't often bother – at least not to me, possibly because I don't ask – so this was just guesswork on my part. But he didn't explain the library shelves to the Harris curators either.

Next, Keith said that he wanted to put some work outside the gallery, in front of the Harris itself, in the empty, paved, central Flag Market. There, said Keith, he wanted to put: a puddle.

'A puddle?' said one of the curators, as you would.

'Yeah,' said Keith.

What Keith would like, he said, was for the Harris' art funding to pay for some council workmen to dig up a few flagstones in the middle of Flag Market square, and then to relay them in the same place but at odd angles, slightly wonky, so that when it rained, a puddle would form.

'How big do you want the puddle?' asked a curator.

'Big enough to cause a bit of a problem. Big enough so you'd have to walk around it, so you couldn't just step over it,' said Keith, helpfully.

I looked at the male curator. He didn't seem at all fazed, which surprised me. Keith had told me about his puddle before we'd come to Preston and I'd thought it sounded ridiculous – funny, but utterly ridiculous. (I'd said, 'Are you going to label it? Will people know that this is a special, art puddle?' Keith had said, 'No'.) But the curators seemed to take the puddle pretty well. They hadn't burst out laughing, which is what I thought they'd do. It was what I'd done. There's no way they'll go for it, I'd said to Keith. If the local newspaper got hold of the plan – which they would, if council workmen had to do the work, and if grant money paid them – then Keith was likely to be found drowned in two inches of his own work. Keith didn't care. Though he did want the puddle to be a success, because he wanted to take it to other towns, maybe even outside Britain: to take the puddle on tour.

Public art always causes frothy hysteria. Art, generally, fosters strong emotions, often resulting from the prices it commands: the '*How* much? my cat could do better' argument. Still, such financial affronts can be borne, if the art is being bought privately (the 'It's their money, they can spend it on what they like' counter-argument). But when the art is funded by the communal purse, then people feel – rightly – that they have a right to comment. And if the work is not to the general taste (if it's non-figurative, or 'unsuitable' which means genitalia-airing), or if it looks like there was little effort put into the making of the work, then people can get extremely annoyed. I supposed that Keith could point out that a puddle was environmentally-friendly, and that he wasn't making any money out of it (the grant would just pay the workmen); but he flunked comprehensively on the 'isn't that pretty' and 'I made it all myself' fronts. I had a feeling that Preston would rip him to shreds. When I'd said so, Keith had replied that he thought it would be funny if people got really angry over a puddle.

You had to admit that he'd chosen a prime site. Flag Market must be the only square in Britain not to be puddled already. I'd looked as we'd walked over it to Brucciani's; although it was drizzling, and had been for some time, there were no pools underfoot. The flagstones had been laid very carefully, in a workmanlike manner, and maintained so there weren't any irregularities. Flag Market was a puddle-free zone.

The curators started to talk about getting the idea past the local councillors. I thought, You'll be lucky. Even aside from the public reaction, the council was bound to be paranoid about being sued for relaying flagstones so they weren't smooth to walk on. All it would take is a tumbling mother with pushchair, or the grazed knees of a half-blind pensioner, or a roller-blading health freak with a bloodied nose and the council would be bankrupted.

I said: 'What are you going to call it?'

Keith said: 'I dunno. Puddle.'

I sneaked a look at the woman curator, but she had the serious look of a true art believer, that rabbit-in-the-headlights gaze of someone awed by genius. I could feel laughter bubbling up, and I didn't want to ruin Keith's chances, so I excused myself and went to the toilet.

When I came back, they'd moved on and were talking about other artists, some I'd heard of, some I hadn't. I couldn't tell if the puddle had been accepted, but I guessed that it had: no one looked disgruntled. The male curator seemed bemused, but he had done anyway. It looked to me as though Keith had succeeded.

After lunch, we went back to the Harris and Keith talked some more with the curators whilst I wandered around the galleries. The displays were varied. On one floor, there was a profusion of perfume bottles, the personal collection of an old lady called Mrs French. There was a 'style through the ages' costume bit, with some hilarious captioning: *Sambo made clothes in the 50s and 60s, which were sold through Miss Selfridge. The brand name chosen by this company shows a naivety about race relations.* There was the Elk. There was some rubbish from the local art college. And there was the permanent collection, the hotch-potch mixture of most regional galleries: pastoral, romantic, some modern photographs, bought when and if the Harris had the funds. The most popular painting in the museum, said the girl curator, was *Pauline in the Yellow Dress* by James Gunn. They got bundles of protesting letters whenever she was taken down. I went to have a look at Pauline. She reminded me of that serene green-faced lady whose portrait was a household staple in the 1970s. I liked her.

Keith was done with his negotiating by now, so we left and wandered about The Most Average Town In Britain for a while. The roads were slick with rain. Most of the shoppers were gone; the few that were left were huddled under bus shelters. Along the main street, a small crane suspended a workman about twenty foot in the air. He was fixing a stop-thief-you're-on-candid-camera CCTV to a lamp-post. Keith and I walked in a large circle, just inside the one-way system. We discovered: a covered market, the bus terminus, several charity shops, a lovely Victorian square, a shopping centre with stalls set up in the middle, where a man tried to sell us roll-back garage doors.

And we found some previously established public art. Outside the Flax and Firkin, once the Corn Exchange, there was a history-aware sculpture. Keith started to seethe as soon as he saw it.

It was a strange sight: four chunky individual figures cowering before the massed guns of a group of others. There was a gap of a few feet between the two factions. Those who were being shot wore comical, Kenneth Williams-type expressions of surprise and clutched favoured parts of their bodies in the manner of footballers in a wall before a free kick. Those who were shooting formed an amorphous, anonymous whole. There was a poetic inscription.

Remember, remember, people of proud Preston
That progress towards justice and democracy
Has not been achieved without great sacrifice
Remember, remember, people of proud Preston
To defend vigorously the rights given to you
Strive to enhance the rights of others who follow

Then there was an explanation. 'In Lune Street Preston, four workers were shot and killed by the military during the general strike of 1842. Several thousands of Preston workers were demonstrating against wage cuts and for the "charter" of democratic rights.'

Well. If this was the kind of art that the people of proud Preston were partial to, then Keith was, without a doubt, heading for a lynching, despite local progress towards justice and democracy. His only chance of preventing them from defending their rights too vigorously and him losing his life in the process was to point out that their ancestors were also fighting to enhance the rights of dilettante artists like Keith. And that, unlike the square-shouldered martyrs, his puddle wasn't permanent. It would go away eventually. As long as the council would agree to put the flagstones back as they were.

Keith looked at the sculpture and said: 'Bet that would be hard to push over.'

Keith seemed gloomy. He hated the Preston martyrs sculpture, as he hated most public sculpture, indeed most things in general. Keith, despite his cheery demeanour, hates a lot of life, not just art. I remember him once getting very depressed about a funeral. Not because the funeral itself would be depressing, but because he hated the ceremony. He despised the way that organised religion always got in there at the end, even if the person who died was an atheist. It was the theological opportunism, not the actual death, that upset him. He's a funny fish.

I had a phone interview to do, so we checked into a business hotel rather than a B&B. A Trusthouse Forte, out by the bus station. It was exactly as you'd imagine: big telly, pastel wallpaper, wrapped soap, trouser-press. (Does any company other than Corby produce trouser-presses? Have the Monopolies and Mergers Commission checked out Corby's stranglehold on the permacrease slacks market?)

My interview was with Bob Cartwright, a man from Whitbread breweries. I'd phoned him to ask about All Bar One, a chain of open-plan food-and-wine-bars which had, apparently, been designed to attract young women – on the premise that if young women went there, then young men would follow. Although there were only a few All Bar Ones, they were proving remarkably successful. There were early evening queues outside the London branches.

Over the phone, Bob told me all about All Bar One: the consultancy team, the focus groups, the lifestyle research, the demographic changes in the drinking market. I got a real feel for the place. Bob explained that Whitbread had identified several different drinking types. No longer was there just the two: the drinking and the drunk. No, in the late nineties, entirely new groups of pub-goers have emerged. These were identified as a) women b) families c) seniors d) empty nesters. So – before the All Bar One era, everyone who went to a pub was a young, single male. Now, with Whitbread's help, everyone else is allowed to come along too.

The important thing to understand, it seemed, is that not all these new drinkers want to hob-nob with each other. In the Venn diagram of social tippling, there are few who live in the overlaps. So Whitbread have designed a different pub for each category. There's All Bar One, pitched at youngish 'twenties to thirties' women, *vis*: big windows (so you feel safe and can see who's in there before you open the door), hard surfaces (voices carry, seems more lively), mix of table sizes (mingle or remain solitary), large variety of wine on offer (as opposed to just white or red/dry or sweet/screw top or nothing), newspapers on rack (if your date's late you can fob off the lechers by pretending to read *The Beano*), food served on small plates (ancient Weight Watchers tip: looks like you're eating a big meal, when you're just having a measly snack). The All Bar One chain is extremely successful: each of its bars averages over £25,000 a week in takings. Bob spent quite a time explaining All Bar One to me. He'd Venned me as a potential client.

Bob then whizzed through the other categories of drinkers for whom Whitbread catered. Families and couples are served by good old Harvesters. Seniors get Vintage Inns: British country pubs, emphasising 'history and heritage', which serve British food, none of your Johnny Foreigner curries or pizza. Students are provided with It's A Scream, a 'discreetly branded' pub with good value food and 'zany' promotions, such as a free condom giveaway. Those who are young, but not students/coupled off/heritage buffs/women who drink wine, can go to O'Neills, where 'the message is fun', there's live music, and the staff get up on the bar and dance. If you think that this is over-the-top, that you just want a drink, then the Goose and Granite chain can come to your rescue: no smoking areas, no music, beer at a reasonable price.

And finally, in case anyone feels at all left out, there's Edwards, a bizarre joint where the atmosphere, lighting, music, food, staff-uniforms change throughout the day, in order to attract particular customers. Thus, in the morning, there'll be coffee and pastries, papers, a French feel; then at lunch, pub food, friendly chatter; in the afternoon, shoppers are catered for (easy atmosphere, cup of tea); and in the evening, there's a shift between the early, after-work, calming-down drinkers, and the more manic, out-for-the-nighters after 8 p.m. Edwards is Whitbread's 'chameleon brand', said Bob. He told me that Whitbread had just won Brewery Chain of the Year, for all their innovations.

It was strange to talk to Bob in the Most Average Town In Britain. Bob made me feel as though Average just wasn't good enough any more: that, these days, Average had to be broken down, broken up, divided into a family of Averages. There was Ms Average 20–30. There were the Average Geriatrics. The Average Schizophrenic. The Students at the University of Average. And now we'd been recognised and categorised, us Average consumers would no longer be confusing, nor confused. No more time wasted on non-specific goods, on matters unfamiliar, on bewildering, enlightening new experience. Every one of us had each been tagged and targeted and given what we want (on average). Never again would anyone exclaim: Of all the bars in all the towns in all the world . . . because everyone you knew and everyone like you would always be in all the same places.

After speaking to Bob, I really needed a drink. Keith had been leafing through the What To Do In Preston folder and had found, well, nothing that he fancied. So we walked back towards Fishergate, the shopping street, and stopped outside an imposing establishment called Fives. Fives had bay windows and dark wood and looked like a well-bred hotel, from the outside. Inside, it made a chameleon brand look focused. Like Edwards, Fives hadn't been able to make up its mind what kind of bar it was. But instead of changing its tune throughout the day, it had permanently divided itself into five different places. Fives was Tick Tack Toe, Masquerade, El Meson, Sans Souci and No 12. All at once.

The ground floor was El Meson and Sans Souci – a Spanish tapas bar plus a French restaurant. We had bumbled into Sans Souci before we'd noticed any of Five's cute identity crises; it wasn't until the waiter brought us a menu with patatas bravas on one side and snails in garlic on the other that we realised that anything was up.

The waiter was well-scrubbed, round eyes blinking behind metal-rimmed glasses. He was ready for a chat. It was early evening and there were only two other people eating – two glamorous middle-aged ladies – and he knew them already. He launched into an explanation of Fives for us, calling over to the other diners to confirm his story: 'That's right, int'it, Mrs Burrows?' He told us that Fives' owner ran Tiggi's, an Italian restaurant over the road, and that Fives used to be the local Conservative Club.

'It's all fake, this,' he confided, waving an arm around Sans Souci. 'He had it done up just recently.'

Keith and I were quite astonished. Sans Souci looked the real deal: the mirrors had spots on them, the fittings were elaborate, the bar was polished wood. Sans Souci appeared just as genuinely old as Brucciani's, as permanent as the Preston Martyrs. The waiter smiled at our reaction, pleased that we'd been fooled. He said we should have a look around the whole place after we'd eaten: Masquerades was shut, downstairs, but the two floors above us, Tick Tack Toe and No 12, were open until after midnight. He said we should go to the top floor: 'It's a bit special, up there.'

Then he said, 'You've heard of that Trafford Centre opening near Manchester?'

I said, yeah; surprised.

'Well, he's going to have a restaurant there. His'll be the only one in the food hall that's not a chain.'

I was impressed. Mr Fives must be a local player of some note in order to have swung that. Well – he must have some cash, at least. I wondered to myself why no other north-west businesses had been allowed to join him in the vast dining-rooms of Dumpers Hall, but, really, I knew why: because Dumpers Hall was all about quality, and quality meant national and international brand organisations that could afford to pay the rent. There wouldn't be many businesses in Dumpers whose parent company couldn't be found in the FTSE 100. It was a finishing school for boutiques with the right connections.

We had a lovely tea, Keith and I, and got warmly, winely drunk. By the time we'd finished, Sans Souci was filling up, so we decided to venture upstairs. On the first floor was No 12. It was a sports bar, a chrome and glass extravaganza, with tellies everywhere, all showing the same football match. There were even screens set into the floor, which was lit in squares, like a seventies disco. We did a spot of stupid Thriller dancing, trying to get the TVs to change channel by balancing on our toes (it didn't work), and then exited to try the next bar up.

Tick Tack Toe was very different: the kind of discreet niterie Mick Hucknall would frequent when accompanied by latest flame. Sensually lit (to ensure that morning-after vision couldn't set in too early), expensively sofa-ed, with *faux* candles, fireplaces the size of council flats and a chandelier that thought it was the Milky Way, Tick Tack Toe had more than a touch of class. It grabbed chichi with both hands and shoved it down your throat until you gagged.

The central bar was circular and lit from below, so that the rows of bottles glimmered like small, radioactive rockets. Around the bar sat a handful of people, their chins and nostrils blazing chicly in the underglow. Outside the bar's searchlight, the room was almost black. There, in the gloom, couples lounged upon fully upholstered leather sofas in fully upholstered leather trousers. You could tell they were there because when they shifted their weight, the air was rent with squeaking.

All in all, it was like a Depeche Mode promo. I wished I still smoked: Tick Tack Toe was just the place for a sophisticated Sobranie Cocktail. Keith and I thought we'd better order cocktails. I wanted a Flaming Lamborghini but Tick Tack Toe was far too cold-blooded for such a fire-breathing concoction, so margueritas it was.

We stayed until closing time, well after midnight. I don't remember what we talked about, although I know that Puddle was a part of it. I understood that one of the reasons why Keith wanted to make a puddle as a piece of public sculpture was that it was fleeting, that it might not arrive (unlikely, in the sodden north-west), and then that it would soon be removed. Also: its removal would be a good thing – people would be happy to see it go. Another aspect was that, unlike most public art, Puddle had no overbearing memorial purpose or weighty opinion of itself. Keith also pointed out that it would be hard to vandalise. The spray paint would dissolve.

I'm sure our conversation was perceptive and hilarious and that our wit impressed the not quite middle-aged not quite middle-management and their tipsy girlfriends who were enjoying the ambience of Tick Tack Toe along with us. But, like I said, I don't recall much of the evening. I remember looking around and wondering what kind of Average all us Tick Tack Toers were: maybe we were Haven't-You-Got-An-Average-Home-To-Go-To types.

Of course, Keith and I didn't: we had a Trusthouse Forte. We bumbled through the rain, admiring puddles, until we reached the hotel, where the lights were fluorescent and the bar was still serving. We made a move on the pool table; our opponents were Mick and Gareth and they were IT consultants from Peterborough. They were very good at pool. Keith potted quite a few. His drunkenness had turned him into James Coburn; he leant against the wall between shots, and when it came to his turn, he pushed himself away from the wall and into position on the table in one smooth motion. Sadly, my drunkenness had turned me into James Tarbuck. My game tactics consisted of poking the opponent in the bum with the end of my cue whenever he lined up for a sitter. We won one game and lost two and celebrated our pathetic victory (they fouled the black) with a glorious lap of honour around the pool table with cues raised high above our heads.

Mick and Gareth said that they had been in Fives too, in No 12, the sports bar; they said that Preston was better than Peterborough for nightlife. They came up a lot, because they were helping with the new computer system for the hospital. They made a few weak jokes about nurses, and we made a few weak jokes about computer nerds and then the barman started flashing the lights on and off. We all shuffled out of the bar and into the lift and along the padded corridors and then we each fiddled with room keys and went to bed.

The heating was set to roast, but I couldn't work out how to turn it down. My teeth felt like they belonged to someone else. The rain battered against the picture window. I wasn't sleepy.

So I lay on my bed and I thought about being Average: how complicated a concept it seemed to have become, how over-analysed and harassed, constantly redefined, endlessly prodded and examined under the bright, harsh light of marketing prospects. I thought of how when you try to pin someone down, they wriggle free and confound you; how if you want to see something clearly, you have to look at it out of the side of your eyes.

And I thought about Puddle. At least it was something that everyone could agree on. A puddle is a puddle is a puddle. It has universal appeal; maybe not appeal, exactly, but it is universally understood. You couldn't target a puddle so it was more appealing to one type of Average person than another. Not unless you made it out of Sunny Delight, or Lemon Hooch, or your own urine, or something. No: a puddle was a fundamentally everyday thing. Ultimately, a puddle was Average. And Keith's Puddle would be a free, all-encompassing and indiscriminatory gift, given, briefly, ludicrously, to each and every one of the Average people in Britain's Most Average Town. I wondered if they would be grateful.

11

searching for Britland

I'd gone to York. I'd arrived quite late and had spent the night at a respectable B&B. It was respectable, I knew, because it did not stint on the chintz. I've always found that the more frequent the ruffle, the more righteous the establishment; and this place boasted a bow on every possible surface. Everything that could be was swathed in billowing flowery fabric. The room and en suite were a profusion of rose prints, a riot of pastels, a heart attack of ruching. There were frilled soap-dish mats, and a flouncy cover for the spare toilet roll. If I'd worn a ra-ra skirt I'd have been lost forever.

I'd gone to York for a couple of reasons. First: I fancied a longish off-motorway drive, and the A road between Preston and York was a good one. It skimmed under the Yorkshire

Dales, skipped over the cities – Blackburn, Burnley, Halifax, Bradford, Leeds; it's a fast, high, scenic spin, free of the lorries that rumble up and down the country and thunder across England at its narrowest driving point, a few miles north. (If you're making notes: A66, Penrith to Scotch Corner, wig-raisingly frightening in an elderly car.)

The second reason I'd gone to York was Heritage. If I was trying to locate suburbia through my own experience of it, then it was my own past I was sourcing. But my knowledge of my personal pedigree goes no further back than my Granny, and I'd already been to visit her. I'm aware that there must have been others who went before, but I've never known much about them; I'm from a long line of un-noteworthies, and I bet you are too. (Although once, my mum was contacted by a man writing about Middlesbrough's Good Old Days: he told her that some of her distant relatives had been in a successful turn-of-the-century Middlesbrough performing troupe called The Cycling Elliotts, who patented an enormous table that span around at 500 times a minute. Whilst it did so, The Elliotts performed cycle tricks upon it, to much Victorian applause. The man sent my mum a picture.)

But aside from The Elliotts, the only past I'd ever known about was the national, jingo type. School gave me Kings and Queens of England and Scotland, Battle of Trafalgar, day trip to Fountain's Abbey, fin. My educationally minded parents tried harder: dragging me and Toby around museums, churches, art galleries, local historical centres like Styal Mill and Chester, as well as their preferred destinations of shopping centres and building sites.

From such trips, I'd deduced that my heritage is the same as everyone else's. You get the history you're given; and unless your name is listed in the reference index of real, written-about History, or unless you or your parents travelled a long way to settle in the UK, then your heritage is the same as my heritage is the same as your dippy second cousin and her screwaround husband's is the same as that bastard who stole your car stereo's is the same as – agh – Jeffery Archer's. Though he will keep denying it.

I'd been trying to look at suburbia through the window of my childish past – that of Sunday driving, going to see my Granny, going to the supermarket, aiming to be Average – but my history was wider and more all-encompassing, more general than that. I decided to locate it. It wasn't as if it would be difficult. These days, British Heritage is brown-signed off motorways, blobbed on maps, housed in Visitor Centres, given page after page in Sunday supplements.

And York is a city that is stuffed with history. I knew if I looked around there, for a single afternoon, I'd stumble upon mine. And that of every other Briton.

In my ruffled room, on the occasional table, there was a plastic file of Things To Do In The Local Region (Please Leave For The Benefit Of Other Visitors). I was delighted to discover that, yes, York fairly bristled with Heritage, and with attendant Visitor Centres. Which one should I try first? The Trees To Treske Visitor Centre, which promised to give 'all ages an insight into the world of wood'? Or The Hawes Ropemaker, where I could appreciate that 'part of the fascination of watching ropes being made is the satisfaction of seeing the complete process, in which many thin strands of yarn are rapidly twisted into a strong rope'? Or how about the Brontë Weaving Shed, which didn't explain itself at all, but where, no doubt, I could gain an insight into the world of weaving, which was the favourite pastime of the famous sisters (other than moaning on about their lack of rich boyfriends), and be enthralled by the process, in which many strands of yarn are rapidly threaded into a crap bathmat.

There were many, many officially-pamphleted distractions in the area, all of which seemed to offer some Heritage value for money – or if not, a good knick-knack shop. But how to choose? I couldn't, so I decided that I would set out and let Heritage lead me where it willed. I decided that whenever I saw one of those brown Heritage signs, I would turn off the road and visit the indicated attraction. Once I had absorbed its historical relevance, and perhaps sampled its teacakes, I would continue with my journey, until I saw another brown sign, when I would turn off, and so on. I would thus traverse North Yorkshire on a Heritage Trail, like Michael Palin or that bloke who Trod In The Footsteps Of Alexander The Great or, indeed, my mum and dad on an extra-long Sunday Drive. I was pleased with this plan: I felt sure that its very randomness, its lack of bias, would give me a true picture of my country's Heritage – and therefore, of mine.

So, after a breakfast you could call hearty, or you could call piggy (it was mostly bits of pig), I got into the Peugeot and set off. It was a horrible day. The rain clattered down on the roof with an insistent, intimate rattle. The windscreen fogged as soon as I sat down. The heater creaked. Not a day for a soft-top. I felt as though I were in a two-man tent on skates.

Still, I refused to get in a bad mood. The Peugeot was happy to be on A-roads again; and I continued to be happy to drive it. A modern car might have all those fancy doodads, like multi-speed windscreen wipers, and a carpet, but you can't pretend you're Grace Kelly in a M1-matey Micra, can you? No. But you can in my car. Not that I'm after a strawberry jam ending, of course, but I am after a rosy-hued life. And even if it is hailing and the heating's blowing ice and the only radio station you can find is Natalie Imbruglia FM, where every other song is by Natalie, or Elton John, or The Lighthouse Family, and where every advert is for replacement windows – even then, even now, driving a good-looking car on clear, scenic, two-lane roads is enough to heighten your life's colour by quite a few degrees. Anyway, how could I be downcast? I had a project! I had a Heritage Trail to follow! I turned up Natalie Imbruglia FM (it was playing Hanson's 'Mmm Bop') and swooshed through the wet towards York's ringroad.

Within half a mile, I saw my first brown tourist sign. The graphic was a choo-choo train. The sign said: *National Railway Museum*. Well, there was a thing. I was pretty sure that I'd been to the Railway Museum as a child: so my first stop on the Heritage Trail really was part of my past. I span off the main road and followed the brown choo-choo signs until I arrived at the National Railway Museum car park. Unsurprisingly, the parking fee was astronomical (though, of course, nowhere near as dear as travelling anywhere by train these days), demanding a unwelcoming £2.50 on top of the £4.95 admission into the museum.

The museum itself was in an old train shed. Airy and modern, with a huge central floor turntable for hauling locomotives round to whichever way you wanted them, and, I was pleased to see, more than a few press-me buttons about. I pressed all the ones within reach, quickly, one after the other. Each started what seemed to be the same video of behatted people on a railway station, emerging through stormclouds of steam to wave hankies at one another, speedily, jerkily, black-and-whitely. I looked closely at the screens to see if anyone was flourishing their knickers, à la Jenny Agutter, but no one was. Shame. I'd always enjoyed the idea of pretty teenagers treating train drivers as though they were Robbie Williams. Good old Jenny and her out of *Robin's Nest*: the world's first, and last, railway groupies.

There were plenty of impressive locos about, dominating the vast space. Powder blue ones, racing green ones, ones with chimneys, ones without; brass-trimmed, shiny-plated, ding-dong-belled. Each came with accompanying middle-aged trainspotter (male), lurking shiftily, stroking the wheel trim with shy lust. When you approached the object of his affection, the worshipper would vanish, hide behind another train, returning to his caressing post only after you'd moved on.

From time to time, an official voice would crackle over a tannoy, inviting you to demonstrations in other rooms: out of some skewed devotion to realism, this was as impossible to understand as a genuine rail announcement. 'Txxxxzzscrkle 11.04 video on hrgggrrrggipflip developments from the Victorian era to the poobakkakxxxch approximately flugley minutes late . . .'

You got a lot for your fiver. I saw the 1829 Rocket (or at

least something that looked very like it), which, in its day, was the fastest train on two tracks; I meandered through a Royal Mail section, complete with Auden poem; I dondered at old photographs and marvelled at two middle-aged lady 'Explainers' who hauled gamely at heavy mechanisms to set the turntable in motion, even though there was a train the size of a council estate atop it. I bought a railway bun and a cup of tea. I pulled faces at small children. I decided not to attend the talk in the lecture room entitled, I think, *'Stroking The Boiler: Trains I Have Known,* by A. Perv'.

In all, I lasted about two hours, which isn't bad for someone who's about as interested in trains as they are in having their toenails pulled. When I left, I felt stimulated, informed; and a little downcast over the systematic governmental destruction and ruinous business negligence of a public service and industry that really was our nation's Heritage. Then I returned to the full-to-bursting car park, revved the Peugeot, thought, Thank Chrysler I don't have to walk to a train station in this weather, and continued with the Heritage Trail.

I'd been sluicing along the A64 for only a few minutes before some more brown signs pointed me to Castle Howard, a few miles on and to the left. Castle Howard was the stately home used in *Brideshead Revisited*; it was old, grand and beautiful; still lived in by the Howard family, who could trace their descendants back to Tudor times, and further. Castle Howard was genuine British Heritage, and as much mine – or yours – as the Lloyds Building. Still, I'd seen its brown sign now, so I had to turn off. I did so, parked up, and went straight to the Castle Howard shop.

The theme tune to *Brideshead Revisited* was playing on loop, and the tapes were available to buy. So too, was an entire skip's worth of other *Brideshead* paraphernalia, plus shelves and shelves of cake-tins, bookmarks, rulers, mugs – all stamped with an official Castle Howard stamp. And there was all that other random, useless, Laura-Ashley-goes-ramraiding-at-Woolworth's detritus that you only find collected in knick-knack shops: paisley-covered notebooks, packets of dried flowers, pocket-sized wind-up toys, concertina postcards, plastic pencil sharpeners, tiny china animals, fridge magnets that read BEHIND EVERY MAN IS AN AMAZED WOMAN and LIFE'S HARD ENOUGH WITHOUT HAVING TO GIVE UP CHOCOLATE. A young woman was pointing at the chocolate-epigrammed fridge magnet, and nudging her husband. She was laughing. She thought the fridge magnet was funny.

I was quite struck by this. The laughing girl was younger than me. Still, despite her youth, she must have heard better jokes than that one. What on earth had happened to her to make her lower her humour threshold so? She was really guffawing. She genuinely thought that the magnet was funny. Perhaps she'd never heard the one about the chicken crossing the road, either. I looked at her husband. He wasn't exactly roaring, but he was sniggering a little too. Aha, I thought. They must have a little chocolate fetish thing going on together. She's laughing because it's a reminder of their smear-the-Milk-Tray love-making. It's the titter of tender trufflers. I wondered what would happen when they actually reached the sweet counter. She might not be able to control her hysterics.

I stared at the couple until I realised that they had stopped laughing and were looking right back at me. From their expressions, it was clear that they considered that I was the mad one round here. I felt like shouting, Well, it isn't me that can't control her public sweet-toothed sexual innuendos, but then realised that would appear a lot more strange and perverted than laughing at a fridge magnet. I smiled at them and dashed out of the shop. Maybe that swinging party had left an impression, after all.

Castle Howard itself could have hosted an orgy for the population of Italy and still have had room for France. It was enormous. Room after gargantuan room of florid fortunes beautifully spent, on jewel-like art and curly furniture and great golden mirrors; let down only by recent investment forays into tacky glassware, such as – this is true – a plate decorated with an engraving of bacon and eggs. Each stuffed parlour was manned by a doughty old duffer in a suit, or a tweedy lady in skirt and jacket, who, when prompted, would launch into a history of any furnishing you cared to point at, always in the manner of an impatient teacher: 'This is a Holbein portrait of Thomas Howard now Howard as you no doubt will recall was the uncle of Catherine Howard and the advisor to Catherine Parr thus the Protestant side of the Howard family can trace their lineage back directly to the wife of Henry VIII stop fidgeting at the back if you've anything to say you can share it with the rest of the class.'

The house was dazzling: an entire world in a single family's ancestry; a castle, a story stuffed with History, art, passion, travel, and Trump-like spending sprees. And all because one of their great-greats shagged a blue-blood. The wind howled and the rain smashed against the scores of panelled windows. I sprinted back to the car.

The next two brown signs I saw led to Eden Camp and Flamingo Land. But I didn't go into them. I did pull up outside, first one, then the other, but both looked so hopelessly unwelcoming that I couldn't face either. Eden Camp was off the A64 near Malton: a depressing collection of one storey buildings that shivered behind a sign that read 'Eden Camp. The People's War. 1939–45. Allow three hours for tour.'

Three hours? It was still sheeting down. There was no way I was going to spend 180 minutes traipsing between bunkers in a blizzard playing at *Dad's Army*. On my own. And that sign annoyed me. Since when was World War II 'The People's War'? Was it meant to indicate that lots of people died during the War? Or that lots of people should be interested? Or that our dear departed Di, the acknowledged People's Princess, was somehow a direct descendant of the conflict? And if it was the People's War, did that make Winston Churchill the People's PM? If so, who is Tony Blair? Or for that matter, who was Hitler? It's not as though Adolf was swept to power when a couple of German farm animals gave the nod. A whole load of people voted for his party, too.

I talked myself out of going to Eden Camp easily enough, turned the Peugeot around, and struck off on to a side road, aqua-planing northwards towards the east coast and Whitby. Flamingo Land was next to be brown-signed. Dutifully, I followed the signs around the small, empty town of Kirby Misperton until I pulled up outside some large gates. I switched off the engine and checked my watch. Four o'clock. And it was still chucking it down.

Flamingo Land was an amusement park, or so I'd guessed from the carousel graphic on the brown sign. But there was no evidence of anything remotely amusing around here. Scrubby bushes, empty car park, iron gates, memorial plaque. The plaque read: *Robert Dewar Gibb. 1937–1995. The owner and founder of Flamingo Land. He will be greatly missed by thousands of people. His memory and his work live on.* I looked about more closely to see if I could spot some of Robert's work. There! Look! Behind that hedge! – two full-size water buffalo *en plastique*. Not bad, as life's works go. No doubt the theme park and camp-site were also living on in Robert's name beyond the gates. It was just that I didn't particularly want to check. Big dippers are fantastic things, but not in subzero thunderstorms. I turned the starter key and set off again.

My Heritage Trail had gone slightly wayward, I felt, so at the next brown sign, I slammed on the brakes with purpose. The sign announced: *The Dalby Forest Drive.* I pulled across the road in the direction of the arrow and drove until eventually, I came across what the Dalby brown signs wanted me to. Which turned out to be another road. Just an ordinary B-road that meandered smoothly through a forest to Scalby, near Scarborough. There were fee-boxes for you to insert the £2.50 charge for the privilege of driving down this special road, and a small map that showed you where you'd end up. I put the money in the box.

I don't know if you've been on the Pepsi Max ride at Blackpool – it's the enormo-roller-coaster that the American bloke rode continuously until he'd got into the *Guinness Book Of Records* – but anyway, it's terrific, except it doesn't last half as long as you think it will. The Dalby Forest Drive was similar in one respect. It was over and done with before I'd quite realised. Thrills-wise, though, it wasn't quite up to the Max's standards. You know, a tree is a tree. A road is a road. I saw nothing to tell me what I'd spent my money on. I didn't even see a bench. There weren't any car parks. No shop. The road was the same as every other one I'd driven on that day, except it was a little twistier, and there was less traffic. I don't know where my £2.50 went. Maybe the trees got together at the end of the week and blew their collected loot on pints of rainwater and nubile young saplings.

I emerged from the Dalby Forest Drive on to the coast road to Whitby. It was nearly five. I'd started the day feeling happy and invincible. Seven hours later, I was thoroughly vinced. I was starving, and tired, bored of driving and fed up with Natalie Imbruglia FM's wittering advertisements and happy-sap pop. I decided to drive straight to Whitby. I used to holiday there as a child, so it was without doubt a part of my history: since then, Whitby had been made a Heritage Town, which made it even more relevant. Just by staying there, I'd be continuing the Heritage Trail. I could take up with the brown signs again tomorrow.

On the way to Whitby, I thought about being a tourist in your own country. I had a travel guide to Britain in the back of the car. It was like all the other travel guides that I'd seen, in that not once did it make this country sound like the place where I grew up, where you grew up, where we live.

The problem is our Heritage. According to the guide books, if you don't want scenery, or London, then Britain is just cathedrals and estates: estates meaning the property inheritance of society inbreds, as opposed to the property inheritance of society's outcasts. Every guide book I'd looked at was stuffed with lingering descriptions of stained glass and oil paintings, of royal tombs and ruined remains, of formal gardens and classical architecture. All the books told you was: Britain is heritageful. Britain is heritagabulous. Say what you like about knackered old Britain, but it's always been good to its Heritage.

To be honest, I preferred my own brown-signed trail to Britain: far more diverse and relevant. The guide books would only have given me Castle Howard. But if the weather had been better, and my stamina longer-lasting, my brown signs would have had me stroking steam trains, studying the Second World War, gambolling round a fun-fair and rallying through a forest, as well as cooing at my lords and ladies' chambers. And that was with just five signs. Think of all those I'd missed! There was one now: for the Old School House Restaurant. Brown signs were deregulated by the last Tory Government. Originally, they could only point to tourist attractions with over 20,000 visitors a year: now they can point to whatever attraction they like, as long as someone, somewhere, pays to stick them up. Which explained the Last Drop Village. Well, it didn't, but it explained the Pied Piper signs.

Around this part of Yorkshire, brown signs were everywhere. They peppered the landscape. And you could think the brown signs patronising, or you could consider them an eyesore, but there was no doubting their seductive effect. Your gullible mind believes that if something has a sign pointing to it, it must be worth seeing. Even if, as in the Dalby Forest Drive, you could see the same thing about two hundred yards further on, and not pay a bean for the privilege.

I thought that, when it was finished, Dumplington Hall should have its own brown sign. It was bound to attract more than 20,000 'visitors'. Or, if not now, then in the future, when shopping had moved on and Dumpers was left empty, a listed building, a respected architectural representative of the late twentieth century, typical of its type. When families would drive there on a Sunday, for Shopping! The Experience, and little boys and girls would spend two minutes pressing buttons to see videos of how people used to shop in ye olden days, and then they'd run off to bicker in the café and break the towel-roller in the toilets and go shopping for souvenirs of shopping.

I arrived in Whitby about an hour later, checked into a B&B on top of the cliff, and went out for the evening. I wanted a drink, and some fish and chips. The weather was getting wilder; as I walked down the steep roads to the town, I was forced to curl my back and lean into the cutting, blinding wind. The rain slashed at my face. My eyes felt as though they were about to be prised out of their sockets and be flipped behind me into the night.

At the bottom of the hill, in the town itself, I walked straight into four teenagers, drunk, giggling, teetering on their heels. Each one was swathed from hair to there in long and swooping garments – lace and velvet, mostly – all in the same eye-catching shade of black. Their heads looked like a Furby warzone:

tufty tresses were dyed white or black, backcombed and stuck out all over; their faces were thick with co-ordinating make-up (white for cheeks, black for eyes), applied à la Addams Family. They were Goths.

I asked them where they were going. They told me they were off up the hill to 'the Goth Convention'. I started laughing.

'I dunno what's so funny; we come every year,' sniffed one girl, resplendent in full-length black doily and buckle boots.

'Twice a year, spring and autumn. It's only been going three years, and we've come every time,' said her boyfriend (top hat, dress coat, eyeliner, fake-blood lips gone smudgey in the wind).

Apparently, the Convention – 'there's bands and a club, and other Goths' – was going on in the Whitby Pavilion all week-end. It took place in Whitby because of the town's Dracula connections (Bram Stoker wrote the book whilst staying in a local B&B; and in the story, the Count, the original Gothfather, had paid Whitby a quick visit whilst disguised in the form of a dog). I said I might pay a visit to the Convention the following night. The Goths looked me up and down.

'You will dress up, won't you?' said the doily girl, pointedly.

I said I might. The Goths tottered off into the wind, clothes whipping round them like ragged bat-wings, waving back at me politely with long nails in fingerless gloves. I remembered that another Goth guru, Robert Smith of The Cure, came from well-mannered, suburban Crawley.

And then I carried on down the hill, to bright and cosy Trenchers, where I had a plate of cod and chips amongst cheerful family weekenders. Afterwards, when I was forcing myself back up the hill to the B&B, I saw a man, not a Goth, in his early twenties. Short hair, no coat. He was standing, swaying a little, in a sheltered alcove outside a pub. There was blood dripping down his face and spattering on to his polo shirt. I didn't blame Dracula.

12

a conventional experience

The next day dawned dry, but dark. The grey sea and the dense sky blurred into one. The light, usually luminous on the north-east coast, was flat, colour-sucking, lifeless. On the far cliff, across the little harbour, over the water slashed white by the wind, ruined, imposing Whitby Abbey was a charcoal sketch against the sky. A befittingly Gothic scene.

Before I donned a high-collared cape and turned my hair into angry candy-floss, however, I was going to make a final effort to tackle the Heritage Trail. I'd read some more tourist-tempting pamphlets and there was one in particular that had caught my eye. I got into the Peugeot and set off for Goathland.

Goathland is a village atop the North Yorkshire moors. It

spreads itself wide, its low-browed, long-lived buildings waving at each other across a prairie of flat dark green, with the straightened ribbon of a B-road splitting the green in two. Once, sheep grazed there; these days, there's herds of tourists munching through commemorative Yorkshire puddings as they follow each other from craft fair to car park via fancy goods shop. You see, Goathland is otherwise known as Aidensfield, the village in ITV's *Heartbeat*. *Heartbeat* is the drama/sing-song series in which Nick Berry plays a simpleton local bobby of the 1960s whose decency and dimples win the hearts of the nation, and the purse of Yorkshire Television in doing so. Over eighteen million Britons watched *Heartbeat* at its peak, including my gran. The *Heartbeat* tourist leaflet at my B&B showed a sketch of the rolling Yorkshire countryside, with a huge, hill-sized policeman's hat nestling between the moors. That did it for me. What woman could resist a glimpse of Nick Berry's massive helmet? Count me in.

I arrived at Goathland in a state of high excitement. No sign of Nick, though, nor of his awe-inspiring helmet; nor of 'lovable rogue' Greengrass, nor 'machoman' PC Bellamy, though *Heartbeat*, the newspaper, on sale in the newsagents for 50p, did inform that Bellamy, and every other cast and crew member, thought of *Heartbeat*, the programme, as 'a great big happy family'. It also informed me that, in fact, Nick Berry had departed *Heartbeat* for pastures less blasted, and had been replaced by a fresh-faced nonentity with fade-away features. Nice helmet, though.

I had hoped for a *Heartbeat* Visitor Centre, but there wasn't one. A little disappointed, I walked into the local tourist shop,

and poked about for a bit, fiddling with the snowstorms. One –
of a skating lady – slipped from my grip and fell to the floor.

'Lucky it bounced,' said an old man, who was fingering the
officially licensed aprons.

I was about to make some wry but warm reply when he
jabbed a scaly digit at a sign beneath the china shepherdesses.
The sign said *Thieves Will Be Prosecuted*. As though I'd bother
nicking a knackered knick-knack. Horrible old git.

'I wasn't going to steal it,' I riposted, cleverly. It's great when
a witty reply comes to you, isn't it? 'I WASN'T GOING TO
STEAL IT YOU STUPID YOKEL COFFIN DODGER.'
No, I was going to shove it in the direction of your festering
tonsils, turtle-face. I might look like a thief, but at least when I
watch *Heartbeat* I don't need a pacemaker to make sure mine
continues to do so. I thought of redangling his dewlaps with a
limited edition Nick Berry truncheon, but decided to go for the
exit marked 'dignified' instead.

I left the shop and crossed the road to a craft fair. There was
a small admittance charge, 'for the upkeep of the village hall'.
Lucky there was, or they'd never have made a penny. The place
was groaning with tat, with awful items that no one, not even an
eccentric millionaire macramé collector, would want to spend
money on. Why aren't all craft fairs banned by the Trades
Description Act? There's no craft involved in gluing little
seashells on to big pebbles; nor do toilet-roll holders become
any better-hewn just because they're made from wood, instead
of plastic. A piece of driftwood with two hooks screwed into it
is not a key-holder, even if someone's painted the word KEYS on
to it. And why bother crafting a key-holder anyway? Who has

ever, ever wondered, What is it that this kitchen, this family, this life really needs? – and then thought, A key-holder?

Goathland's craft fair was the same as every other one in Britain. Fridge magnets fashioned from glazed dough. Home-made cardigans with Teletubbies on the front. ('Laa-Laa,' said a toddler, obligingly, though how he could tell, I don't know. It looked like Scary to me.) Flower-pots bristling with those pearlised pebbles that people display in bowls with pot-pourri. Kit-made dangly earrings set with stones which weren't even halfway semi-precious. Chinese pinboxes, for Chinese pins. All for prices that would shame Gucci. £300 for a jumper knitted by a blind dog with two rolling pins? Oh, well, if he lives locally . . .

Most rubbish of all were the Plastic Bag Holders, made from a tea-towel with the two long sides sewn together to make a sausage. You stuff the sausage with your plastic bags (not pro-vided). Then you pull the bags out as you need them. Price: a mere £5. That's £5 for handiwork of such a pre-pre-school standard that even a loving parent would bin it in embarrass-ment. You'd get arrested if you tried to flog that kind of rubbish in any other market; Nick Berry's helmet would appear in a matter of seconds, and his official fingers would descend upon collars, immediately and willy-nilly. Yet, just because the so-called plastic bag holders are stuck on a trestle table by some comely housewife with too much time on her hands and a field for a backyard, we're supposed to be shamed into handing over the rent. It's a national disgrace.

Heartbeatland wasn't turning out to be as great as I'd hoped. So I wandered down to the railway station, where the steam trains ran. I remembered that the North Yorkshire Moors Railway had come out number 1 on the Top Ten Steam Railways section of the British Tourist Board results. Its station at Goathland certainly looked the part. Nice and olde worlde: rickety little bridge connecting two well-kept platforms, bloke in pre-war ticket-collecting regalia blowing a whistle, genuine steam out of genuine chimney atop genuine train.

But I had no time to chuff: I had to be back early to Whitby. In the morning, I'd overheard a chat in a charity shop (which, like all the clothes stores in Whitby, had shoved its Goth clothes to the fore, in honour of the Convention: green velvet dress, shocking pink lace number, black suit – all hanging off geriatric window mannequins in their usual mumsy wigs). The chatterers were in casualwear – frilled shirts, long-tailed dinner suits, full slap – but they were talking about their evening outfits. 'Well, it's going to take me at least three hours to get ready tonight,' said one, and yes, it was a bloke speaking.

This had worried me a little. Goths were used to getting into their get ups; how long would it take me? I wasn't taking any chances. It was time to leave Goathland, to go home and change.

My landlady was excited that I was visiting the Goth Convention – 'Oh, I think it's great they make such an effort with their clothes, and they're actually very sweet when you talk to them' – but, in the end, I disappointed her in my choice of outfit. I'd rooted through my bag but failed to come up with anything appropriately Conventional – no pointy boots, no crimpers, no Bridesmaid of Dracula little black number – so I'd decided that it was better not to compete in the mourning dress department, but to go for another look entirely. I'd nipped out to a charity shop and bought some trousers. Shiny and white, baggy, with thin blue piping and ankle zips: the bottom half of a shell-suit. I teamed them with a white T-shirt and lemon tank top, plus white trainers. I looked like a snowman, with site-specific jaundice and varicose veins.

I was pleased with my cosy, practical get-up, and a bit miffed when the landlady looked me up and down and said, like the Goths I'd met the day before, 'Aren't you going to dress up?'

I said: 'At least I'll stand out.' I looked down at my trousers. They looked as though they might be luminous. I said goodbye and set off down the hill.

The sky had darkened at about six, and now the moon was smudging through the night. Dark clouds scudded over its face, swirled by the wind: it was an appropriately Gothic evening, though it lacked a thunderstorm. I wished that the Goths were holding their meeting outdoors, on the beach, round a fire, with hot mead, virgin sacrifices etc. My trousers made me very warm. They crackled with static as I walked down the hill. As I scritch-scratched to the Whitby Pavilion – a glass box conference centre clinging to the cliff-side, which boasted forthcoming attractions such as King Lollipop's Party Time and a sixties Music and Dance Night – I began to worry that perhaps I wouldn't be let in. Trainers can cause problems at most nightclubs outside big cities, and tracksuit bottoms – especially ones that showered sparks when your legs rubbed together – always fail the smart-casual entrance exam too. And there was no way I'd pass the dress code of the snobbish undead either, being more Angel of Whiter Than White than

Ponce of Darkness. Oh well. I could always go back to the B&B and change.

Outside the conference centre, a tussle-headed collection of small boys were practising their skateboarding. They were shouting at the Goths as they arrived.

'Are you one of *Them?*' one boy asked me, standing on the end of his board, flipping the other into the air to catch it.

'No,' I said, as another boy yelled: 'No way she is! She's got no cloak!'

I told them I was writing about the Goths. ('Can you write that everyone needs to support the Whitby skaters?' said one.) The boys told me that they'd been watching the Goths go into the centre for the last hour. They thought they looked 'brilliant'.

'Look at him,' yelped one, pointing at a new arrival, who'd gone for the funeral-director-with-finger-stuck-in-socket look. 'Is he the leader? Look at his hat! And his coat! He looks cooool!'

Actually, the Goth looked nervous. It made me laugh. There he was, got up like The High Priest of Hell and Pointy Boots and he was frightened of a bunch of small boys. You'd think he'd mutter the curses of Beelzebub at them, or turn them into ravens or earwigs or something. From his reaction, I knew I'd have no problems getting into the Convention. Goths were scared of anyone who didn't look like a horror show. I said goodbye to the skateboarders and went in.

The entrance hall was very light, lit by fluorescent tubes, like the foyer of a sports centre. It reminded me of the Ideal Home Exhibition. There was a bar at the back and tables set out before it: on offer – Whitby Gothic Weekend mugs and T-shirts, plus Spice Goth mugs, fanzines like *The Gothic Times* and a few flyers. One read: NEKROMANTIC ARE DEAD. WE ARE DEKO-LETTE EROTIKA. Nekromantic were one of the bands appearing in the main hall. I had thought that being dead was about as good as it could get for a Goth group, but clearly the band members had not been satisfied with this result, and resurrected themselves almost immediately as Dekolette Erotika – a name I'd have patented on the spot for fear that a vibrator manufacturer would want to use it in the future. ('Ladies! Try the new battery-powered Dekolette Erotika! I liked it so much I bought the company!')

A quick glance through the *Gothic Times* revealed that most Goth bands were brought to you by the letter 'K' (Dekolette Erotika, Inkubus Sukkubus, Manuskript) and by anything tangentially morbid (Die Laughing, All Living Fear, Corpus Delicti). And a quick glance around the over-lit Whitby Pavilion revealed, well, a load of Goths. But Goths, of course, are like any other social subset: trainspotters, politicians, students, swingers, Inner Wheelies, journalists. If you're not part of the group, you think that all the members are impossible to tell apart. If you're in the group, you think you're completely individualistic, and don't look like each other at all. So, after availing myself of a drink, I set about trying to find out who was who.

A round-faced girl in a lace bustier and granny specs attempted to help me. She was American, training in London to be a lawyer and working in Highgate Cemetery to support herself whilst she did so. She didn't say as what. Perhaps she hid behind gravestones and said 'Boo', to frighten the tourists. Her skinny friend, dressed as Miss Haversham dipped in cochineal – 'This is my Red Death look' – said she'd help me too, which she did mostly by dishing out her co-ordinating Red Death cocktail.

'Here,' she whispered through lips like glacé cherries, passing me her hip-flask. 'Try it. It's my own recipe. Sloe gin, Amaretto, Southern Comfort, vodka and cranberry juice.'

The Red Death girls said that they themselves were Net Goths, meaning that they were Goths who were familiar with the workings of the Internet (as opposed, I supposed, to those who weren't, who were Not Net Goths). They told me that you could divide Goths up into different types.

'There's Pony Goths, Vicky Goths, Fetish Goths, Doily And Docs,' intoned the girl in the bustier, whose name was Karina, before explaining that Pony Goths were the ones with long straggly pink or white pigtails, so called because they looked like the children's toy My Little Pony. Vicky Goths were interested in Victoriana, and dressed appropriately; Fetish Goths were pierced and PVC-wrapped; Doily And Docs were the girls who wore Dr Marten boots with their nighties. I was impressed by her efficient categorisation – it was the work of a born market researcher – and said so.

'Oh, that's nothing,' she said, modestly. 'I worked out how you can define a Goth, too. You know what all Goths have in common? There's five interests they all share. Shall I tell you?'

Karina, counting off the categoried on blood-nailed fingers, told me that the defining characteristics were . . . One: Goths liked the same type of music. Two: they liked the same style of dress. Three: they all had an obsession with romanticism ('you know, poetry, things like that'). Four: they were all obsessed with death. Five: they all felt alienated from society.

I thought, myself, that her definitions were a little broad. To me, they included every single moony teenager you ever met, if you allowed a slight leeway in dress and musical taste. But Karina was very pleased with her categories. 'It took me about half an hour to work them out,' she confessed.

I said that I thought that most Goths were very well-mannered.

'Oh yeah,' said Karina. 'They mostly come from good homes, you know? But, you know, they can be very cliquey.' (She pronounced it 'clicky'.)

'Don't tell me that the Ponies toss their manes at the Doilys? The Fetishists walk all over the Vickys?'

Karina smiled. She said: 'Mostly everyone's friendly. Goths are open-minded. There's just the odd one or two who are up themselves. More Red Death?'

When I first started going to nightclubs in Manchester, in about 1984, some of the nights I went to were called 'alternative'. There the clientele was mixed: there were psychobillies, Goths, Joy Division fans, mods, cowpunks, Smiths obsessives . . . essentially, every white kid under twenty-five who didn't go to Rotters down the street. People who went to alternative nights wore black and stuck their hair in the air; people who didn't wore white and had moustaches. The two groups were eventually brought together by soul and house music and – in Manchester – The Haçienda; but I can remember those alternative nights – the monkey boots, the pints, the pale faces and dark clothes, the odd mix of music (Curtis Mayfield, New Order, The Pogues, Lee Dorsey's 'Working In A Coalmine').

So when I pushed open the doors into the main room at the Whitby Goth Weekender, it was like walking back in time. It was exactly like those nightclubs of fifteen years ago. Which is a strange thing, given that most nightclubs pride themselves on being up-to-date, and given that most nightclub goers aren't much older than fifteen anyway. I looked around. Excepting that the clientele wasn't as mixed, that there were just Goths, no Smiths fans any more, everything was the same. There were the same straggly groups sitting around on stack-able chairs and on each other's knees; there were the same dancers, dancing the same Goth dance (there're two meth-ods – either: throw hands alternately in front of face, over and over, like a bad juggler, whilst turning head to regard each hand in amazement, or: pretend to unscrew a lightbulb); onstage, there was the same chubby girl in black velvet moan-ing and swaying and looking out significantly from beneath her pink split-ends. And then there was me, looking like I'd wandered in from Rotters down the street. I thought about offering someone a fight.

Instead, I started talking to Carl and Martin, two Brummies with long hair and paisley waistcoats. I asked them if they wanted a drink and, before they specified, I knew they'd want cider. All Goths drink cider. Carl was a computer programmer; Martin ran a warehouse. Martin said he lived in 'darkest sub-urbia'. Like most Goths, I said, because they're frightened of townies, and he agreed.

'There's a weekday Martin and a weekend Martin,' revealed Martin.

What's the difference?

'Weekday Martin ties his hair back.'

I told them the five qualifications of Goth. They scoffed. They saw my trousers. They scoffed some more. They told me terrible jokes. I liked them. They were funny.

I asked Martin about weekend Martin.

'Oh, I'm like everybody else,' he said. 'Ramblers, fish fanciers, DIYers. Everyone lives for the weekend, don't they? And at weekends I let my hair down. Drink too much, try and find music I like. Difficult business, in Brum.'

After a while, they went off to find some friends and I wandered back into the foyer. I talked to quite a lot of people. Everyone was terrifically polite; most were well-spoken; nearly all had come from the north of England. A lot were students. And without exception, all the Goths banged on about the 'narrow-mindedness' of something they called 'conventional society': which made me laugh, given that we were at a Convention where everyone looked and acted the same.

I saw the top-hatted Goth that the skateboarders had shouted at, so I went to talk to him. His name was Dean. He told me that there was nothing that connected Goths except for 'a dark aesthetic'. Emboldened by Red Death and vodka, I told him he was pompous. He didn't seem to mind.

I asked him if he would ever wear a shell-suit.

Dean said: 'But people have to look at you in it! Think of them, poor things.'

I said: 'Are you offended by the sight of my trousers?'

Dean assured me that he could cope. Then he introduced me to Gavin. Gavin had a skinhead and two small rings through his neck, at Adam's apple level. The holes in his neck looked scabbed and sore.

'That's nothing,' said Gavin, when I pointed this out. 'Look at this one.' And he pulled back his mouth to show a short metal rod, poked through the little strip of skin that connected his front teeth to his top lip.

'I've got twenty-nine piercings, every one done with no anaesthetic,' he growled. 'I'm a hardcore biker, me, not a Goth. I reckon it's shit here, full of ponces. You go to the toilet and there's some prick next to you in lace and a skirt . . .'

I blinked at him.

He continued, a man possessed: 'I like Metallica, Megadeth, Motörhead. You've got to respect Lemmy. You've got to respect someone who drinks two bottles of Jack Daniels a day. I tried it but I only managed half a bottle.'

I said: 'I think you came to the wrong weekend.'

Gavin said: 'It's my boss's wife, she's why we're here. That's her over there, the one who looks like Maid-fucking-Marion.'

I felt that Gavin had a few anger issues that he needed to sort out, and his neck was making me feel sick, so I excused myself. I went to the bar and tried once more with top hatter Dean, who burbled on about the Goth scene needing to move on, how it needed to accept other elements like fetishists, or people who liked harder techno or thrash music, 'darkcore'. As he explained, I became mesmerised by his purpley mouth, by his bloodshot eyes, his shiny black hair. He really did look odd. He reminded me of a toy I had as a girl: a plastic head, with nylon hair and a wipe-clean face that you could make up anyway you wanted. The head was called Girl's World. It was meant to coach little girls in the feminine art of beauty or the art of feminine beauty or something. But after a while the blue eyeshadow and pink lips colour-combination became boring, so you scrawled over the plastic face with felt-tips in all the wrong colours. That was what Dean had done to his face. Except he called his look 'the dark aesthetic' and I used to call it Witchy Face.

He didn't half go on, old Witchy Face. And with his 'the scene mustn't stagnate' and 'we must encourage younger people to get into the scene', he could have been speaking at a wife-swapping party or the last Inner Wheel Conference. In fact, my granny had shown me the text of the Wheelies' Conference presidential address, and it had been full of the stuff that Dean was spouting. There was really little to choose between the Dean and Madam President: both on a weekend gathering of like-minded people; both thinking they knew best how to take their elderly organisation into the next Millennium; both out in their nicest outfit, with hat and shoes and full-on slap. Maybe Madam President had been a little less haphazard in her lipstick application. But otherwise, she and Dean were soul-mates. I wondered if Dean had a girlfriend, and if he was into older women.

I realised that I was drunk about the same time as I realised that I was very bored with Dean. I twirled unsteadily on my trainer and left.

Outside, the night was dark and wet and salt. It intensified my heady state, pinpointed it, compressed it into a thin flash behind the eyes, a shove in the small of the back. Then I was running down the hill towards the town. My feet slapped on the tarmac. I ran with my arms outstretched like an aeroplane, like a bat, like Caped Count Dracula. I lowered my eyebrows and tried to do his laugh. I stuck my front teeth over my bottom lip, for fangs. I practised barking, in case I had to change shape. Then I opened my mouth as far as it would go and ran faster, to catch the sea in the back of my throat. Then I was at the bottom of the hill.

It was after closing time. I could hear the muffled thump of music from a hidden nightclub; laughter, from the far cliff. Probably some Goths climbing up to the abbey. I walked along, squinting my eyes, trying to spot them; then I gave up and just ambled for a time, bumbled along the twisting streets, turning off into the narrowest, the darkest, the highest-sided passage-ways I could find, stamping and yelping for the echo. There was no one else about.

After a while, I stopped. I was outside what seemed to be a shop, though it was larger and boarded up more completely than most of the showy little Whitby emporiums. I looked up at the sign. In dripping, important letters it announced: BRAM STOKER'S DRACULA EXPERIENCE. The *Dracula* was in bigger letters. I gazed at the sign for quite some time. I thought that you could get quite a good Heritage Trail going if you started in Whitby. From Gothland to Goathland. I tried saying it aloud a few times: 'From Gothland to Goathland. From Bram Stoker's Dracula Experience to Nick Berry's Helmet. Several centuries and many miles travelled between the lives of two mythical figures.' But I kept stumbling over the several centuries bit. I gave up and went in search of the sea.

I walked to the edge of the harbour. Peered down at the depthless ink water, out to the silvery masts that chimed in the wind, out further to the racing, tormented clouds. Seagulls scolded from above. I sat down – bump – on the flagstones, dangled my legs over the side. They were ghostly, greeny white. They looked like radioactive sausages. I hooked the wall into my knees and lay back; looked up past the street lights to the purple blanket night, until the cold seeped into my spine, and after.

13

chocolatey cities

Only four miles from the concrete and walkwayed centre of Birmingham, Bournville is a different world. A quaint place, with duck pond and village green, bell-towered school house, tall trees, clippered gardens, perambulating mothers. Spacious, timbered and sparrow-brown houses cluster along litterless cul-de-sacs and curving lanes. Bournville is not quite a picture postcard market town – despite appearances, it's still a suburb of Brum – but it certainly appears closer to Chipping Campden than it does to Spaghetti Junction.

I was in Bournville to visit Keith my puddle artist friend. Bournville was where he grew up. And Keith's take on Bournville was like mine had been on Wilmslow: not quite look back in anger, but certainly look back in a bit of a bad mood. He'd left when he was nineteen, so his view of his old home was stuck in resentful adolescence. Suburbia is one big bore when you're a teenager. Like trousers with elasticated waistbands, suburbia is a brilliant idea, but only for the under-12s and over-35s.

I'd come to visit Keith because I'd decided to face facts. I'd seen how Britain's long-established provincial clichés had buckled and smudged (revving, not washing the car; living through golf, not playing at it; wife-swapping as a means of making new friends, DIY to impress them, clubbing as an alternative to DIY); and now I'd explored my personal experience of an out-of-town existence. And I'd learnt that things had changed since my childhood. Now, being middling did not mean being bored. Far from it: these days, Averages were acknowledged, targeted, carefully catered for. New developments were built with the suburban in mind: Vegas-style drive-to shopping centres, for my Granny, for my parents; über-groovy All Bar One and genteel Fives for me. The collective history of the normal was picked out by useful brown signs, gathered and contained within clean, quality buildings, with café, knick-knack shop, rows of glistening toilets – contemplate your heritage, buy a mug and a cake, hop back in the car and motor home. All our hobbies, our interests, our lifestyles: respected, researched and furnished by Exhibitions, Experiences, Conferences, Conventions; and we trotted along to them so we could meet ourselves in replica and cease to feel alone.

Suburbia was strong; it was taking over. I had to accept its new, modern image. I had to see where the suburbs were really at; what Middle Britain was spending its time and its money on as one millennium shuffled into another. If the snapshot had faded, then where was the new picture? If the truisms weren't quite true, what was? If the out-of-towners weren't just driving, nine-to-fiving, paying off the mortgage and saving for a rainy day, then what on earth were they getting up to, the frisky little gits?

Well. At least I knew where a good number of them spent their afternoons. Ten thousand people a week were off to the same place. That's Britain's Most Popular Visitor Centre: Cadbury World, in Bournville, South Birmingham.

But before I went there, I wanted a tour of Bournville itself. Keith reluctantly agreed. We wandered through the tree-dappled roads to the local school and central green. I exclaimed at their picturesque dinkiness. Keith said: 'Hmmph.'

For my benefit, though, he reminisced for a while: he remembered getting caned by the head at Bournville Junior School for ringing the school bell at the wrong time; he recalled failing his art foundation course at Bournville Art College. This last is quite a hard thing to do, and not just in Bournville: across the nation, all art students pass their foundation year, unless they don't bother to make anything at all. Keith actually came up with quite a bit of work, but then locked it in a box. He put the box on a plinth in the middle of his designated exhibition space, and then covered the rest of the space with A4 photos of himself. There were a few spare photos next to the box; if you wanted a picture, Keith would hand one over after signing it for you, celebrity-style. It seemed to me that this type of Gavin

Turk antic would get you straight on to the Turner Prize shortlist these days, but maybe, in 1984, Keith was ahead of his time. Anyway, they failed him.

We walked on, and found a small shop entitled the Bournville Trust Office. I went in; and fifteen minutes later staggered out again, reeling under a library worth of local information. And from that I can now inform you that, despite its chocolate box cuteness, Bournville's origins are firmly new town.

In 1879, George Cadbury moved his chocolate factory out of Birmingham's inner city, slap bang into the surrounding green belt, and built sixteen cottages near by, to house factory workers. He called his little hamlet Bournville, after the local river, the Bourn; it was 'ville' rather than 'town', because France was considered the home of good food. A few years later, in the 1890s, George bought up more of the surrounding land and began to build Bournville into a proper village, to provide housing for what he called the 'labouring classes'. So far, so Harlow. But the difference between George, and, say, Barratt Homes, was that George was a Quaker, and thus far less motivated by a year-on-year financial growth plan than by his conviction that working people should 'own houses with large gardens, secure from the danger of being spoilt either by the building of factories or by interference with the enjoyment of sun, light and air'. He had been appalled by the living conditions of the poor in industrial cities. So he commissioned an architect, Alexander Harvey, to design a town that would provide a decent alternative; and he set up fair mortgage terms for buyers. Later, he built homes to rent, too.

On arrival, each new resident of Bournville was issued with 'Suggested Rules Of Health', drawn up by the inimitable George. At the top, he proclaimed, with the doughty conviction of a New Age devotee: 'If you will follow the rules below you will be healthier and therefore more cheerful. You will probably live ten years longer than those who ignore them.' The Rules contained such advice as 'do not take flesh meat more than once a day. The German army before Metz suffered much from disease; they were compelled to have largely a meat diet.' George also recommended that residents should: 'breathe through the nostrils with the mouth closed'; 'wear strong boots and keep your feet dry'; 'never allow water to stand on tea for longer than three minutes' and should not forget that 'anger and worry will wear you out much more rapidly than hard work'. So, keep smiling if you're on the dole. Being a Quaker, George couldn't resist a couple of no-fun clauses: under 'Sanitary Arrangements Etc.', he cautioned that it would be far better to 'furnish your sleeping apartments with single beds; double beds are now little used in civilised countries'. Well, not for sleeping in, anyway. George also prohibited any pub or off-licence from being built in Bournville: it remains a dry town to this day.

Despite, or because of, George's Rules, Bournville flourished; and in 1900, George created a Trust, which devolved his interest in the estate and handed affairs over to twelve trustees, so that the village could expand after his death without recourse to unscrupulous builders and property developers. And the Trust is still going strong. By 1905, it had 315 homes on 330 acres; a few years later, over 900; now there's 7,500 homes on 1,000 acres, housing 23,000 people. The remarkable Trust also built and owns the largest solar village in Europe; in 1982, it bought 65 acres to the south of Bournville and constructed 300 properties, aiming to 'maximise the energy saving benefits of solar gain and energy conservation while keeping in character with Bournville Village'.

I proclaimed all my new information to Keith, who nodded and said, 'Are you finished yet?' a lot. I was telling him nothing he didn't know already. He wanted to go to Cadbury World. And he wanted to go now.

Cadbury World was just round the corner from Bournville's village green, in the original Cadbury factory. It was opened in 1990, its construction hotly opposed by local residents, who thought that the crowds it aimed to attract would destroy their peaceful *faux* village. Which seems a little churlish, when it was Cadbury's who created their idyll in the first place. Still, the residents have calmed down now, and since Cadbury World has opened, it's gone from strength to strength; Keith's mum had told him that it had been recently much improved and expanded. She'd been on a tour and found it 'quite entertaining'. She said that, really, all ages could enjoy themselves there; that there was something for everyone in Cadbury World.

Well, there was something for everyone if everyone was fond of purple. Cadbury World was a fiesta of lavender, a symphony in mauve. I'd never seen anything like it. The colour started with the factory railings and ended half a mile away at Bournville railway station, and included all points in between. Everywhere was painted in that shiny, hard, seventies purple that packages Dairy Milk. The signs, the litter bins, the benches, the kerbs: it was like a prank, an elaborate practical joke that had had an entire village painted overnight, just to film the residents' reaction for Jeremy Beadle. Except, of course, that with telly, such jokes are rectified free of charge – with Cadbury World, the indigo won't go. The violet is inviolate.

Outside the purple entrance to the purple World's purple foyer were two enormous Cadbury's Creme Eggs: mostly purple, but with red and gold bits too. The Creme Eggs were actually cars, but when we tried to get in for a test drive, we were shooed away by a purple-clad security guard. In fact, we were sent away from Cadbury World almost as soon as we entered: we coughed up our £13.00 (£6.50 each) only to be told that as it was a busy day, visitors were being staggered in shifts, and we should come back in half an hour. So, Keith and I wandered about Bournville for a bit longer, admiring such local landmarks as the pool where Keith learnt to swim, and the back of the Cadbury factory, mercifully grey through its purple railings. All about, the air was heavy with chocolatey smells. It was like walking around with a Quality Street shoved up each nostril. I remembered *Charlie and the Chocolate Factory* and felt very excited.

In the end, though, Cadbury World disappointed: no Oompa-Loompas or Augustus Gloops or entire meals contained in one piece of chewing gum. Just armies of screeching, over-sugared brats; smeary fingers and smudgey faces provided courtesy of Cadbury. That was one thing you could say for the tour: plenty of choco-freebies. In fact, you were accosted on almost every corner by a smiling representative eager to press more cocoa products upon you: Aeros, Ruffles, Crunchies,

Dairy Milks, Flakes. We'd barely got past the first, chocolate-is-made-from-cocoa-which-comes-from-far-away-places-like-Mexico educational section before one toddler puked all down his mother's front: brown sweet-smelling, liquid sick, like a chocolate drink left to go cold. Cup hands, Mum, here comes Cadburys.

The tour consisted of three sections: history, then factory, then scream-at-Mummy-and-Daddy. The last section was actually called Cadabra, and was a tiddly fun-fair ride, but the queue for it was far too long for a couple of hundred children to cope with, wired as they were on sugar and E numbers. So they pelted up and down the corridor, fell over their booties, smacked each other, demanded more chocolate, puked, yelled, cried, sat down and refused to budge. One winning little mite, just in front of us in the queue, kept pulling wobbly lip faces and backing away from his mother when she offered her hand. The queue moved forward. He reversed into my legs. I smiled indulgently. He turned round and walloped me in the kneecap. This pattern continued for half an hour, until, finally, half-crippled, I overtook him at the entrance to the Cadabra ride, where he burst into tears and refused to get on the train. We left him thumping his mother whilst we trundled for approximately two minutes through various moving tableaux involving Mr Cadbury's Parrot and the sexy Caramac Rabbit (not as interesting as you might have hoped). All around, the ankle-biters either bawled in fear or passed out in boredom.

I said: 'They should video this and run it on a loop in family planning clinics.'

Keith said: 'Oh, I quite like it when they cry.'

If the Cadabra section was upsetting, the previous, factory section was almost worse. The tour wiggled past a huge, high-ceilinged room, with machines and conveyor belts and flashing lights working busily and ostentatiously. But the machines didn't fill the room, far from it: there were huge gaps between appliances, yards of winding belt between the machine that put the chocolate in the wrapper, and the one that turned the chocolate so it faced forward, and the one that lined the chocolate into two queues and the one that piled the queues up into stacks of a certain height. The general effect was of Heath Robinson without the jokes: there was an awful sense of overelaboration, of a long, twisted, mimsy process for a result that could be achieved in the real world with a mechanism no more complicated than a paper stapler.

A handful of workers, in shower caps and overalls, put the chocolate stacks into boxes, sealed the boxes, put them in a corner. A few others wandered about, checking that the machinery didn't get in a fangle. The visitors filed past at a trot, desperate to get the kids on the Cadabra train. The visitors outnumbered the workers by about ten to one.

When Keith and I emerged from Cadbury World, tripping over the disorientated children, drugged and reeling from chocolate fumes and lavender vision, it was four o'clock. Keith suggested a quick trip into the centre of Birmingham. He was on a committee to oversee the redesigning of east London's Whitechapel art gallery, and he thought that a visit to Birmingham's own Ikon Gallery, which had just undergone a very expensive facelift, might give him some tips.

We walked to Bournville's purple station, ten minutes away, guided by the purple signposts. I had a strong desire never to see another Dairy Milk again, at least, not unless it was corking the blubber-mouth of some mithering little whelp. I still had four bars in my pocket. I thought of giving them to a couple of children, but realised that such actions could be misinterpreted. These days, you can't even ask a six-year-old if he wants to sniff your bicycle seat without the social workers getting their Birkenstocks in a bundle. So I skewered the chocolate on to railings, like the heads of traitors, just far enough out of reach to be a source of real frustration to anyone under thirteen.

Keith and I had a pleasant train journey into town; we tootled gently alongside one of Birmingham's famed-but-actually-quite-hard-to-locate canals, and pondered the thorny problems of Visitor Centres. I was pleased to have finally made it right round a VC, and the country's most popular at that. But I had been disappointed. I don't know what I was expecting – well, I do: Willy Wonka's Chocolate Factory – but Cadbury World was far from being it. Even the knick-knack shop had been disappointing: there had been all the merchandise you might expect – Mr Cadbury's Parrots, purple mugs with *Chocolate Is A Way Of Life* on the side, printed tins of 'Victorian' sweets – but everything had been badly displayed, over lit, chaotic, crushed into the floor, messed up by children and not sorted out afterwards.

We chatted for a while and came to the conclusion that it wasn't the commerciality of Cadbury World that had grated, but the educational aspect. It was obvious that not a single visitor had come for the history section: its automated voice-over, meant to guide you through ye olde cocoa genealogy, was still wittering on about poor old George Cadbury long after every punter had stopped listening and was hanging about waiting for the automatic exit door to open. No one was bothered. Similarly, most people pelted through the factory section; some did stop and watch the machines, but they were too clunky and old to hold interest for long. What people came and coughed up for were the Cadabra ride, the free chocolate and the shop. Really, Cadbury would do better to dump the clever stuff and concentrate on creating the world's most exciting specialist chocolate shop. Cadbury World could be like a Niketown or a Warner's store, full of entertainment as well as the shopping; they could keep the Cadabra ride and Mr Cadbury's Parrot, and add video walls and a proper, supervised play area for the small and additive-raddled to hyperventilate within whilst Mum and Dad fed their bulimias. If it was considered essential, there could still be an educational element, just scaled down some-what: an informative mural, perhaps, or a reproduction factory conveyor belt around the edge of the shop; they could sell spe-cial edition place mats with artists' sketches of old Bournville, or, for the grown-ups, a locally historical Trivial Pursuits (avail-able next to the chocolate penises).

Keith and I were pleased with our revamp idea. But we realised that there could be snags. You see, Keith and I aren't parents. Parents don't like to feel that they're just taking the children shopping. They want to think that they're broadening the rug-rats' minds: feeding their little imaginations as well as their big gobs. A Visitor Centre is proud to create that illu-sion – but a shop has no such pretences. Cadbury World

doesn't care that the kids are bored throughout its history section; as a VC, it will push its educational appeal as hard as it
can. Not for the kids, but for the sake of the parents. Parents
would also be pleased by Cadbury World's choice of today's
pro-active learning techniques: voice-overs, push buttons,
moving figures, non-stop videos, out-of-work actors handing
out chocolate bars etc. And another Cadbury World plus: that
whiff of Old Heritage that people find so reassuring. Observe
the ancient competence of the chocolate packer, his skills
passed from generation to generation! Marvel at the authentic
labouring classes busily a-labouring! You wouldn't get that at
Cadbury's the Megastore, even if it did have floor-to-ceiling
tellies.

The train was pulling into Birmingham New Street as Keith
and I came to our conclusion. What Cadbury World managed
was to soothe the parent – educational element, support of
long-suffering British artisan – whilst satisfying the child –
chocolate, fun-fair ride. And perhaps this is what Visitor
Centres are about: something for everyone, as Keith's mother
said. Not quite a museum (low on entertainment: kids won't
go), not quite a superstore (high on expenditure: parents won't
go), but a happy marriage between the best of both. Aw. What
a luvverly, family-friendly concept. How modern and inclu-
sive. I felt quite overcome. I wiped a tear from my eye, elbowed
a pre-teen in the mush, barged before a young mother struggling with the baby buggy, knocked an elderly man through
two compartments with one deft rucksack manoeuvre and followed Keith off the train.

*

The Ikon Gallery was in an old warehouse area of central Birmingham, by a canal lock, near to where Keith had had a studio when he was young. The whole area had been recently revamped and pedestrianised: the cobbles gleamed; the canal brickwork was free of rust and lichen; the old works buildings had been painted and plastered and pointed and primed and divided into lots for suitable commercial ventures. The lots held a Pizza Express and shops that sold china fruit.

The Ikon Gallery stood a little back from the canal, between the boutiques and a rubbly wasteland.

'Prime brown field development potential there,' I said to Keith, and so it proved. In fact, a lady at the Ikon informed us that the developers had been so excited about the prospects for the wasteland that they had provided a good deal of the money for the Ikon make-over, reasoning that a modish art gallery gave added chic to the area, i.e. they could probably whack an extra £5,000 on to every two-bedroomed flat.

The Ikon itself was an elderly warehouse which had been given a modern glass and metal tart-up. The warehouse still stood, cleaned and almost unadorned on two sides. As to the other two: a see-through lift clung to the outer wall on the left of the entrance; to the right, an airy café-bar with hard-edged chairs and a well-labelled clientele was displayed through huge plate windows. Both were part of a half-cage of silver tubes and glassy curves that hugged the front and left sides of the warehouse like a disco octopus.

Inside, the floor was polished, the lines were sharp, the have-a-little-sit-down benches were of a functional, yet cool and classy design that could earn them a nice big pic in an interiors mag. When you clambered up the shiny metal stairs they clanked, like a fire escape in a nightclub.

In order to get to the galleries you had to walk first past the café, then past the shop. Keith started to seethe.

'You should be forced to look at the art before you can get to the shop,' he said. 'The shop should be at the back, behind the galleries. I hate it when people can just pop in and treat an art gallery like a bookshop.'

We wandered around the whole building, inside and out. Keith absolutely loathed it. He said, rightly enough, that the glass-and-tubular-metal bit was nothing but a lazy imitation of what was once daring design. That doing up a building in such style these days was just as dull and crap as clipping on a pseudo-Victorian extension.

Keith's funny when he doesn't like things. His 'I abhor this' mood is almost indistinguishable from his 'this is great' one. He went off to talk to one of the gallery workers – a friend of his – and I could hear him as they wandered away to look at the gallery offices: 'What do you think?' asked the Ikon girl. 'I hate it,' said Keith, pleasantly. 'I absolutely hate the whole concept of it.' From his tone you'd have thought he'd just put an offer in on a brown site apartment, because he loved the all-new Ikon so dearly.

I had a quick skip around the two shows (Young-British-Artist-goes-to-toytown, plus 'I am woman see me roar' wall-stencilling, both rubbish), then went to the café to have something to eat. Scrambled eggs: £3.50. Clearly, the Ikon weren't about to use their snack prices to tempt in passing punters. Though I could imagine that the café would make rather an enticing bar in the evening: it had the cocktail chic of Eskimo's, plus the massive windows of All Bar One. All the Ikon had to do was seal off the gallery and put some bouncers on the door. Actually, maybe they could open up the gallery after last orders, in case any particularly flush drunk wanted to invest the price of a few rounds in a nice sculpture for his back-yard. They could call the bar Art Attack. Or Art Less. Or Art-y Bar-ty. It would make thousands. Especially with a Pizza Express round the corner.

But hang on a minute. Hang on a minute. What was a Pizza Express doing round the corner, anyway? I was in the middle of Britain's third largest city, in an area considered scummy, dodgy, squattable until just a few months before, and it felt exactly as though I were in Wilmslow. The pedestrianisation, the chic little café, the upmarket ornament shops, the Pizza Express. I looked round at my fellow snackers, and yup! clocked one smartly cut skirt-suit, two pairs of court shoes and some frosted highlighting worth the better part of £100.

What was happening? I thought that the suburbs were meant to pick up on city fads, that it took a good five years for trends to filter out to the gormless satellites. Yet here it had happened the other way around. Birmingham had been in for a wash and scrub up and come out smelling of Surbiton. Even the way that the Ikon had been made over was utterly out-of-town: the attempt at high fashion style that was years too late; the thrown-in executive apartments; the sodding cobbles.

I was seized with a sudden fear that everywhere in Britain was going to go the same way; that no longer would you be able to visit cities for rough-edged excitement and scabby potential.

That everything would be cleaned and polished and turned into Wilmslow, or a no-roof Dumplington Hall. After all, cities had to compete. And if you wanted to tempt in the people with money, the people who thought cities were nasty, rough places, with nowhere safe to put the car, then what could you do but turn the cities into suburbs? Light the dark alleys, shut the scary clubs, turn the ancient caffs and elderly shops into something bright and brand-y. Turf out the wasters and the wall-eyed scum. Lock the truants in a children's home. Provide supervised parking, pedestrianised areas, easy-access shopping, almost trendy bars, discount meals, family tickets, a fresh approach, a bright environment, a litter-free, fret-free, life-free life. Keep things buzzing, but not wanton. Exciting, but not fierce. Then watch all us punters turn up and put out.

I finished my coffee and walked outside. The sun glittered on the Ikon's glass lift, and the water in the lock was rising.

14

middle of the road

One of Cadbury World's less endearing traits had been the piped music that wafted over your wait for the ultimate fun-fair fiasco. Not only did you have to endure the humiliation and pain of being beaten up by cocoa-smeared toddlers over a period of hours, you had to do so to a background accompaniment of The Best Nursery Rhyme CD in the world . . . Ever! It was the kind of torture I thought had been outlawed when we signed all those human rights treaties. No imprisonment without access to a lawyer; and no forced listening to Rod, Jane and Freddie for longer than two minutes.

But what do I know? The suburbs are tuneful places – musical hotbeds, if you love your pop. Every textbook and memoir of British popular music, from The Stones to speed garage, via punk (especially punk) and house (especially house), advances the same, long-accepted theory: that all our best musical revolutions are not city-bred, but come tearing out of the suburbs.

They pelt out with such passionate velocity because the musicians are desperate to escape. 'When you're seventeen you want to fit in and have friends, but you know deep down you don't want the dull life. The Escort XR3 and the bird with the biggest tits in the pub, and getting your dad to get you a job,' explained Suede's Brett Anderson, who grew up in Hayward's Heath. 'Going through all that as a teenager makes you frustrated enough to break out and find something else.' So he and his band hopped on a train to London. As did an awful lot of other popstars. David Bowie came from Beckenham. Paul Weller from Woking. Siouxsie Sioux was a Bromley girl. Dexy's Midnight Runners based their fanclub in Sutton Coldfield. More recently, Radiohead were out-of-town Oxford boys; The Prodigy grew up in suburban Essex. The mutations that spawned contemporary speed garage (or UK garage, or whatever you want to call it) came from the late eighties split of house music into garage (cool, urban) and acid (corny, suburban), and how the traditionally white acid sound was subsequently warped and interpreted by black musicians, such as The Dream Team.

When Paul Weller was a teenager, he used to go to central London on the train, and then walk along the city streets with a whirring tape recorder, trying to capture the buzz and the tumult of urban life, so he could take it back with him to boring

Woking. Back home, he wrote songs called 'In The City' and 'Down In The Tube Station At Midnight'. Suede upped and left Hayward's Heath for London, where they made a glamorous sound and sang about concrete and council estates. You couldn't blame them. What else were suburban popstars going to do? Write songs called: 'Down At The Cash And Carry At Midday'? Or 'In The Covered Market'? Sing about bathroom extensions? Or garden gnomes? (Don't mention David Bowie.)

But, aside from all the urban wannabes, there's another sound of the suburbs out there, a different song, a new tune. It's whistlable, it's listenable, you could call it likable. You hear it every day on Natalie Imbruglia FM. It's the commuter chorus. The middle of the road sound for those in the middle of the road.

Driving means that you listen to music in a certain way. A very concentrated way, essentially. Unless you're carrying a passenger whose verbals can drown out guitars, if you play music in a car it will fill your environment. Whilst you're driving, in fact, is one of the best times to listen to music: your sub-brain is focused on the mechanics of motoring, leaving the rest of your mind to fixate on those little twiddly flute noises that you never noticed when you played the same Hooked On Classics tape at your last dinner party.

Of course, if you drive a lot, you soon run out of tapes. And that's where Natalie Imbruglia FM steps in. Local radio, and national radio that pretends to be local radio e.g. Talk Radio, Melody, Heart FM, is a potent force in popular music. It's a potent force for advertisers too: half an hour's traffic jam and your product will be drummed into the collective captive consciousness. Listen to local radio as you motor around the country and you'll hear adverts for items that you never knew you wanted; items that never merit a telly mention but can keep Natalie Imbruglia FM going all day. Like 'replacement windows'. I thought the nation's glazing obsession died with poor old Ted Moult. Remember Ted's finest moment? 'Fit the best. Fit Everest'; feather floats gently shagpile-wards as gale blusters beyond French windows; Ted collects cheque; everyone leaves. But it hasn't. Replacement windows are an advertising stalwart of Nat. FM. One ad follows another – 'Fit Posh Windows!' 'No, no! Fit Easyfit!' – until they join forces and start to roll around your mind, trouble your tiny brain with thoughts such as: just what are replacement windows, exactly? Are they windows to replace ones that have been broken i.e. are they panes of glass? Or are they windows to replace ones you don't like any more i.e. are they the whole thing, sills, sash and all? Who knows? Frankly, who cares? Whatever – there're ads for replacement windows on every local radio station across Britain. And nowhere else.

Similarly, there's a whole genre of pop music on Natalie Imbruglia FM that you would never hear on the national stations. Well, okay then, you would; but nowhere near as often. It's mostly easy-on-the-ear, no challenge sap-soul-pop: Natalie herself, The Corrs, M People, Louise, R Kelly (with the rude words taken out). There's a fair sprinkling of old stalwarts, too: Elton John, Wet Wet Wet, Barry White, Luther Vandross, Sade, Wings, Sting. Natalie Imbruglia FM is the only place that will play 'I Just Called To Say I Love You' more than once a year, and do so with pride. Not even Radio 2 can manage that.

I have to say that I've a soft spot for such naff soul-lite: it gets me right in the sentimental, and I'd certainly rather hear it than Gomez. When I was younger, before I went to Manchester nightclubs, or found John Peel on the radio, it was all Shalamar and Sade and Wham! for me. Smoochy, oochy-coochie numbers; or mindless feel-good dance music. I never liked Joy Division until they turned into New Order.

Whatever – these days, the undisputed music kings of Natalie Imbruglia FM are The Lighthouse Family. The Lighthouse Family are staggeringly popular: their two LPs, *Ocean Drive* and *Postcards From Heaven*, have clocked up over 3 million sales between them; and though you might not recall the name of any of their hits, you know them really. You will have whistled 'Lifted', 'Ocean Drive', 'So High' to yourself; you just didn't know you were doing it. The Family met in Newcastle and they are Tunde Baiyewu – black, beautiful, honky-voiced singer – and Paul Tucker – white, moose, singalong songwriter. Their music is warm, relaxing, conversational soul music, and they sing of what they themselves have called 'normal people's lives'; their lyrics are optimistic lines like ''Cos we are gonna be/Together, you and me', and the darker 'He left you black and blue/Without a word of explanation'.

I once spoke on the phone to The Lighthouse Family's manager. He said: 'The Lighthouse Family's songs are about trying to be positive. Within reason.' Which is a reasonably positive ambition, I suppose.

After miles and miles of driving, up and down and across and around Britain, I had been thoroughly indoctrinated with

Natalie Imbruglia FM, and with The Lighthouse Family in particular. I found myself humming their tunes in the bath, tra-la-la-ing them as I traipsed round the supermarket. More strangely, I started tutting when they were slagged off in the trendier of magazines. (Many music journalists regard The Lighthouse Family as the devil's work. Clearly, they aren't: the devil's work would result in a product far racier than the sensible Family, who make a block of lard look like it needs a muzzle.) Eventually, when I'd picked up their CD in a record shop for the umpteenth time, still without bringing myself to buy it, I decided that there was nothing for it. I had to go and see them live.

Naturally, for such a popular group, The Lighthouse Family were playing to a sold-out Wembley Arena. I trundled over there on the crowded tube on a Friday night; yomped across endless, slabbed, pedestrianised areas with thousands and thousands of other Family fans. They appeared remarkably well-behaved for concert-goers: clean, nicely dressed, mostly couples; a few ladies-only groups; one or two teenagers. No one was screaming or getting worked up in any way: if any of them were excited about the gig, they weren't about to vocalise it. Everyone was enormously, thunderously quiet. I'd been to many concerts at Wembley – The Smash Hits Poll Winners' Party, The Pet Shop Boys, Pulp – but I had never before been to one where the crowd was actually *silent*.

Even inside the arena, you could have heard a popcorn drop. Just the odd cough or squeaky chair revealed the polite presence of 12,000 punters on the edge of their seats. Perhaps they were too thrilled to speak. Or to move. When The Family and their backing group came onstage, bang on time, the audience did stir itself a little: there was sustained clapping, a few cheers. A hundred or so devotees near the front jumped to their feet. But they soon sat down again. In the end, the only way that Tunde could get anyone to stand up was by informing them, about a third of the way into the concert, that he was about to sing the National Anthem (the entire audience rose dutifully; he didn't sing it).

From then on, things got more energetic. At one point, the man in front of me quite lost it: he danced and danced and clapped along, occasionally giving it a double half-clap on the off-beat. The groove was in his heart; Riverdance was in his kneecaps. He sang with gusto. He pummelled the air between claps. His bottom bumped like an executive toy. His girlfriend moved away, slightly.

Unfortunately for me, The Lighthouse Family didn't get me like it got the happy dancing fellow. I felt like I was listening to a CD, with 11,999 other people. Excellent sound quality, but too quiet, too polite, too crisp, too note-perfect. Not even Tunde shaking his neat little tush could stop me yearning for a sofa and a remote. The stage set wasn't an attention-grabber, either: just a couple of road signs and a huge photographic projection, which changed from song to song. Variously, it showed: a lighthouse (geddit?); an industrial estate; the Angel of the North; and – the highlight for me – a drive along a motorway.

That did get me excited. Not because of the film's drama, or beauty: the drive was shot without artiness, no smudgey car lights or colourful filters; and it was filmed in real time, through a windscreen, to make it look as though you really were driving.

No, what got my attention was the journey it showed. It took me a couple of verses to make out the motorway signs, but it came to me all of a sudden. It was the turn-off for Warrington that did it. I was watching a video of the journey from my mum's house towards my granny's. Up the M56 to the M63, follow it round to the M62, take the Preston turn off to the M61, and at Junction 9 you'll bear on to the M6 North. There were the signs, there were the slip-roads, the familiar curves and bridges.

Well. I couldn't believe my eyes. I was utterly overcome. The driving video appeared to have exactly no relevance to The Lighthouse Family, nor to the song they were singing, but it certainly made me feel at home. Suddenly, I was hurtled back into the Peugeot, listening to Natalie Imbruglia FM, singing along to the Family. It was all the reasons why I'd come to Wembley. I almost wept.

Another musical aspect of driving round the country comes from the boom and bump of the provincial nightclubs. Sometimes, when you're overnighting in an unknown town, the walls of your B&B start to move in on your mind and you have to get out, to where there's noise and where the other people are. During my suburban sojourn, I went to clubs in Stevenage (Vogue), Peterborough (5th Avenue), and Douglas, the capital of the Isle of Man (Toff's).

The clubs were all huge and shared certain similarities: no trainers, no sportswear; no black people, except for one or two; no obscure tunes. The music that was played was strictly mainstream, and it matched the girl clubbers' bleached hair-dos, i.e.

it was white, with black roots (boom boom). The DJs played uptempo chart house, with the odd old soul or R 'n' B track.

It's very easy to be snobby about such melodic club-pap: it's bland, it's clichéd, it says nothing; it's a pale imitation of the true music that comes from the heart and the soul. But the tunes that thump, muffled and distorted, through big, busted speakers, across dancefloors steamy with bodies and sticky with spilt alcopops – those tunes are just as much a soundtrack to life as noodly *Urban Hymns* by the moany old Verve. And you're far more likely to cop off to Toni Braxton's unashamedly snogfriendly 'Unbreak My Heart' ('Unhook My Bra', as it's been called), or the ever-popular grind-and-grope of Color Me Badd's 'I Wanna Sex You Up'. If Pizza Express is the location for the drama of your life, then Simply Red is the music that will always take you back there.

So – let me tell you about my night out in Douglas. I'd gone to Douglas because I'd reasoned that if modern suburbia consisted of satellite towns, then the Isle of Man, as a satellite of Great Britain, must be the ultimate UK suburb. Plus, a friend of mine, Clint, had a part in a film that was being shot on the island. It may surprise you to hear it, but the Isle of Man is very supportive of British film: due to its financial breaks (it's a tax haven), the island can offer very competitive prices to the small budget movie-maker. I saw an advert about it in *Manx Tales*, the inflight magazine of Manx Airlines, amongst other ads for personal off-shore banking consultancies. The advert said 'Let's Make The Movie Here!'

And they do: when I touched down and was picked up, I was

told that around twelve films that year had chosen Douglas as their backdrop. The one that my friend Clint was in was called *Everybody Loves Sunshine,* a drugs-and-guns-and-clubs flick, and was set in contemporary urban Manchester. Of course, real-life contemporary urban Manchester was far too expensive and dangerous to provide a convenient filmic backdrop; in order to create the correct gritty ambience on the Isle of Man, the film was being shot in an abandoned hospital.

That's not to say that Douglas itself didn't have a grittiness all of its own. Imagine a Liverpudlian Bermuda Triangle. Now take away the sense of humour and the Barry Manilow singsong. Add freezing rain and the enlightened attitudes of a place that only made homosexuality legal because the European Court Of Human Rights forced it to do so, and you just about get it. It's only a 35-minute flight to the Isle of Man from Liverpool (which is why all the Manxers have Scouse accents), and yet – cue Bermuda Triangle spookiness – somewhere within that short distance everything warps. You lose all mobile phone and pager connections, even the ones that work in America. Then, money magically changes into special Manx notes that spew out of one of only two cashpoints in Douglas. And, strangest of all, George Formby and Norman Wisdom transform into entertainers worthy of bronzed immortalisation. George and Norm are the Isle of Man's most famous sons, and there are statues of them, standing proud on Douglas's pedestrianised main shopping street. Well – George leans (on a lamp-post, how 'funny'), and Norman is sitting on a bench. Seagulls use Norman's lap as a lavatory. Judging by his expression, he thinks that this is pretty hilarious news.

All this I discovered within half an hour of arrival. I'd checked into the ugly, square Stakis hotel, on the seafront, at around 4 p.m. By a quarter to five, I'd done the sights of Douglas. Apart from Norman and George, and the crashing, thrashing sea, and the holiday steam train (shut), there was really nothing to see. Still, perhaps things would get going later on, when Clint and I were off out on the town. It was Saturday night.

Of course, Saturday night – at least, according to that old Natalie Imbruglia FM favourite, Elton John – 'Saturday Night's Alright For Fighting'. And when Clint and I did venture out, we found that Douglas agreed wholeheartedly with Elton. At 10 p.m., the seafront pubs were thronging with mini-skirted teenage girls and their pastel-swathed swains. Bumpy house music spilled out into the air. And the atmosphere in Douglas shouted: Fun Fun Fu . . . Fucking What You Looking At Dick'ed?

You could feel it everywhere. Violence was just a joke, a drink, a glance away. Clint and I didn't dare risk any random body contact: if you brushed past someone to get to the toilet, they instantly turned into Joe Pesci (but with Scouse accent). We grabbed a couple of drinks, then decided a nightclub might be better. As we tottered along the main drag, the air rang with the sound of the sea smashing on to the shore, bottles smashing on to the ground, heads smashing into blunt objects. The wind smashed into our bones. We had to get smashed just to join in.

On the recommendation of a group of wobbly holidayers, we'd chosen to go to Toff's nightclub. Conveniently, it was in the Stakis Hotel, where we were staying. At Toff's, there was the usual trainers-and-jeans border control, plus an odd sign at the cloakroom: *No Bags Accepted*. I kept mine slung across my shoulder, and elbowed my way to the bar. I made the mistake of pushing past a heftily-buttocked chap to get there. He turned on Clint. The next quarter of an hour was spent with hands in the 'I am unarmed' position, apologising for being so out of order and offering to buy fat boy a drink too. There is something very wearying about constantly saying sorry in order to avoid full-fisted confrontation, especially when your chosen nightspot is packed so full of people as to make sardines look like they enjoy loft living.

I had a bit of a dance to Run DMC with a girl called Carol who worked at Marks & Spencers. When we started chatting, I said something mildly derogatory about Norman Wisdom, and she said, with an eagerness bordering on the certifiable, 'Oh, he came into the shop the other week. I couldn't belieeeeve it! I kept saying, "Is it really you?"' Carol was eighteen. I couldn't belieeeeve that an eighteen-year-old could find Norman Wisdom in any way exciting, especially given that she knew he lived on the island. I mean, where else but M&S would he purchase his Y-fronts? Anyhow, me and Carol jumped around on the dancefloor with her chums for a while, to The Venga Boys and other music for aerobics classes. I put my bag on the floor, next to the DJ booth. A girl came up and put her bag right next to it, in the textbook 'look-away-and-I-will-walk-off-with-your-bag-as-though-it's-mine' nightclub nicking manoeuvre. I picked up my bag again. I asked Carol if there was any other club worth going to in Douglas. She said: 'Oh no, Toff's is the best.' I asked her if she knew many people in Toff's. She said,

'Oh yeah. Everybody.' I felt as though I had 'Rob Me, I'm a Foreigner' written on my back.

I went to find Clint. He was sitting in a booth, being depressed. The film had an all-black cast, and the Isle of Man had very few black residents, so everywhere he and his fellow actors went, they were clocked as being 'filmstars'. This meant that a) all the island girls made a play for them and b) all their boyfriends got annoyed about it. Clint was worn out from all the hassle. Plus, he felt that he had thoroughly availed himself of the Isle of Man's entertainment options, but was yet to have a good night out. Clint was tense with frustration and simultaneous confrontation avoidance.

So we left Toff's and went to the Stakis Casino. To the sound of chinking fruit machines, and Frank Sinatra, I lost a lot of money and Clint won some. Then, at 2 a.m., when the casino shut, we went to the Hotel Castle Mona. A wedding party was still limping on. Smartly suited bodies were dotted about the foyer bar, slumped in chairs, eyes shut, mouth a spittle waterfall. But the music played on, in the background: a selection of appropriately wedding-friendly tunes, such as Stevie Wonder's 'You Are The Sunshine Of My Life' and 'Love Changes Everything' by the (mercifully) long-lost Climie Fisher.

A handful of die-hards were up and drinking and we struck up conversation with three: a Mancunian lad and his girlfriend, plus the lad's uncle, who came from the Isle of Man. They told me and Clint that you couldn't get work on the island unless you'd been living there five years. Also that there were 70,000 Isle of Man residents and 20,000 of them were masons. Which is an awful lot if you think about it, given that half the residents must be female, and some must be kids. I asked the older bloke if he himself was into apron-twirling. He said no; but from his carefully level gaze, I guessed he was lying.

After we left to go back to the Stakis, at about 3.30 a.m., the rest of the night was spent trying to calm an increasingly hysterical Clint. He kept pacing the floor and walking into furniture and muttering, then shouting, about how he understood how people ended up wrecking their hotel rooms. He brandished a chair at the sea. He hurled abuse at the wind. He wouldn't let me leave. Clint, in healthy frame of mind, is a happy-go-lucky person who makes friends in seconds and then charms them into staying up all week with him. He'd turned into a misanthropic hostage-taker and he'd only been staying in Douglas for a month. In desperation, to stop him ranting, I turned on the television. Bizarrely, it showed a live picture of the entrance foyer to the Stakis Casino. There was background music playing over the picture.

We listened to 'All Out Of Love' by Air Supply, Kylie Minogue's 'Give Me Just A Little More Time', Whitney Houston's yellalong version of 'I Will Always Love You', Celine Dion's yodelling Titanic epic 'My Heart Will Go On'. A soundtrack to cabin fever. I managed to stop Clint from throwing himself out of the window. But only just.

15

orf my land, out of my azaleas

When Swampy came to Wilmslow, in 1997, he was already as famous as a filmstar. He'd been on all the front pages, all over the TV, his mucky baby face as cute as DiCaprio's, his skinny fringe flopping like a doll's misplaced pull-string (yank on it and he'd wet his combat trousers: if you were a security guard, anyhow). Swampy was a national figure, a household name. And it was all because he lived in a hole. Or sometimes, a tree.

Wilmslow's citizens, usually so finickity, so snobby about property (where you lived being their shorthand for who you were) were surprisingly welcoming to Swampy, despite his living circumstances. They diverted their dog-walking routes just to tramp by Swampy's camp: not always stopping to talk, but often leaving food, or spare jumpers. They wrote support- ive letters about him to the *Wilmslow Express Advertiser*; they gave him and his dreadlocked friends lifts in expensive cars, to and from the protest site.

But it wasn't Swampy's celebrity that made Wilmslovians so friendly, though of course fame always counts for something in the footballer belt. No – it was what Swampy was doing that clicked. Swampy and his chums were dug in to protest against the construction of a second runway at Manchester Airport: they believed that the runway wasn't needed, that it would ruin the countryside, pollute the environment, kill flowers and ani- mals and tweety-pie birds – and encroach upon the green belt. It was this last that hit the Wilmslow nerve. If you drive south out of Manchester on local roads, as opposed to the motorway, you won't see much greenery before Wilmslow. At the moment, Wilmslow really is a suburb, an edge-town between city and countryside. Turn one way and you get the shops, turn the other and there're fields. And that's the way the locals like it. They might not have agreed with everything that Swampy blathered on about, but they were with him on one point. They didn't want a runway to spoil their view.

'*Holy Mother Earth The Trees And All Nature Are Witness To Your Thoughts And Deeds*. A Winnebago Wise Saying.'
And no less wise for having been felt-tipped on to a pink bal- loon and fastened to a multicoloured rucksack, eh? The sagely lettered balloon bounced about in front of me, an orb of inspi- ration, a small rosy sun of hope in a drizzly and downcast

environment, namely Stevenage. Stevenage isn't exactly Rome, and in the rain it gives Douglas a good fight for the title of Great Britain's Armpit.

Still, the balloon, and its owner, a chubby woman in tie-dyed trousers and velvet Rubette's cap, seemed upbeat enough. Mrs Tie-Dye strode along an open, flooded underpass in her wellington boots, balloon bobbing behind her, wise saying aloft, gamely witnessing Holy Mother Earth's Deeds: which appeared, at that precise moment, to consist of rustling up a weather system to widdle upon her grateful children and smudge their sloganeering. Not to worry, though. All discomfort was in a good cause. Mrs Tie-Dye, and I, plus a few hundred others, were traipsing along Stevenage's sopping walkways in order to register our protest at 10,000 houses. These particular 10,000 hadn't actually done anything as yet – they hadn't actually been built as yet – but they were destined to desecrate quite a piece of green and pleasant, just outside Stevenage, on the far side of the A1(M). We were marching to the not-yet-building site to stand about and say no! at the field where the houses were meant to take root.

But we hadn't yet managed to get there and start protesting. In order to do so, we had to yomp from Stevenage railway station through miles of scrambled pedestrian alleys, whilst cars thundered above our heads. When we did poke our heads above ground, Holy Mother Earth was nowhere to be seen. There was just the undulating rural landscape of Glaxo factories, the twittering sound of traffic.

Eventually, after about half an hour's trudging, we emerged on to a proper field. Nearly there now. We clambered over a stile, and sploshed through a small copse scattered with burnt tyres, rusted bikes, plastic bottles, children's clothes. A landslide of a hill stretched out before us. The rain fell like iron filings. Ah, bucolic idyll! We took a few tentative steps. The sodden path sucked at our boots.

'It'd be better for Tarmac or some crazy paving,' muttered Lizanne.

Lizanne lives in Hitchin, the next village along from Stevenage, and I was staying with her and her family for the weekend. All of us – Lizanne, her husband Phil, their children Flo (11) and Harry (8), and I – had come on the West Stevenage housing protest, in a spirit of national fraternity. Across the country, respectable folk were up in arms over Big Bad Developers threatening their tightly buckled Green Belts, and we had decided to join in their protests. Extra houses were a topic *du jour*, for those who lived on the outskirts of a town; I'd collected quite a few newspaper cuttings about 'How Green Was Our Valley', and 'The Case Against Despoiling Our Countryside'. The proposed Stevenage expansion was the biggest so far: 2.5 miles long by 1 mile wide, the largest loss of the green belt planned anywhere in Great Britain for the past fifty years. It had inspired protest poetry (*how can I explain to everyone/about habitats that will soon disappear/why we mustn't lose the meadows and fields/which are home to the hare and the deer*: Annie Palmer, the Bob Dylan of Langley); impassioned letters in the local paper (*I've never read such a load of balderdash in all my life . . . why didn't you carry on living in Harrow!* – steady on, Mrs M Brown of Hitchin) and had attracted a capped and Barboured William Hague for lamely opportunistic 'I love the countryside, me' photo.

Actually, I was curious to see why people were so worked up over a few extra cul-de-sacs. After all, Stevenage itself was only young: created as an overspill from London in 1946, it was a new town built specifically to house post-war families living five to a bedroom in the old East End. An overspill town that subsequently provided its own work – at factories that made plastic bags, or Platignum pens, or at British Aerospace, or Glaxo – along with spanking, spacious, personable housing and facilities. Stevenage boasted Britain's first ever pedestrian shopping precinct, and a spider's web of car-free walkways. Its housing estates were colour-coded: you got there by following the green or red or yellow blobs on the signs along the ringroad. Stevenage was people-friendly; it was very definitely modern.

So it seemed strange that the local residents were so bothered about the proposed development. Stevenage is a big bright town, that supports those working in it and those who travel to London. It's commutersville, not countryside, so you'd think people would understand if there was a need for new houses. But that, apparently, was the problem. According to the protestors' calculations, there wasn't the need. Ten thousand was far too many.

The last Conservative Government had insisted that 65,000 houses be built within the whole of Hertfordshire, over a twenty-year period from 1991: and 44,000 had been knocked up in seven years. Local authorities reckoned they could find 15,000 homes within existing towns. Which left just 6,000 to be created.

So what was with the 10,000? Even the 6,000 was based on the now somewhat suspect predict-and-provide idea of housing. You'd think that the county council would make the bulldozers hang about a bit, given that there were thirteen years left to run on the building period, just to check that all those houses were needed. And why would you put them all west of Stevenage anyway? There were other places within Hertfordshire, places that weren't on the wrong side of the M1. Places that didn't require a new tunnel or bridge to be built so that residents weren't forced to play motorway chicken to get to the shops.

I'd tried talking to local councillors and protest organisers but the phone conversations had soon degenerated into what sounded suspiciously like personality-based bickering: 'Have a word with so-and-so if you want a laugh'; 'Well, if you knew a little more about it you'd realise that that is typical of the man'. It was proper handbags at dawn stuff, except, of course, that these were adult men, who disdained city wusses, and were proud of their countryside connections. Gro-bags at dawn, then.

The more I tried to make sense of the Stevenage Expansion Problem, the more warped it became. The maths seemed clear enough – 10,000 didn't add up – but the blame-sharing was complicated, contradictory and unceasing. It was the fault of the old Tory Government. It was the fault of the new Labour councillors. It was Stevenage local council holding the entire county to ransom. It was just two men on Stevenage local council; it was the developers; it was the activists; the houses were needed; they were not; the green belt would be moved, recreated elsewhere; it could never be replaced. The lead-up to the protest was so densely twisted that it made Stevenage's underpasses seem open-plan. This was a bitterly contested, long-standing war: the Battle for Langley Valley.

So. From where we were standing, I have to say, Langley Valley didn't seem worth all the fuss. Lizanne, Phil, Flo, Harry and I stood in the drizzle and gazed out at the moist, mucky prospect of the contested land. It was just a field. No patches of wild flowers, no gambolling lambs, not even a teensy crop circle. Nothing to write home – let alone the *Hitchin Comet* – about. We trudged on.

'Uuuuurgh!' squealed Flo, dramatically, standing stock still mid-field, with one boot wobbling above the sludge. 'A woooorm.'

'You're lucky to see it,' said Lizanne. 'It's been the only wildlife so far.'

It was true. The protest had direction signs that said *Follow The Hare*, with appropriate picture, but the cartoon was the only flop-ears we'd seen – much to Flo's disappointment. Flo loves rabbits. She has two, and has trained one to race up the stairs like it's the Bionic Bun.

'The rabbits have all gone back to Glaxo's for a fag,' said Phil, consolingly. He then launched into a whispered narrative, out of the kids' hearing, of what Glaxo is rumoured to do to its lab animals. It sounded terrifying: a living Damien Hirst sculpture.

'Thanks, Phil,' said Lizanne. 'Nip of fruit juice, anyone?'

The fruit juice was grapefruit, pepped up with a good deal of vodka. A night out – a day out – with Lizanne is not a half-hearted affair. You're just about okay if you never venture from the house, but if you do, if you try to mix it with people, you'll always end up in a situation: a show-your-pants competition, or a thump-the-bouncer row, or a never-ending pestering of some defenceless half-celebrity. 'I'm easily led,' shrugs Lizanne, as though she's a bystander.

A quick example: a hen night. Not Lizanne's, but Julie's, another woman with a high stir-it-up capacity. About twenty of us were booked into a restaurant in Streatham, one of those that comes with free Elvis impersonator. It was a few days after Princess Diana's death, and I had a pair of short-leg trousers on; Lizanne decided that these were 'half-mast for Lady Di', and that everyone else had to join in, 'as a mark of respect'. This meant that during the meal, and for the postprandial teeter along the Streatham High Road, most of our party dropped, and kept, their trousers around their ankles. When Elvis came on stage, Lizanne donated her bra to him: went up and fastened it on – over his shoulder-pads and sequins and Las Vegas padding – whilst he was giving it 'Hound-dog'. She joined in for a time. At one point, she grabbed the mike; at another, Elvis grabbed Julie. Then there was the dancing on the chairs; the appalling vibrator incidents; the losing of the shirts (temporary); the losing of the money (permanent); the assaulting of the taxi-drivers; the arrival at the nightclub and, well, whatever happened next . . .

I passed the grapefruit juice back to Lizanne. She grinned at me.

'What do we want?' she shouted, tramping rhythmically

through the slime. 'Come on everybody! What do we want? Ten thousand houses! When do we want them? Now! . . . Ooops.'

A bibbed protest organiser was giving disapproving looks. We smiled at her and changed the chant.

'What do we want? Ten thousand houses! Where do we want them? Over there! A bit of a way away! Just where we can't quite see them!'

'How much further?' moaned Harry, whose small legs had disappeared deep into what used to be Mother Earth. We were making our way along the top of a low hill. Our destination was an airfield at the bottom. It was a bit of a way yet. I looked about and wondered where the 10,000 houses were supposed to go exactly. I'd had a glance at a map, but the rain had made it smeary and I didn't know the area, so it hadn't made much sense. Anyhow, from what I had seen of the local countryside, it didn't seem that 10,000 houses wouldn't brighten things up: the landscape was hardly dramatic, or animal-packed, or even that clean. Every few steps we tramped litter harder into the mud. Maybe it wouldn't be so bad if they concreted over the odd hillock. It would make it easier to walk on, for a start.

Actually, having driven from London, through Luton, Bedford, into Hitchin, on to Stevenage, I'd come to the conclusion that you might as well do the job lot. Just turn everywhere south-east of Northampton into a car park. It would be about as scenic as it is now, and think of all the pay-and-display revenue you'd create. Perhaps the profits could be diverted into good causes. Or maybe the whole area could become a twenty-lane motorway, connecting London with the Midlands. Commuting would be far speedier and there'd be an instant increase in leisure and service investment opportunities: all those hungry drivers, those road-wearied lorry-men, the crowds of bored kids wanting arcade games and sugar fixes. Visitor Centres would sprout like bluebells; safe play areas like faeries' grottoes; knick-knack shops would glitter at every slip-road. There'd be a choice of food franchises in variously themed snack plazas across the land. We'd all be Burger Kings of the Road.

When we arrived at Rush Green Airfield, a lady clicked us in on a hand-held counter. She said there'd not been as many through as had been hoped: 'The weather put people off,' she thought, and we agreed. 'It's still a lovely family day out,' she continued, smiling at Harry, who ignored her. Harry was so hacked off that for the past thirty minutes he had refused to speak or look anywhere beyond the end of his wellies.

Flo was still cheerful, though. 'Is it here that we stand to stop them building houses?' she asked, gazing around, as though fleets of reinforced concrete mixers were revving up round the corner.

The airfield was much like the field we'd just tramped across – grassy, soggy, wildlife-free – except that this one was a lovely family day out, and thus boasted a marquee and a small stage to break up the view. Also green anarchists, Socialist Workers, the odd fire-eater and, inside the marquee, a group labelled as a 'soul-fusion band' by its leader, with some pride.

'We're going to have a great day today, because we don't want 10,000 houses here, do we?' shouted the band leader at the sheltering crowd. There were a few cheers. 'Do we?' he insisted, like a pantomime dame. A few more cheers.

Lizanne said: 'Shall we spread a rumour that Oasis are playing?'

I grabbed a home-made flapjack and went out to talk to some of the protestors. Mr and Mrs Yards carried a placard that said *Infrastructure Before Homes*, which was specific, at least, if not exactly catchy. Fresh-faced, earnest, with the freaky zeal of Born-Agains, they were pleased to elaborate on their slogan.

'We mean schools, jobs . . .' said Mr Yards, gravely, from behind his owl specs.

'It's no good just plonking down houses and Tescos,' said the well-combed Mrs Yards.

'They've not thought it through,' said Mr Yards. 'We don't usually get a lot of rain around here, and there won't be enough water in the reservoir for them all.'

'Not everyone works in London,' said Mrs Yards. 'Those that stay local will have no facilities.'

'And what about hospitals?' boomed Mr Yards, suddenly. 'I've been waiting eighteen months for my operation!'

Trembling, I dared to ask what kind of operation he needed.

'Hernia!' barked Mr Yards, disconcertingly and very loudly. 'My hernia operation! Eighteen months it's been! My hernia!'

Mr Yards was getting upset. People were beginning to stare. The fire-eater was struggling to keep his audience. Small children were pointing and asking their parents what the funny man was shouting about. 'My hernia!' boomed Mr Yards, again. Oh dear. We had definitely strayed past social chit-chat into that queasy 'too much information' area. I decided that it was beyond my remit to spend an afternoon listening to a detailed run-down of Mr Yards' troubles with his waterworks, with or without a cheer-leading crowd. I excused myself.

I wandered over to the outdoor stage, where supportive local VIPs were sprucing themselves up for the photographer. Minions rushed about, floating umbrellas above well-connected pates and shiny suits. The VIPs lined up to stand next to a sign that read: *I saw the news today, oh boy/10,000 homes in north Hertfordshire/And though the homes were rather small/They had to count them all.* The verse didn't continue, which was a shame. It would have been good to see what the local dignitaries would have made of 'I'd love to tuuuuurn youououououou oooooooon'.

I had a quick chat with other protestors, but they were either NIMBY ('this land has been locally owned and used for generations') or Fotherington-Thomas ('hello birds, hello sky'). There certainly wasn't much of a feeling of anger, or action. There were too few of us and we were all too wet and cold. Far from confronting the antis, we hadn't seen anyone other than fellow protestors for the past hour. A protest needs an enemy, someone to shout at: when I used to go on marches, we always stopped outside the entrance to Downing Street, for an energetic venting of our collective spleen. Then we'd mooch into Trafalgar Square to squint at the supportive speakers, then split into Soho for a pint. Whereas there simply wasn't enough to do in Langley Valley to keep you hanging around. Though I did realise that was the point. If we'd walked all this way to arrive at an entertainment complex, then Mr and Mrs Yards really would have something to get upset about.

Anyway, the countryside is all about making your own entertainment. So we went back to Hitchin to whack gangsters on the PlayStation.

What is it about houses that gets people so het up? The good burghers of Stevenage would not have been so ready to march if the council had proposed to put a wildlife sanctuary or a dog's home in Langley Vale: what's the problem with housing people, as opposed to fluffy bunnies or ickle puppies? I suppose you could argue that kennels take up less room than homes for humans (unless the houses are built by Barratt). But I felt that there was something more fundamental bubbling under the protest, under all the modern anti-housing demonstrations. It was the nature of property. Property gets the British going. It stirs their juices. It hits a special nerve.

I once phoned up the *Daily Mail* and asked a journalist just where, exactly, Middle England was. He thought for a moment and said: 'An executive housing estate just outside Swindon. A house with a Rover in the drive.'

I went to find it: whizzed round Swindon's one-way system, hauled the Peugeot through umpteen mini roundabouts, in and out of retail estates, around entertainment complexes. I located Middle England at about 4 p.m. The houses were modern, built to the two-thirds size beloved by Barratt; but they were Tudoresque and there were fancy cars about, often two to a drive. Some kids were mooching on the communal grass: not-yet-teenage girls singing a Boyzone hit, their little brothers whacking each other between kicks of a football. I parked up and walked into a cul-de-sac.

The first house I saw with a Rover had nobody home; still, I could see a china ballet dancer behind the lace curtains, so, according to Dr Cliché, I was on the right track. Then, across the way, I saw a woman – about my age, dressed in smart, practical jacket, carrying a baby. She was walking past her husband's Rover to get into the Clio. I ran over and said: 'I was thinking of moving round here and I wanted to know what it was like.'

The woman smiled and told me all about it: how great it was living in the area; how the kids all played together round the back and the mothers helped each other out; how west Swindon was only fifteen minutes away, if you wanted entertainment. I thanked her; then I asked a couple of men, out walking their dogs, and they said much the same thing: great for kids, everyone very friendly. I went back to the Peugeot and asked the mooching kids. They said 'there's nothing to do', but then they were kids and that's their job.

Why did those people live there? Because of the property; because of the location. Property means all sorts of things to all sorts of people, but essentially, it just means home. And home is a grave and significant business. The nerve that property development touches is not the same one tickled by *Changing Rooms*. Interior decoration makes us all light-headed, excited, giggly with potential and plans. But property – the bricks and mortar, as opposed to the wallpaper and throw cushions – is far more serious. It's about boundaries, and safety, and defending yourself. About what's yours, and what's theirs. The *Daily Mail* man defined Middle England by its housing; Wilmslow judged people by theirs; and Stevenage was distinguishing itself in the same way.

The housing protest wasn't really about the green belt; it was about the houses. The ones that already existed, and the ones that might be built next door. It was understandable: for most people location is a major factor when making a property purchase, and they don't bargain on it suddenly changing. Imagine buying a *bijou* loft in the cool heart of a city, and then waking up one morning to find all the other buildings had been razed to the ground, and flower-studded meadows put in their place. You'd certainly feel disorientated – and where would you go to buy the paper?

The Stevenage protestors and the Wilmslow Friends of Swampy and the rest of the middle-class protestors dangling from tree-houses and clamping themselves to bulldozers on the British front line, on the edge between city and countryside, they all had the same thing in the forefront of their minds. Their home. Their own property, that they worked to pay for, where they brought their kids up and lived their lives, the place that kept everyone out that they didn't decide to let in. The protestors had their backs against the wall, but the wall was their own. Nowadays, it is property rights that stirs the passions of the suburbs: because if they didn't, then the suburbs would no longer exist.

16

does your mother know you're out of it?

Ah! A sunny day in Romford town! God brushed and flossed and gargled with Listerine, then bared his glistening teeth into the brightest, most dazzling of smiles. He smiled on to the tattered railway station, on to its car park that opened on to the vast shed of Hollywood's – Romford's landmark nightclub. He beamed upon Romford's centuries-old open-air market, stalls laden with fresh fruit and fluffy towel-sets and three lipsticks for a fiver; he warmed the well-kept houses, out towards Gidea Park, sent a breeze to shuffle the gravel on the raked front drives; he let his sunbeams glint back along the cracked tarmacked roads around the Waterloo Estate, and batter the traffic on the blazing freeway out towards Chelmsford, back towards London. That day, God smiled upon Romford.

Romford, naturally enough, gave God a blank stare back –
What's that big beardy bloke think he's looking at? – and carried on with its day-to-day business. In the main shopping
precinct, set back from the market, office workers sat on the
edge of the defunct fountain and ate their pick-and-mix salads
from clear plastic boxes. Elderly ladies compared small pains;
young mothers ditto. Outside the entrance to the public toilets,
a *Big Issue* seller slumped in the shade.

In the centre of the precinct, local teenagers hung out, chatted, mooched, smoked. Chris and I sat and watched them for a
bit; we were working our way through our pick-and-mix salads,
catching some sun as we did so. Chris knew most of the kids in
the Romford area, but there were some there that he'd never
seen before. He went over for a quick chat. The teenagers
stopped laughing when he approached, but they didn't stiffen,
or move away, they turned their attention to him without sneer
or threat. The wiry, crop-headed boys seemed to do most of the
talking; standing amidst them, Chris, with his wavy hair, his
gone-to-Goa shorts, his personable face, looked like a floppy
Labrador amongst a pack of close-haired, race-hungry whip-
pets. He handed out a few leaflets. After a while, he loped back.

Chris was a senior detached youth worker for the London
Borough of Havering. I'd read about his job in one of the many
leaflets he had handed to me over the morning (public sector
jobs come papered in leaflets – glossy, multicoloured, tatty, pho-
tocopied). In social work speak, Chris helped young people
'unable or unwilling to fully relate to existing opportunities and
provision', 'primarily . . . aged thirteen to nineteen years, on the
streets, on "their home ground", in cafés, clubs, cars, parks etc'.

The leaflet demanded that he accepted teenagers 'as they are', and it observed that 'visible groups of young people are often seen as a threat to the community or a risk to themselves. A non-judgemental approach is essential'. I looked back at the visible group of young people on their home ground of the precinct. I tried to accept them as they were, although, as I hadn't met them, I wasn't quite sure what that was. Were they unable to fully relate to existing opportunities? Were they a threat to the community? Or were they, like most teenagers, just a big pain in the non-judgemental arse?

Chris had been doing his job for the past eight years. He munched on a banana and said that he wasn't sure how much longer he'd continue. Recently, he'd been wondering if he ever actually achieved anything, if any of the 'young people' he 'targeted' really gained from his efforts, or if he himself was advancing, growing as a person (Chris's natural speech was more yoga than social work; although he had the trained negotiator's 'yeah?' at the end of most sentences). Chris was thinking of jacking it all in. But before he did, he'd agreed to show me just what he would be jacking.

Chris said: 'So, we'll take you to the drop-in information centre, yeah? Spend half an hour there, get to know what that's about. Then you can meet James at CDAS, that's the Community Drugs Advisory Service, yeah? Then we can maybe take a quick scout around the flats, see if we run into this little group I'm working with, and maybe go down to the park, where I said I'd see another group. Okay with you?'

Okay with me.

*

I'd come to Romford because I'd driven through it and something about it had reminded me of home. It was the flash cars and the pedestrianised shopping, the scrubby parks and scowling adolescents, the train into town and the glitzy discos and the teeny council estates and the clippered almost-countryside. I'd also come because Essex and drugs seemed to have been wound up with one another for quite some time, in a front page manner usually confined to the inner cities and sink estates of Manchester, Glasgow, Liverpool. There'd been the shotgun murders of the two drug dealers in 1995, then the enormous palaver over Leah Betts' death (she'd taken one ecstasy tab at her own eighteenth birthday party, held in her parents' house near Basildon; her father was a policeman, her mother an anti-drugs worker). There was The Prodigy, the best and most influential group (at least in terms of hair-style fantasies for the under-eights) to come out of rave: Essex boys and biscuit munchers to a man. To be fair, these days, The Prodigy are without chemical whiff. But they still live in Essex.

Anyhow, I had this vague media-fuelled idea that the young people of Romford, in common with the youth of the entire county of Essex, were bottle-fed liquid MDMA from birth until they got a job – taxi-driver or dance-act vibe controller – whereupon they immediately switched to snorting cocaine. So I thought I'd come and have a look at them. Maybe it was because their parents were all off protesting against property developers, but Essex kids seemed to be free to have a lot more fun than I'd ever had as an adolescent.

When I was a teenager, my kicks were limited. Still, during the day, they did exist: traipsing through the shops, sitting on benches making bitchy comments, going to the park, going round a friend's house. At the friend's house, you spent five agonising parent-appeasing minutes talking about school and stuffing McVitie's in your gob; and then you hurtled upstairs to work out dance routines to Michael Jackson or Duran Duran, or you played with puppies. At night, though, options were more limited. Either you went to the cinema (which I did, with my friend Tracey, every single Friday night from the age of twelve to fifteen. We saw: *Arthur*, *Tootsie*, *Kramer Versus Kramer*; *Chariots of Fire*, *On Golden Pond*, *The French Lieutenant's Woman*; *Fame*, *Flashdance*, *Police Academy*, *Private Benjamin*, *Porky's*. Our budding imaginations were pickled in syrup, sexism and show-offy dancing). Or: you stayed in, locked yourself in the bathroom, spent two hours with Shaders or Toners wash-in-wash-out dye plastered on your fringe, then spent another two fiddling about with ice-cubes and a needle (sterilised by a good blast with the hairdryer) trying to pierce your ear. The evening was rounded off in style by hanging out of your bedroom window puffing on several of your mum's B&H.

So, as you can imagine, the idea of a modern adolescence spent gambolling in a beatific haze between under-age rave and talk-your-way-in nightclub seemed an appealing one to me. Especially as Essex would allow you to do so within striking distance of some dinkily pretty scenery. NB: Before anyone decides to report me to the authorities for promoting drug use to children, I should like to quote the government-approved Institute for the Study of Drug Dependence in its publication, D-Mag (purple and yellow glossy magazine-style leaflet 'produced for people aged thirteen and upwards'). It reads: 'There is nothing in this which condones or encourages drug use. But if you are thinking about it, you should have all the information at hand to make an informed decision.' So, kids, be informed: with my teenage entertainment choices, I took the risk of lung cancer, tetanus poisoning and a fringe like a Bridget Riley painting. But I didn't risk instant death. Except the social version.

Actually, I did try drugs when I was a teenager. But I thought they were rubbish. They didn't work. This was because I was so worried about hallucinating (I had no idea what this was, but thought it would be like the Pink-Elephants-On-Parade scene in *Dumbo*) that every time I took any drugs – spliff, speed, poppers, pills bought over the counter – I would only allow myself the teeniest amount. One toke, one dab rubbed into the lower gum, one sniff, three Do-Dos. No way were those freak elephants going to stomp on my head and blow bubbles in my ears, I would think; but afterwards I'd be horribly disappointed that the elephants hadn't even bothered to turn up. Not even the scary dwarf one in the tutu. Another factor in my narcotics disdain was that, being a teenager, there was nowhere comfy for me to go to try drugs. It was always on a park bench, or a railway station, in the freezing cold and rain. You have to smoke a lot of something stronger than dodgy Red Leb in order to override such adverse circumstances. I went back to the more conventional Benylin and vodka mix, until I could get to go away without my parents. Then there was a brief phase of ridiculously elaborate drug taking: hot knives, blow-backs, vodka bongs, pipes made out of Coke cans. Drugs as fiddly gourmet cooking, as look-at-me ritual, as BUPA surgery (always performed by pompous youths; I could barely roll a

joint). That lasted until I got into nightclubs. You can't smug-
gle an African hubble-bubble with embossed brass stand past
club bouncers, not even under a Mancunian-sized puffa jacket.
Nightclub drugs necessarily involve less paraphernalia.

Chris didn't actually work directly with addicts; that is, he
wasn't part of a unit designed specifically to help drug depen-
dancy. He was a Youth Worker. But working with Youth meant,
sometimes, working with drug abusers: especially because, in
social work leaflet terms, such abusers included boozers, ciga-
rette-smokers, glue-sniffers, steroid-freaks – as well as those
partakers of the more media-friendly recreational drugs that
peppered Essex in my mind.

Actually, to judge by the leaflets that Chris handed over,
such news-friendly drugs formed a very small part of what was
on offer: one pamphlet listed fifteen *categories* of drugs, from
the traditional mind-looseners of heroin, cocaine, LSD, through
to tranquillisers, barbiturates, poppers and GHB. There was
even a category called Snidey Drugs, the stuff taken by gossip
columnists and Jeremy Paxman. Not really – snidey drugs were
those annoying ones that weren't what the funny man said they
were. This includes most drugs these days, in my experience
(admittedly somewhat limited, judging by the leaflet). Of
course, drugs, being illegal, have no enforceable consumer guar-
antees, so you can't run griping to Anne Robinson when you
don't get what you paid for. This means taking drugs is like
cooking your tea from a selection of tins with the labels taken
off. There you were hoping for tomato soup and sponge pudding: what you got was pear halves in syrup and Mr Dog.

Anyhow, that morning Chris had taken me to see a fellow youth worker called Andy, who had set up Romford's drop-in centre for fourteen to twenty-year-olds, The Information Shop. Andy talked fast and Scottish: he attended courses to improve his theoretical knowledge, he ran youth clubs, he worked at residential programmes, he knew every scrap of relevant legislation. Andy also talked social worker: using phrases like 'moving from a wants-based to a needs-based work relationship'.

It was hard to get him to talk specifics (it was hard to get a word in), but eventually, Andy said that one of the techniques he used to increase young people's drugs awareness was Drug Trivial Pursuit. Essentially, you swap all those poncey Arts and Literature, Science and Nature, Geography, History categories, and replace them with ones entitled Smack, Crack, E etc. The kids set the questions and answers. It sounded like a winner for the Christmas board games market to me – students would love it – but that was me thinking commercially, as opposed to public-spiritedly. Drug Trivial Pursuit was only for those youngsters who wanted 'to take things deeper', said Andy.

'How do you know when they want to do that?' I asked.

'Oh, they'll just express an interest. Not all of them do. There are those who'll never be interested, because they're not interested in taking drugs,' said Andy.

Very true. Some people are interested in taking drugs and some people are not. But one of the things that Chris and Andy have to deal with is that those who are interested in taking drugs can change the mind of those who aren't. Not because they say 'ner ner ner let's point and laugh at Miss Straight or Mr

Cleancut', but because, when you're young and daft, then the people who are interested in drugs can appear to be the most interesting people out there. Look at *Trainspotting*. It doesn't matter that the film-makers were careful to show that heroin is disgusting and messy and can result in you being dive-bombed by a mutant plastic baby: the drug-takers in *Trainspotting* were glamorous, sexy, funny, *interesting*.

Of course, if you've got more than two brain cells to rub together, you'll soon work out that whether someone is interesting or not is a personality facet, not a cheekbones/sleaze thing. And you'll also realise that, actually, there isn't much that's fundamentally interesting about drug takers in the same way that there isn't much that's fundamentally interesting about, say, sitting about laughing at a cornflakes advert. Or, indeed, sitting about thinking you're a cornflake in the cornflakes advert, or banging on for hours about how much better you are than a cornflake, or dancing to the cornflake music, or thinking, I really fancy a bowl of cornflakes and then having to eat them with water because you're far too skint and/or doped to go and buy the milk.

Andy only goes to the authorities if a teenager is dealing, or being abused. Otherwise, he just tries to keep his young chums informed, tell them that they can be put away for carrying just three Es, that some people die from sniffing solvents, that you can't go and get your money back when someone sells you a wrap of baking soda. His difficulty is getting information out to those who aren't going to walk into The Information Shop, or come to youth clubs, or read leaflets in a library. He tries to think of things he can do that will grab young people's interest, and then, once he's got that, he can give them drugs knowledge. I thought it sounded a bit like those recent sneaky Christian techniques: you know, get the kids down a rave-up and then tell them they're dancing for Jesus.

But I was being mean. Andy clearly worked very hard. He handed me a CD called *Crave*. It had a picture of a young, worried-looking androgyne on the front, and a list of bands on the back – all local to Romford, all part of an enterprise called the Havering Bands Project, all asked by his local drugs action team to write and perform a song 'with a drugs awareness theme'. The CD was recorded, pressed and released in 1997: the bands staged a concert, there was a lot of local publicity.

I listened to *Crave* when I got home. It was bad, but no worse than many of the CDs that you get sent as a pop critic: just sub-indie whining and guitars. Which is just the stuff to send me screaming to the drug-cupboard, but there you are. No nose-bleed horror show techno, sadly. In between the yearning, heartfelt, terrible lyrics – 'a taste so sweet, without a care'; 'blood-stained minds lose it every day'; 'I cry so loud that no one hears' – was leaflet-type information on drugs. I remembered how I used to read and reread record sleeves in my youth. I looked at the CD notes and thought: I didn't know that magic mushrooms were Class A if you cooked them.

Chris also took me to meet Steve. Steve worked in the local YMCA, which was a place that served a multitude of purposes. It was a probation hostel overflow; it was accommodation for homeless people, and, I suppose, tourists; plus a local gym and a place for young male Christians to practise their synchronised dance routines. Steve had turned up at the YMCA after a spell in prison 'for something I didn't do'. After his release, he'd been dossing on friends' floors until someone had mentioned to him that the YMCA 'was like prison, except the doors opened'.

Steve was big, tattooed, skinheaded, with beautiful blue eyes in a face like a bruised melon. I wasn't quite sure of the reason why I was talking to him, except that Chris had mentioned that he was a YMCA success story: Steve had an NVQ youth work qualification which he had completed whilst working on building sites and living at the YMCA. Now he was helping with local kids too, though his job was with younger children, five to eleven years old. Steve said that there wasn't too much trouble with drugs when they were that age, although he thought that there might be a bit of marijuana smoking amongst the older ones. Discipline was more of a problem with the kids he worked with: 'You can see that some of them are disturbed,' he said, 'with their kicking and biting. I say, "you can carry on as much as you like, because I'm not going to hit you back." Then I put them in a squash court to cool down, let 'em take out their frustration on the walls, deprive them of their fun. They get better after that.' Steve didn't talk social worker.

I asked him if he thought there was a general drug problem around Romford.

'There's a big, big problem,' said the big, big man. 'In the clubs, you can see it. There's pills and a lot of coke about. Heroin, you don't see so much, 'cos they keep themselves to themselves. Puff, I see as different.' (Steve lowered his voice.) 'I think, myself, that they should legalise puff and come down hard on the rest. You know, bang someone up if they find any-thing, anything at all, on them.'

Steve did admit, though, that in his long-gone wilder days he had tried drugs stronger than a joint.

'Didn't do much for me, though,' he said, and went back to his job.

His colleagues at the YMCA, and Chris, were more circum-spect about drug-taking: only one admitted to having taken drugs themselves in the past – 'I had a phase of doing trips in my teens', he volunteered; and they were noncommittal as to whether they thought that drug laws should change – one ven-tured: 'I think it should be discussed, at least.' What they had to worry about was the nature of any governmental directives that were handed down to them. Drugs were just one factor in the many that they had to consider when trying to do their job.

Whilst he was driving me to our next assignment, I asked Chris whether he ever had to deal with child abuse, and he said: 'You come across it.' He also said: 'You need a lot of evidence to accuse someone of child abuse. Sometimes, we can tell when a child is being abused; well, we can guess, from their behaviour, yeah? Like, you get a boy who keeps trying to hit you in the nuts. We know the vulnerable kids, we can put them on the 'at risk' register, but we can't be with them 24 hours. We can't live inside their homes.'

It's not until you meet a professional drug specialist that you witness the zeal of a true addict. James worked at CDAS. He was very busy: he only had a few minutes to squeeze me in between clients, or customers, or whatever the current term is.

James worked with people whose lives were dominated by drugs, and so was his: he had so many narcotic statistics that if you stuck them in your crack-pipe, you'd be smoking for a week. Here's a selection:

- Britain could fill six of its prisons solely with convicted cannabis users
- 60–80 per cent of Britons who test positive for Hepatitus C are intravenous drug users
- There is an 80 per cent chance that whoever stole your car radio was a drug abuser
- There has been a study in the US that worked out that for every dollar's worth of treatment for drug addicts, society was saved seven dollars in prison charges and loss of property

Before the whole conversation degenerated into a rapid-fire Drug Trivial Pursuit, I asked James if he had seen any recent changes or trends in the drug-taking of his clients. James got very excited.

'Over the last two years, we've seen about a 300 per cent increase in the problem cocaine users,' he gabbled. 'Whereas before, cocaine was seen as an exclusive drug – *was*, in fact, an exclusive drug – now we're getting a flood of people with serious cocaine problems.'

What was different about these coke users, said James, were that they were ordinary, working-to-middle-class people; that is, they weren't exceptionally rich, they didn't work in television or the music industry or the City. They worked in construction, or technology, or 'business'; they were boozers by nature, who went out on a Saturday night for a session with the lads. Then they started taking coke, and the sessions turned into binges – the cocaine meant that they drank more, more quickly and for longer periods – and the binges lasted all night, and then all weekend. And then the weekends started on Friday night, and then on Thursday; until people fetched up at CDAS with a cocaine habit of an ounce a week. There are 28 grammes in an ounce. About £1,000-worth of cocaine a week, if you bulk-buy. Plus all the drink. That's a whopping hangover you have there, sir. Especially if you've got a mortgage and a family.

James said that there had also been an upswing in problem cannabis users: those who smoked an ounce, two ounces of psychotic skunk every week. And recently, CDAS had been helping people in trouble with anabolic steroids: young men proud to be fit, who wouldn't touch 'regular' drugs, who worked out every day and played sport and built muscle. And then flexed that muscle until the veins stood out so they could find a nice fresh one in which to jack up their Sustanon.

It was late afternoon. Chris and I had been visiting social work institutions all day. Chris still had a job to do. Whilst I'd been talking to Andy and Steve and James, he'd been nipping out to local council estates, checking on stuff like how the new football pitch was going on the Waterloo Estate, chatting to the kids there (who thought the pitch was rubbish: it was tiny and had wooden boards instead of goal nets), introducing himself to their mothers, seeing if any of the younger kids wanted to come on a day out swimming, or quad-biking. He'd been making phonecalls, writing reports, helping some older teenagers with housing problems, checking that his fellow workers were coping with their day out orienteering in a local park.

I asked him how he felt about his job. Chris said: 'I feel tired.' But he'd bumped into Wayne, a lad who used to come to activities that Chris had organised, and Wayne, now twenty, was doing well. He was a kids' entertainer: magic tricks, balloon animals, juggling. Chris had remembered the weekend away when he had taught Wayne how to juggle, and he'd felt the best he had all week.

At the end of the day, Chris and I went down to Cotton's Park, a big, flat, green park with swings at one end. There were two small groups of teenagers sitting close together on the grass. Five girls, in their late teens, two with babies; and four younger boys. As Chris approached, one of the boys looked over and shouted, 'Fuck off home.'

'Hi, Billy,' said Chris, mildly, and we sat down with the boys. I felt very awkward, in a schoolgirl way, and a familiar, long-forgotten tension came hurtling back into the present. Sitting down with the hard lads, looking for something, waiting to see who'd be funny, or who'd be picked on, what would happen, whatever. Thinking of things to say, but biting your tongue anyway. I was glad I was no longer a teenager.

Billy was a stocky lad, in Adidas snap-pants and muddy T-shirt, and he paced around us like a tiger in a tantrum. Chris told me that Billy had been excluded from school for the past two years. Billy talked a lot, but didn't look anyone in the eye. He paced and paced. I asked why he didn't sit down. He said he was stressed.

Chris said: 'I'm stressed, too.'

Billy said: 'Fuck off, you nonce.'

Chris, to me: 'Nonce is the latest insult.'

A thin boy, with a wandering eye and a slackish mouth, asked: 'Chris, what's a retard?'

Chris said, gently: 'That's another insult. That's what cruel people call people who are mentally handicapped.'

The thin boy, who was called Paul, said: 'Oh.' He looked a bit upset.

Chris said: 'Miranda's from Manchester. Do you know anything about Manchester?'

Paul said: 'Crap football team.'

A littler lad said: 'Don't they play rugby there as well?'

Billy barged into the circle and stuck his face right up to Chris's. He said, loudly: 'David Beckham's a wanker.'

One of the girls said: 'Fuck off, Billy, Beckham's lush.'

A discussion followed amongst the girls as to which footballers they fancied: top scorers were Alan Shearer, Michael Owen, David Beckham, Ian Wright.

Chris: 'What does anyone here know about drugs?'

Billy: 'Have you got any? Give us some.'

A girl said: 'If you want drugs, I know where you can get 'em.'

I talked about nightclubs with her for a while: she told me about the different nights at local club Hollywood's – 'hippy night, nappy night, grab a granny' (student night, under-18s night, over-25s) – but she said she could only go out now if her mum let the baby stay over. She said she didn't mind not going. I played with her baby. His name was Jamie.

Billy was pacing again; alternating between berating all footballers for being 'fucking Cockney nonces', and muttering
about 'smoking black hash'. Paul kept asking Chris if he could
go on a bowling night that was being organised. Chris said no,
Paul had been banned by the bowling alley because of the way
he behaved the last time. Paul said: 'It was boring. I lost con-
centration. But I've been good otherwise, ain't I?' Chris said
that perhaps Paul could turn up early and Chris would help him
talk to the bowling alley owner to see if he would change his
mind.

After a bit, Chris and I got up and went to talk to another,
older group. Again, the boys were in one spot, the girls in the
other. The boys – eleven of them – were all skinheads, and they
were all stoned. Most of them were lying down. Three joints
were going round. I noticed that the four girls weren't smoking.
Chris gave me a drugs leaflet, so I gave it to the girls. Their
names were Gemma, Katie, Vicky and Laura, and they were
quieter than the boys, pretty in their T-shirts and jeans. They
put their heads together to read the leaflet.

One of the boys started to read it out loud: 'What's XTC
stand for?' he asked. He said the letters phonetically: 'Ex-tuh-
cuh.'

'It's ecstasy, you *prick*,' said another boy.

Vicky said to me: 'We don't take drugs.'

Laura said: 'We get pissed though! Lemon Hooch!' The girls
giggled and buried their heads in each other's shoulders.

17

weekenders

A fter all those drugs, those protests, that grating musical accompaniment, all that long-distance driving to all those short-attention-span Visitor Centres, the modern suburbanite can end up feeling weary. Worn out, fed up, ground down, cynical. At such times, you cast about for something, for someone, to believe in . . .

At the end of August 1997, Diana, Princess of Wales died in a car crash, and the world united in grief at the untimely death of the Posh Spice Princess, the one who used her good looks and unique fame to obtain free designer shift dresses to wear at starstudded premières and whilst performing her many and effective charitable works. Like 90 per cent of Britons, I thought

283

Diana's death was sad: I moped outside Kensington Palace for a good ten minutes, I stayed in and watched the funeral, I blubbed for her motherless sons and for the people I loved who were dead.

As you might have noticed at the time, the press went a little bonkers over Di's death and its consequences; there was much trumpeting of 'the end of cynicism', 'the dawn of a new intimacy', 'a slight wobbly movement detected in the stiff upper lip'. There was also an obsessive desire to identify Diana's mourners: were they all of us? Were they New Labour voters? Were they women/black/gay/northern/cat-lovers/ half-wits/C1s and 2s/lapsed vegetarian *Guardian* readers with MPV, PEP and fifteen years still to go on the mortgage? No one knew. Everyone, even the marketing consultants, was confused. There was a classic quote from a (sadly unidentified) former member of the last Conservative Cabinet. 'I walked through the crowds in St James's,' he commented, to the *Telegraph*'s political correspondent, 'and realised that this was no longer a country I truly understand.' In other words: who *were* these people?

Well, I went to St James's, too, and I had a look; and I watched the telly, and studied the swelling, welling crowds. And, after careful analysis, I can reveal that, in my expert opinion, the majority of Princess Diana mourners were shoe-wearers. Most sported some form of clothing. A high proportion were human, I think, and several were male. Or female. I forget.

Actually, what I did notice about the mourners was how much they looked like they were just off to the garden centre, or the supermarket, or to pick up the kids from school. They looked like a lot of people do in suburban towns: slightly hassled, but neatly dressed and resolute; patiently showing the world that they know what the right thing is and how to do it. Television had demonstrated the acceptable manner of expressing grief at Diana's death: buy a bunch of cellophaned daisies and a Family Saver Return; get little Natalie to draw a card; queue for the afternoon to sign the condolence book; secure five seconds on the *Six O'Clock News* being inarticulate in BHS pastels, go home. Yes, television – as it's supposed to – had shown us how to behave in extreme circumstances (death of a royal, nuclear attack, unexpected appearance of husband in lipstick on the *Jerry Springer Show*). So out we all went, and behaved.

Later that year, Earl Spencer announced that he would hold a tribute concert for Diana, at his Althorp estate, in June 1998. I bought a ticket, because . . . actually, I'm not sure why I bought a ticket. I think I thought it might be a funny day out; but none of my friends would come with me. They refused to spend £40 to sit in a field for a day and listen to Chris de Burgh, The Lighthouse Family, Lesley Garrett and Duran Duran. Instead, they wanted to spend £80 to sit in a different field for three days and listen to Pulp, Blur, Tricky and Robbie Williams. Glastonbury Festival was being held on the same weekend as the Diana Tribute. In vain did I try to entice them away by reading out the delights listed on the Diana ticket: 'picnic-style concert . . . situated between Northampton and Rugby on the A428 . . . complimentary car parking facilities . . .' But they just looked at me as though I'd said 'I know, let's all chop off our toes and thread them together to make a string of very personal Diana tribute pearls.' I was upset. I only wanted to go to the concert. I wasn't asking them to snivel in four-part harmony with Chris de Burgh or anything. But they weren't having it. My boyfriend took me aside, and said sternly: 'This suburban thing has gone too far. You can't want to go and see The Lighthouse Family *twice*.'

But he was wrong. I was quite happy to see them again. I was searching for today's suburban adventure, and devotion to Diana seemed to provide a large part of such an experience; more, even, than the estimably average Lighthouse Family. The mourners at the Palace gates had all travelled to get there; it would be out-of-towners that attended the Tribute, I knew. This would be Middle Britain's grand gathering of the year, its big day out, its proper party. I was determined to go.

But no one would come with me. I decided to compromise. I would join my friends at Glastonbury for the Friday night, then drive cross-country on the Saturday afternoon to arrive at Althorp House for the Diana Tribute at 7 p.m. I'd stay at least until The Family sang a couple of crooners, then bomb it back to catch Blur's encore, if I was lucky. Thus, I could do an effective Compare And Contrast concert experiment, and give the Peugeot a nice long run into the bargain. I told my friends of my fantastic idea, but they looked at me as though I'd said 'I wasn't joking about the toes.' Oh, well.

So, the Friday came, and with it the kind of sheeting, freezing rain that makes most people abandon a visit to the corner pub, let alone a long weekend outdoors. That's a long weekend outdoors *the whole time,* except when 'under' 'canvas' (read: suffocated by collapsed Wendy House); a long weekend outdoors without flush toilets, or any form of seating, or any guarantee that any band you wanted to see would actually be bothered to traipse through the state-of-emergency horror-sludge to perform. I looked at my Glastonbury ticket, to see if there was an enforceable money-back clause, or a contractual promise of a gilt-edged good time. But the only warranty pledged that 'in the event of inclement weather, we hereby guarantee that your miserable mud-bath will be shared by at least 80,000 students wearing bin liners'.

I didn't know how the rain would affect the Althorp event. Having endured more than a few wet festivals in my time, I had come prepared (essentials: bottle of vodka in every available pocket, hotel booking); but I was unsure as to whether the Diana Tribute was going to be like anything I'd ever attended. I mean, I'd never before been to a concert that forbade 'umbrellas and awnings which obstruct the view of other patrons' and 'the use of barbecues'. Awnings? Barbecues? What on earth did they imagine people got up to at festivals? Were they worried that the 'patrons' would suddenly rise up as one to stage a spontaneous village fete? Did Earl Spencer get his security guards together and say: 'Listen boys, I think the plebs might want to roast a suckling pig; unwant them, all right?'?

I also wasn't sure as to how the Peugeot would react to the rain. On the radio, solemn-voiced announcers were detailing the extent of the 'extreme weather conditions': it sounded as though the whole of the southern half of Britain had sunk into the sea. I was concerned that even if I did manage to aquaplane the Peugeot to Glastonbury, I then had to persuade it that it didn't want to drop anchor and stay put. That, instead, what it would really like would be to set sail once more on a round trip of 200 miles for no proper reason at all. I had the awful feeling that the car would just play the get-lost-I'm-over-25-which-is-at least-100-in-car-years card and not start again once it had stopped. Plus: there was the further complication of England playing Colombia in the World Cup. The match was scheduled for Friday evening and John, my beloved, was insistent on being before a TV screen at least fifteen minutes before kick-off.

It would have been so much easier to stay at home. But I'd read plenty of articles that insisted that what everyone under 50 needed was a bloody good war to stop them moaning; and what with all the mud and the cross-country reconnaissance, this was as close to the trenches as I was ever going to get. We set off.

It took five-and-a-half hours to get from my house to Glastonbury's car park, and John was spitting with frustration when we got there. The football had started, and I'd tuned in the car radio; but unfortunately, the rain and the Peugeot's dodgy electrics had resulted in the radio making an ear-splitting crrrzzxxxzrkksss noise every single time the wipers moved across the windscreen. John and I had a small contretemps as to whether it was more important to hear the football match, or see the road. I was reminded of my gran – her hearing aid is too big to wear at the same time as her specs – and in the end, like Granny, we'd settled for alternate blasts of each faculty. See no evil, hear no evil. See no evil, hear no evil. Our speaking of evil, of course, remained pretty much constant.

When we arrived, it was only ten minutes into the first half of the football match. But then the stewards sent us round the full circumference of the site, a distance of approximately 5,000 miles, because our tickets didn't match our car-park allocation, or because the stewards were too cross-eyed to see beyond their booze-blown hick noses, or something. And then we had to queue to get in. So, by the time we'd swapped our tickets for wristbands, our shoes and clothes for flippers and wet suits, and our good humour for the sort of sulky obstreperousness that would make Ian Paisley seem like an eager Boy Scout, it was half-time. And we still hadn't got to a telly.

There were two humungous screens either side of the main stage, but it was a million miles away, across a mud-ocean. There would be a TV somewhere in the backstage area, but that was a million and one miles away, behind the main stage. John gave up on the football, and we went for a walk. Walking is what you do at festivals, after all. You tramp from stage to stage, via food stalls and beer tents and ooh-let's-have-a-look-at-the-bungee-jumpers, and then you lose your friends, so you walk around a bit until you find them again. By the time you do, you've all forgotten what you set out to see, and anyway, who-ever it was will have stopped playing by then, so you wander round for hours longer, gradually losing each other, until you're on your own again. And it's at that very moment that your drugs start kicking in and you walk smack into Satan, i.e. that bastard who you used to go out with who still owes you all that money. Festivals are like life – a confused meander towards death – but on disconcertingly fast forward.

Rain-soaked festivals mess with the speedometer, though. If

it's raining, you start out walking very slowly and carefully, to keep your plastic trousers nice. Despite this, each step flicks enough mud to provide a power-shower of slime. Within minutes you look like you're having head-to-toe skin-softening treatment and your cautious tiptoe gives way to a nonchalant cavort, a flippant skip, a high-kicking, cartwheeling, splash-it-all-over frolic through the septic tank of the Great British countryside. Until all the mud cakes solid on your boots and the weight forces you to slow-trudge once more. Then you hit a particularly deep and liquid patch, the caked mud is washed away, and you begin gambolling again.

By the time we made it to the cosy backstage area – well, there was a covered beer tent – we were moving like Mogadoned bears in moonboots of lead. We stayed put for hours, with our feet cemented to the ground, leaning forward and back, like Weebles. Eventually, we made it out to see the Chemical Brothers in the dance tent, but it was hard work. Every pathway was a sewer, every field a lake of shite, and when we finally shoved our way into the tent, the heat inside concreted our body clabber so we couldn't move without cracking. I thought: I am too old to do aerobics in a concrete overcoat. So we went for another walk.

I have to say though, that I did enjoy myself. I always do, at Glastonbury. I'm not sure why: it's to do with the hugeness of it all, the chaos, the ridiculous amount of people. You never see that many British people together without a corresponding number of bricks. Crowds don't come without buildings: stadiums, shopping centres, stations, high streets, high-rises, housing estates. That's what's wrong with crowds: the buildings squish them in. Crowds of people should roam free, like wilde-beest herds; and midge, er, herds. Except, of course, that crowds can't. Not for longer than a weekend anyhow: after that, they start missing all the interesting stuff they keep in their buildings, like carpets and bubble bath and their CDs, in alpha-betical order. And all the interesting stuff in other people's buildings: beer, frocks, chicken tikka masala. But, anyway, if you can manage without such fundamentals for a couple of days, then Glastonbury Festival's one of the best places to be in a crowd: as long as there's a vehicle handy to whisk you away to a nice, warm building when things get too messy.

At about 4.30 a.m., there was. We managed to blag a lift from a friend who was going to Wells, where we'd booked a hotel. John and I bumped about in the back of a van, like dogs, except dogs have a homing instinct and might have given better directions. We did three tours of the one-way system and got to bed before six. Just.

The next day was Action Althorp. I awoke at midday to find that the bile lake in my stomach had risen like the Glastonbury mud and my brain was drowning in acid. Still, after a breakfast of baked potato, cheese and baked beans, I felt a lot worse. But I was determined. Althorp was calling, in a thin, high-pitched whine, although that could have been my stomach again. Or tinnitus. I got a lift back to Glastonbury, started the Peugeot (first time!) and off I went.

I looked at the map before I set out. God, it was a long way. I could either drive back to London on the M4, and then up the M1, or I could go cross-country. I couldn't face going back to

London – too much like defeat, and I was worried that the Peugeot might just drive me home once I was there – so A roads it was. I won't tire you with the details of the journey, except to say that it involved a lot of stopping on laybys to reconsult the map, and a few unexpected tours (Chippenham, Oxford and, towards the end of the journey, a detailed surveillance of the goods ways of Sixfields retail village, near Northampton). I arrived at Althorp at 6.30 p.m.

There was a queue to get in: a long, chugging, patient queue of cars that trickled along the high-hedged country lanes and filtered through the vast iron gates and crawled along the drive to Althorp House. The queue didn't bother me: it was a gorgeous evening. The rain had stopped, at about five o'clock and Kidlington, and I'd taken the top down and let the wind brush the slurry from my hair. Glastonbury's slough of despond seemed a very long way away: Althorp's grounds were green and lush, trees awhisperin', house aglistenin', grass abloomin', dreadful scrapey noise of Julian Lloyd Webber and the BBC Concert Orchestra awaftin' on the air. I parked the Peugeot amidst rows of shiny Mondeos, Vectras, Sierras, Range Rovers. Compared to the mud-splattered camper vans and multi-hued huckster buses of the Glastonbury crowd, the Althorp concert-goers had arrived in style.

Unfortunately for them, though, they'd also arrived in peep-toed sandals. And once they'd tripped past the ticket-checkers, and dallied on the gravel path around Althorp House ('*There will be NO ACCESS to the House, Visitor's Centre and Lake*': so remove that snorkel now, madam), they were presented with a sight that, whilst not quite a twin of Glastonbury's swamp, looked a lot more like it than the daisy-strewn meadow for which the Tributers were prepared. The Diana Tribute Concert was a lake of mud. Its surface rippled in the evening breeze. The peep-toed masses ground to a halt at its edge, terrified. Suddenly, my Gore-tex all-in-one looked really big and clever, as opposed to just really big. With a nonchalant, experienced air, I saluted the security guards, winked at the horrified ladies, and strode into the quagmire.

When I emerged, dripping, on the other side, where the mud had solidified into a sticky brown beach, I discovered lots of middle-aged people sitting on fold-out seats, like cake decorations stuck in chocolate icing. They were all stuffing their faces with food and goggling at Julian Lloyd Webber. I realised that I'd discovered the Contrast in my comparison of Glastonbury and the Diana Tribute. The only real difference between the two was how their audiences catered for their perceived festival needs. Glastonbury-goers came with drugs and plastic trousers. Tribute 'patrons': deck-chairs and pies.

Sadly, though, several of the Althorp brigade hadn't come properly prepared: they huddled, quivering and bootless, on cardboard boxes, marooned around the swamp's edge, miles from the stage, far too worried about getting their frocks dirty to dare to sit down. Novices are not unusual at festivals, but, unlike Michael Eavis, who organises Glastonbury, Earl Spencer hadn't bothered to provide the Tributers with stalls which might have helped them out. At Glastonbury, there had been a shop (called, for some reason, Joe Bananas) which sold blankets; and there were other outlets offering wellies, plastic ponchos, bin liners, umbrellas, torches, alcohol, headache pills. At

Althorp, the stalls sold champagne (£34 a bottle), official programmes (£7), official Diana key-rings (£5), official Diana
address books (£10), official Diana teddy bears (£18). But no
fold-out chairs. No tarpaulins, no blankets. Not even any bin
liners. You could, however, buy free-standing lanterns (£12).
These were metal cages which hung upon a stout hook. You
paid your £12, lit the taper inside the lantern, shoved the
bottom of the hook into the sludge and stood well back. *Voilà* –
your very own candle in the wind.

Plenty of the concert-goers had bought a CITW and had
marked the perimeter of their territory with it, like a driveway
burglar light. Several of them appeared to have spent the rest of
their entire life-savings at the supermarket before they arrived;
some had even splashed out at Harrods, to judge by the size and
stuffed plumpness of their hampers. All those who had come
prepared were sitting pretty: one family, gift-wrapped in
Barbours and plaid blankets, reclined on fold-out chairs around
a tarpaulin smothered in licked-clean plates and coolers the size
of fridge-freezers. They'd brought a plastic table, too, which
was laden with bottles. The family had settled back to relax. I
splatted down in my waterproof trousers on to a nearby mud-
patch, and listened in, like a tramp at the window of a
restaurant. The conversation consisted of favourable remarks
about the wine; observations on the cosiness of the blankets;
comments, one to another, about 'that Lesley Garrett that's on
later, she's the top of the pops on Classic FM, you know. I've
got her CD in the car'. In my mind, I substituted cider for
wine, and Robbie Williams for Lesley Garrett. And it was as if
I'd never left the mud-flats of Glastonbury.

After a while, I went for a walk and a chat with the patrons. Some of those on the edges were disappointed with the Tribute. One woman had won her ticket in a works raffle and had come over from Dublin: she perched on a piece of fencing and said, 'You'd think they'd provide seating, at least, like in the concert halls.' Others didn't mind: 'I'm just here for Diana,' boomed a glamorous thirty-something. 'I'm not bothered about who's performing. The last concert I went to was twelve years ago: AC/DC. My boyfriend forced me to go.'

One mumsy old dear told me that 'we've come for the atmosphere'. I looked around and tried to soak up the aforementioned. There were a few thousand people at the concert: not a football crowd, but not a C of E congregation either. And several wore very loud T-shirts, that read *English Teddy Bear Company* or *Florida*. Despite this though, everything was quiet: there was no movement, other than chewing; no noise, apart from that coming from the stage. The sky had clouded over again. To me, the general ambience was of, well, a wet weekend in Northamptonshire; 'limp' would have over-emphasised the thrills. Frankly, you could have cut the atmosphere with a crisp packet.

But again, that was no different from Glastonbury, which is remarkably silent away from the stages. I looked back at the lady. 'It's exciting, isn't it?' she grinned at me, and raised her arms to join in with a Mexican wave.

The Mexican wave had been started by the hilarious Midlands comic Jasper Carrott, who had wandered onstage to compère. As a joke, (I assumed) he was behaving like a complete git . . .

Jasper stopped his rib-tickling Mexican semaphore, and made a gesture for calm. Then: 'Oggi Oggi Oggi,' shouted Jasper, wittily. 'Oi Oi Oi,' replied the dutiful audience. This full and frank exchange of views went on for ten minutes, until Jasper decided to tell some real gags.

'So, we won the football yesterday,' he boomed. 'That means it'll be England versus Argentina in a week or so. Well,' (here Jasper paused, for comic timing), 'there won't be any trouble at that match, will there?'

Good grief. That was a joke? Pass the needle, Mother, for me to mend my split sides and trouser-seams. Or for me to sew Jasper Carrott's lips to a motorway.

Jasper must have read my mind, because he then turned his keen observational eye and rapier wit to transport: 'I came from Northampton today,' he informed us. 'How many of you came that way?' About a quarter of the audience raised their hands. 'Well,' said Jasper, 'wasn't it easy getting here?' The audience seemed to agree with Jasper: at least, they didn't start pelting him with mud, which was the other, more considered option. But Jasper didn't leave too much to chance. He started another Mexican Wave and sneaked off the stage to make way for T'Pau.

I stayed until 9.30 p.m.; until the sun had set and the night was lit with the twinkling of a thousand lanterns, and the twinkling of a thousand stars – none of whom made an appearance. No, that's not fair. Amongst the troupes of confusing nonenties (Miriam Stockley, anyone? Laurence Gowan?) there were some genuine household names: Lesley Garrett, the cheery northern opera singer, who said down-to-earth things like 'Didn't she touch our hearts, Diana?' between belting out the Greatest Hits of Car Adverts; Chris de Burgh, the poison dwarf of adult-orientated rock, who I thought was wincingly off-key and kept running on his little legs from one side of the stage to the other to stop us from noticing how badly he sang. Chris de Burgh: like a popstar, but smaller. (Chris, incidentally, was hit hard by Diana's death. Here's a few official brochure quotes: 'I just thought she was a very, very special lady . . . I found her very charismatic and feminine . . . I loved her smile and her eyes . . . one of the most illustrious, compassionate, loving and special people of the twentieth century.' If Diana had lived, she could have filed a stalker's order.) Then there was Sir Cliff Richard, who was weird and mesmerising, a cross between a super-keen teenager and a cult leader. And the ever-cuddly Lighthouse Family, who played their huge warm hugs of songs to an audience that seemed a bit confused as to who they were.

I left just before big girl's blouses Duran Duran started playing, although I like some of their songs. But I wanted to get back to Glastonbury before everyone I knew there had disappeared into the night and the mud and the madness. As I drove, I thought about the Tribute. It had come about because Earl Spencer wanted to raise money for the Diana Memorial Fund, whilst celebrating his sister's life and her love of music. Putting aside any nit-picking about Chris de Burgh and the term 'music', I thought it was an understandable thing for him to want to do: when someone dies, it's usual for friends and family to desire a commemoration that's 'appropriate' – 'it's what she would have wanted' (and Diana had notoriously appalling musical taste) – and they often seem to want more than just a funeral, no matter how stately.

So, I could see why Earl Spencer would bother organising a Tribute to his sister. And I understood why all those people had bought tickets: they'd bought them for the same reason that people had bought Glastonbury tickets – because they thought the concert was a special occasion and (a bit) because the money went to a good cause.

In the end, in fact, my Compare and Contrast experiment had revealed very little difference between the two events. Earl Spencer wanted to raise money for a cause he considered worthy: ditto Michael Eavis (Glastonbury profits went to Greenpeace). He chose music that he rated, along with other acts that agreed to turn up. Same as Eavis with Glastonbury. Both festivals were filmed for television. Both made the front page of newspapers. And both, in the end, were attended by the same sort of people, the same type of stoic middle Britons determined to have a good time. The parents and the little kids were picnicking at Althorp; as the just-left-home daughters and the layabout elder sons were rolling in the Glastonbury quagmire.

At the Tribute, death was magicked into good works, a complicated life into the People's Princess, and Chris de Burgh into something to applaud. At Glastonbury, charity and ecological awareness were transformed into a mosh pit, and Tony Bennett metamorphosised, via the miracle of irony, into a modern-day folk hero. For in order for Magic to work, you only have to believe in it, and the people I'd met at the Tribute had the same clear, unwavering belief as the mud-puppets had at Michael

Eavis's farm. They all had so much belief, in fact, that the magic had happened. Hamfisted banality and lumpen tunes, ruined peep-toe sandals and over-priced food, a county's-worth of slime, a wasteland of drowned tents and truckloads of drugs that never had worked and never would – all had been Magicked into something completely different. Into what everyone at both festivals would undoubtably recall as a really brilliant atmosphere.

18

park and ride

I returned from Glastonbury, packed my bags and moved into a semi in Surbiton. No, I didn't. I packed my bags and went for a weekend at Center Parcs in Elvedon Forest, with John and his family. I was disappointed at first. I'd thought that the entire 400-acre site would be covered by the Center Parcs dome: trees, lakes, smile-for-the-camera squirrels all nice and dry beneath their Truman Show rain-bonnet. But the dome is only little. It encloses the sports centre and a handful of themed restaurants and that's it. A shrunken Croydon in a see-through coolie. The rest of the holiday camp – the countryside – is *sans* Las Vegas ceiling. Center Parcs is just a recreation centre that went for a walk in a forest and couldn't find its way back out again.

Still, after I'd got over my Westworld illusions, I spent an action-packed weekend queuing to hire bikes and paying extra to scrap with Competitive Dads (one of whom tried to ensure his daughter's victory in the Treasure Trail by removing all the clues, so no one behind could catch up). You paid extra for everything. Though Center Parcs is a Dutch concept (thus: orgy-friendly open-plan villas; cycling), it has clearly been sent to a Ronald McDonald business school. Nothing was free, except for the swimming pool, and that was hidden amidst fake rocks, gurgling streams and hilariously over-priced shops. There were little bridges and higgledy paths, indoor and out, with enormous, straight-forward people stomping all over them. There were trees everywhere: after a while, I found it impossible to tell when their foliage was real and when it was made from living breathing plastic. Center Parcs was the sort of place that Radiohead fans write cross poetry about; a place for action men, women and children, where reading the menu for too long marked you out as a posey intellectual.

We had a lovely time. We booked and coughed up and sampled a variety of Center Parcs pleasures. We gurgled along Wild Water Rapids, we gambolled midst speciality boutiques. We played golf, went bowling; petted the noses of deer, ate the wings of buffalo. We were trounced in the Badminton Round Robin Tournament by a stout pair of middle-aged ladies, and by a couple of gonky teenage boys, also two passing squirrels and everyone else. We were thoroughly outclassed in the Best-Dressed Contest, too. Well: outcoloured. Center Parcs was a Colour Me Post-Nuclear world of Barbie pink trainers and shorts in mint creme green, of fleeces like an explosion round

Juan Miro's home-decoration business, of suntans to shame a GM tomato. Nature cowered in the face of so dazzling a palette. I noticed that much of the local fauna was sporting sunglasses.

Center Parcs was suburbia as fantasy. It combined the tall trees, tweety birds and fishing lakes of the countryside with the wave machines, sports-casual outfitters and Fruits De Mer pizzas of the city. You drove there along well-signposted motorways and A-roads, but the on-site parking restrictions (no cars allowed except when checking in) ensured that the kids could roam free without becoming road jam. Your enjoyment was directly in proportion to how much money you spent, yet your expensive detached home was exactly the same as everyone else's, with the same foresty, natural-look view, the same modern facilities: BBQ, fitted bathroom, Sky TV. You spent your allotted time doing allotted activities. Archery, aromatherapy, step classes, drama classes, ten-pin bowling, nine-hole golf, five-a-side. Country Club. Nature Trail. Treehouse Shop. Pay for it, do it, stop it, do something else.

At Center Parcs, rain could not ruin things; nor uninvited outsiders. No poor people, no odd ones, no one that didn't own the right stretch-Lycra patterned shorts. Money talking loud and proud. Amenities second to none. Kids safe and occupied. Parents happy and comfortable. A little world of you and your kind. Middle Britain's fairyland.

I thought about my holidaying youth. The only aspects that Center Parcs shared with our camping trips were the driving to get there and the similarity of the living plots – all laid out like a housing estate, everyone separate, everyone the same but determinedly displaying their differences (our fold-away picnic furniture is better than yours). And I thought about a quote I'd read in a newspaper article. 'The suburbs give most people what they want, most of the time.' The quote was from Paul Barker, senior fellow of the Institute of Community Studies. But you don't need to be a senior fellow (or indeed, a fellow) to know that he is right. Nor to notice that those give-the-people-what-they-want suburbs have changed. My short travels had shown me that there had been a seismic shift: one of those that's imperceptible in the short term, but becomes clear over time. And it is this. The suburbs have become confident. They're venturing further. They're spreading themselves about – pleasure-seeking, outward-bound, showing out. These days, even stay-at-home housewives are happy to drive. And because of this – because, now, all suburbanites are in-car with a ticket to ride, taking their much-mocked small attitudes on day-trips – there are places that have sprung up to satisfy them. The suburbs have always had the money: now they've got the bravado to travel to new spots to spend it. In place of the old 2.4 picture, there's a new snapshot, sharp and clear. And the snapshot is of a Visitor Centre. Or a supermarket. Or a nightclub. Or a conference hall. Or a cinema complex. A free-standing structure, modern, indoorsy, compartmentalised; that you drive to, enjoy and then leave. A building of entertainment, of leisure times, of life-times, a building as separate and apart as a detached des. res.

Is this an entirely bad thing? When cinemas were confined to three-screeners-no-parking in city centres, or dodgy one show fleapits in edge towns, only a few dedicated movie-buffs would consider a film as a nice evening out. Now, with multi-screen complexes next to well-swept food halls, with free parking and clean seats and no worry of mugging, cinema attendance is up and thriving. Conference centres, with their attendant shows, mean that citizens who previously united solely through football can join together in shared excitement over free-standing self-assembly hot tubs, or Dandie Dinmont Terriers, or Engelbert Humperdink, or whatever. And with chain restaurants offering near-authentic foreign food experiences, eating out is no longer the sole province of the truly posh. When I was a Wilmslow girl, it was confined to birthdays and wedding anniversaries. Today it's a regular entertainment option, because chain eateries don't intimidate or patronise or talk a funny language and if you've been once, you'll know what to order next time.

Safety, accessibility, value for money . . . And nice clean toilets. Earl Spencer, the Wingeing Ginge of Althorp, pointed out when organising the Tribute Concert for his sister that 'the public' (meaning, the paying public) 'really do notice the standard of loo provided for them'. So we do; and we notice the standard of knick-knack shop too. We notice because these things matter. Hands up who wants a nice, clean, covered-up environment where you can enjoy yourself with the whole family, from Gramps to little Roger, and where you know there'll be parking spaces and a place to change nappies. Who minds paying for the privilege, if you feel you're getting value for money? Who minds travelling to get there, as long as the route is clearly sign-posted?

A few months after I finished my trip, my mum told me that Dumplington Hall had finally opened. The traffic jams brought the motorways to a standstill. There were shots on Granada

Reports of the first Dumpers shoppers: dazzled, overcome, blubbing with joy. 'It's beautiful,' snivelled one lady, when she contemplated the Las Vegas sky-like ceiling, so different from the real, dull firmament. Around the same time, I read a column in the *Independent on Sunday* which got very upset about shopping centres. It compared them to churches where the priests were knife-wielding sacrificial maniacs (as opposed to cuddly tambourinists). The column was entitled: 'Abattoirs Awash With Our Blood. That's Malls'. Oh, save us from the killing fields of Kookai. How silly all those Dumpers shoppers were: so busy enjoying themselves that they didn't notice that the Italian marble floor was swimming in gore, that just by placing a toe into Smiths they were condoning the murder of their fellow human beings, and umpteen ickle piggy-wiggies and lamb-lings. Bloody provincials, eh? They just don't think.

I read other newspaper features too, cuttings on out-of-town topics that I'd collected during my trip. In the press, 'the dream-world of suburbia' (cf Sir Richard of Rogers) was still happily mired in the fifties. Almost every story reinforced the ancient clichés of Middle Britain: snotty prejudices, potting shed, car-washing, care with money, petloving, petty-mindedness, petit bourgeois affectations. The headlines read 'For Real Misogyny, Just Try Playing A Round Of Golf', or 'In Search Of The Surrey Stereotype'. They were easy to read, slip-sliding past your brain without troubling your presumptions. The only jolts occurred when suburbia didn't behave as expected; when it dared to progress, to explore, to change. Then the feature writ-ers came over all heated. '24 Hour Shopping Too Popular', they fretted, or 'An Estate Too Far'.

I went to see my Granny again. Her eye-sight had got a bit worse: she still watched the telly but she could only recognise long-established soap characters, ones that she knew already. I read her letters out loud for her. They were mostly bills. She told me that she'd been on a trip, to Millom with the Inner Wheel, where the salad had been too big ('by the time I'd found the meat, I'd lost my lettuce all over the place-mat'), but the speaker, a woman who ran a hotel in Eccles, had been excellent. Granny asked me lots of questions. She wanted to know all about Dumpers and Goathland and Castle Howard and Cadbury World and the Diana Tribute Concert. I told her, she pronounced them all 'lovely', and then we had a cup of tea and wrestled with such problematic modern concepts as men that didn't have lady friends and telephones that didn't have sockets and Nick Berry leaving Heartbeat so now Granny couldn't keep up with the storyline any longer. Unlike the press and the media *grandes fromages*, unlike me on several occasions, my non-too-cutting-edge Granny seemed quite able to grasp the idea that suburbia had shifted. 'Everything's changed,' she announced, but she didn't mind that it had. 'Oh no, things are much more convenient nowadays, for the young people like you and your mother.' Granny didn't get flustered over the morality of shopping centres, or the educational aspects of Visitor Centres, or whether the Princess Tribute pilgrims were being ripped off. Though almost entirely blind, she could see and accept that her environment had moved on from the pinnyed housewifery of her earlier years. That cars and abattoirs, covered shopping and leisure-pleasure had smudged the picture postcard of ordinary life in an everyday British suburb.

I didn't move to suburbia because, in the end, I didn't need to. Suburbia had moved to me. I had left but it had followed. I couldn't escape, even when I wore stupid clothes or listened to strange music, even when I hid. Run to Manchester, or London, hole up in city drinking holes, scum-soaked gutters, Soho-boho-hooligan art quarters; hunker down with the glamorous, the intellectual, the scary, the disenfranchised, the dangerous, the iconoclastic and still you'll find you're there. Because the only way that cities can compete with suburbia nowadays is to turn themselves into the same experience. Pedestrianise, cobble over, clean up, sanitise; provide decent toilets and crested litter bins and vast, safe parking areas. Make sure that the same shops, the well-known brands that line the Parades and Crescents of the out-of-town Spendvilles are installed gleamingly, conveniently in the new smooth-edged, smoothed-over, calmed down city centres. And then sit back and hope that suburbia will overcome its urban paranoia, and drive in, park up, enjoy, drive home.

Despite the constant media teasing, the chiding of the chintz, the lampooning of the standard lamps, the suburbs are stronger than they ever have been. They don't need the cities. The BBC may announce, modishly, that it is to remove suburbia from our screens; Brookside's Phil Redmond may trumpet that the middle classes are boring – yet Croydon feels confident enough to make a PR bid to become the third city of London. Westminster, City of London, Croydon. It sounds ridiculous, until you compare Croydon's civic aims with those of London.

Croydon wants to 'return our centre to the pedestrian', create a 'café society', with paved shopping areas and a central plaza;

it also plans a 15,000 seat arena next to the railway station, and to 'develop elements of next century's 24-hour entertainment culture'. Now let's look at London. Richard Rogers, who likes 'neighbourly cities', proposes in his book *Cities For A Small Planet* that we pedestrianise Trafalgar Square 'to accommodate cafés'. His practice is already at work on the South Bank Centre, putting the existing open-air spaces under a 'large undulating crystal canopy' (no more nasty rain!) and 'creating new events and facilities' which will 'generate a vibrant 24-hour cultural destination'. Suburbs take the best bits of a city and put them in a greener environment. So cities have to turn into suburbs. And as the new suburbia expands, into the country, into the cities, a particular knack, a peculiar sense of rightness and separation, convenience and cleanliness expands with it. Suburbia likes certainty, it wants to put things – people, pastimes, pleasures – where it thinks they should be.

I thought about Micky and Janet, the spouse-swappers. They'd told me that they were careful not to let their chosen form of relaxation bleed into other areas of their life. They wanted their swinging distinct, contained, filed in a different-coloured folder, tucked into its own Tupperware container so it didn't make the rest of the fridge contents smell funny. Of course, this might have been due to embarrassment; or a fear of being found out by the tabloids, or social services, or unsympathetic neighbours. Or it might have been that they just liked to organise their lives like that. No messy edges. Bedtime, worktime, kidtime, sextime. Doghour, golfhour, DIYhour, AllBarOnehour. Every second counts. Use each one wisely. Suburbia has won. It's got its own way. It's a consumer force to be reckoned with, an electorate that swings elections, and it's taking advantage of its power. Suburbia's desire to drive everywhere, its insistence on hygiene, time-efficiency and overall niceness has created an environment that provides just that. A hold-my-hand culture, where you don't stumble across a inspiring B road, you are led to and made to pay for a Dalby Forest Drive. Where cities pretend to be shopping centres or theme parks so you won't feel too frightened to visit. Where virtual hamlets are made from tarted up old farm buildings because real villages aren't cute or serviceable enough. Where the spark of genuine life or hard work or curiosity that creates a car cruise, a chocolate factory, even an interest in Dracula, is firmly extinguished, cleverly recreated and sold back to you in easy-to-swallow form.

Once upon a time, I felt rootless. Because my roots didn't feel as though they rooted me. They felt instead like irritating bits of stringy gum that would keep sticking to my shoes. It's easy to desert your past when it's comfy and conventional and seemingly boring. Who wants to have an identity stamped Made In The Suburbs? But when I finished my travels, my adventures in suburbia, I went out and bought myself some nice white shoes. And wore them, with some pride. Because Britain was being built by its suburbs and my past was shaping the present. And because I thought they might make me look taller.

My mum shops at John Lewis's on the bypass, though she always said she wouldn't. But when it's really sheeting down, she can park close by and run to the shop without ruining her jacket. My dad still patronises the Last Drop because the signs make it easy for him to find. He's been helping with the design of other out-of-town sports centres. Granny's been back to Asda: her social club, her Big Day Out. I've been to Ikea, for home decoration, and, you know, just to see what it's like. Everyone's doing it. John takes his daughter to Legoland. It Girls shop at Bluewater. The world meets at B&Q.

Because, you know, what Suburbia wanted, it has got. All life's experiences, but in bite-size form. Time to work, time to shop, time to drive, time to play. Life compartmentalised, with no room for anything nasty to slip through the gaps in between. Drive up, enjoy, drive home again. Park and ride.